HOLY DIRT

A CAMINO JOURNEY

OUT OF MY MIND. INTO MY BODY.
SAVED BY SONG.

MOLLY LORD

HOLY DIRT

A CAMINO JOURNEY

OUT OF MY MIND. INTO MY BODY.
SAVED BY SONG.

MOLLY LORD

DISCLAIMER

Dear Readers,

Do *not* try anything in this book without a life preserver, a quick prayer, and Advil.

Holy Dirt was written to enchant, inspire, find humor, celebrate, warn, and perhaps guide you in life's trials. However, repeat after me: this is *not* a map for your *Camino*.

I disclaim all responsibility if you: eat octopus (and hate or like it), drag a fellow pilgrim into a church to tell God she irons her husband's underwear, or risk accepting a tea invitation from two specific elder Polish sisters. And if you ever do walk the *Camino*, and the *Camino* does not seem to "be providing," refer to the Journal Tips found at the end of several chapters. If they're of no help—punt.

To maintain the anonymity of those unable to be reached for permission, the names and identifying characteristics of some people described in this book have been changed.

The author looks forward to being your ongoing resource for tapping into life's ideal trifecta of myth, music, and magic.

FOR BRUCE AND DOROTHY

Your cryptic words planted long ago became an intriguing map:

"You're inside a box, Molly, and

the answer on how to get out is

written on the outside of the box."

Twenty years, 500 miles, a million poppies later,

I finally get it.

Front Cover Artist: Yana Shvets

Artwork: Poppies Sunset

Yana Shvets is a Ukrainian artist with a wanderer's soul. She journeyed the world nonstop for six years, visiting over 20 countries and living in seven, finding inspiration in unexpected places and people. Yana's watercolor paintings capture these emotional imprints, inviting you to relive your own cherished memories. She combines a realistic style with loose elements, bringing a clear understanding of the subject with a touch of fantasy. Since 2016, she has taught watercolor art both online and offline, and her original artwork resides in private collections worldwide.

Website: https://yanatravelart.com/

TABLE of CONTENTS

INTRODUCTION

Hey, are you one of those who skips book introductions?
Trust me. You gotta read this one, or you'll be lost
before the journey begins.
Okay, with that sorted out...push play
on the first song if you wish, then read on!

There's A Place In The World For A Gambler

~ Dan Fogelberg

(NOTE: If unable to read a song QR code, we suggest magnifying your screen.)

MAY 11, 2019, ST. JEAN PIED DE PORT, FRANCE

Standing in the French town of St. Jean Pied de Port, my eyes focused on the loftiest, visible point of the Pyrenees Mountains. Mentally—physically—emotionally, I steeled myself (for two years) to set out from here for the 500-mile pilgrimage of the *Camino de Santiago*. Dog-eared pages in my guidebooks captured this mountain image to help reinforce that I *could* walk over these mountains and across northern Spain (and survive).

Instead, I faced an eleventh-hour injury and a leg dragging like Igor in *The Hunchback of Notre Dame*. One good leg to stand on wasn't a good look in *this* town.

The gall of bizarre plot twists showing up at the *beginning* of an epic tale. They make you wish the end credits would just run already.

GOT MYTH?

Poring through mythical stories and epic films, I don't recall Luke Skywalker ever pulling a hamstring. Princess Leia never opened Google Translate to ensure a menu item didn't contain dairy. Gandalf never inquired, "Geez, what the hell ya got in this backpack anyway, bricks?" And Glinda, the Good Witch, never advised Dorothy, "Hey, in case those ruby slippers give you blisters, have a good pair of backup Tevas."

This realization hinted that my journey may not wrap up neatly like Cinderella's, and Indiana Jones wouldn't be swooping in on a vine in the nick of time. *Stay tough, girlfriend. It's all a gamble. No one is coming to save you.*

Oblivious to the Alchemist archetype's playbook and the elixir it'd prepared for turning my life perspective on its head, I waited restlessly for my leg to heal so my journey could begin. Eventually, it would (and did) sink in. This hassle *was* my journey.

THE HERO'S JOURNEY
(IN COMPRESSION SOCKS)

Beyond teaching and screenwriting, mythology stirs my fascination, as in Joseph Campbell's expansive ideas in *The Hero's Journey*. Give me *The Hunger Games, The Lord of the Rings,* or *The Wizard of Oz*, and my mind automatically maps out the mythological journey unfolding, from the opening scene where things are calm and hopeful to where everything falls apart. The main character, *The Hero,* resists the trouble that looms. At this point, the Hero's motivation level is: "Dang, I didn't sign up for this crap. I'm out."

However, this "call to adventure" (translation: brace yourself, shit's about to hit the fan) keeps knocking, regardless of our resistance. Notice in your favorite story (or film) how the Hero eventually surrenders, predictably befriends a mentor, and sets off on a journey into the unknown—a true gambler.

When our call to adventure comes (with many in a lifetime), we enter a strange Universe, hoping we too can slay the dragon, face the dark night of the soul, claim the magic elixir, and return victorious as a wise, revised version of our former selves. Though sometimes the dragon wins and victory eludes us, the wisdom from the journey lives on.

When it's in a movie or a book, I understand it all so clearly, but still need a hit upside the head to recognize when *I'm* the Hero, and how to trust the perfection unfolding in *my* journey. I discovered the "call to the *Camino*" includes these built-in hits upside the head when you most need them. Helmet not included.

A SOUNDTRACK FOR THE JOURNEY

I blame it all on the Beatles—age ten. You see, beyond my love of story lies a curiosity about the music we love (from Bach to Rock) and how it gives voice to our day-to-day story.

A screenwriter by night, I morph into a music research nerd by day. I'm not a musician. Yet I've devoted over fifteen years to studying the effect of frequency in music (across all genres and generations) and how it influences mind, body, and spirit. My focus is what *really* happens when music crawls inside our heads. How do we harness the frequencies of Mick Jagger and Pavarotti to crank up our emotional state as we live our Hero's Journey each day?

I thought work and music would remain behind when I left for the *Camino*—silly me. Of course, music followed. After all, key songs link themselves to meaningful life events and get under your skin as sacred keepers of memories, learnings, and resolutions. This treasured collection is *the soundtrack of your life*.

Coincidentally (and unexpectedly), my *Camino* soundtrack took shape, song by song, as my walk unfolded. Worrisome and victorious moments often synchronistically resonated with one of the handful of songs that accompanied me. Mostly I walked in silence, but each song eventually informed me when to push play, bringing uncanny relief to the moment.

Other tunes crawled into this soundtrack, too. Sometimes, as a haunting melody in a high mountain café, or music drifting from a pilgrim's backpack speaker along desolate stretches. The rest found their place in the soundtrack once home. All created the auditory photo journal of my *Camino* experience.

If ever you're curious about my state of mind at any crossroad in this journey, listen to the song preceding specific chapters (enjoy with QR code). They voice *my* revelations, and they'll likely resonate with days *you* have walked a challenging road. You may not understand why I've included certain songs. That's okay. Our soundtrack holds precious secrets only we understand.

YOU PLAN, THE *CAMINO* LAUGHS

The following pages introduce the many souls whose steps (along with mine) had an appointment with destiny. They connect decades of defining events that rolled out the red carpet for this metaphorical desert I'd now cross, for the most part, alone. All this led me *here* to stand injured in St. Jean Pied de Port before this unforgiving mountain.

As with all *Hero's Journey* tales, my story is personal, yet universal. Names and happenings appear differently in mine than yours, but I think you'll recognize your footprints crossing these pages. May they speak to the universal joys, self-sabotage, disappointments, wild discoveries, monotony, elation, breakdowns, and rich friendships that have met you on your life's pilgrimage. A toast to our inner gambler!

In a wise Yoda fashion, I followed the guidebooks meticulously, preparing for Spain. Checking all necessary boxes, I dutifully ensured an organized, hassle-free pilgrimage. HA! The spirit of the *Camino* laughed— the kind of belly laugh that shoots Spanish *sangria* out its proverbial nose.

I'd soon discover a chapter never once included in all those guidebooks.

One that's written when you bravely (or not) take the gamble and face unforeseen plot twists, often before your boots step onto the trail's holy dirt.

Alas, such is the way—some would say the magic—of the *Camino*.

PART ONE

AT THE STARTING LINE

CHAPTER 1

ACCIDENT WAITING to HAPPEN

Somewhere

~ Barbra Streisand

MAY 11, 2019, FRANKFURT, GERMANY

My hamstring felt like a steel rod as I limped off our Frankfurt flight, dragging my Igor leg, sleep-deprived and slap-happy. When the customs officer asked, "What's your name and purpose for being in Germany?" it took everything in me to resist answering, *Who am I? I'll tell you who I am, sir…I'm an accident waiting to happen, about to make the craziest mistake of my life by walking the Camino. Who are you?* Fortunately, my better angels talked me off that jet-lagged ledge, editing my reply, "Molly Lord. The *Camino de Santiago*, sir."

This identity of being aligned with trouble or accidents had deep roots. The label "Molly's an accident waiting to happen" started in childhood. Remnants still lurked—especially facing a 500-mile (800 km) pilgrimage. The first strong evidence of how firm (and dangerous) the grip of this label had on me made itself obvious during my teaching years.

1985 COLORADO SPRINGS, COLORADO

Calling my parents in western New York, I should've known the chaos my news would unleash. I, a 29-year-old visionary and special education teacher, was headed for the stars. Literally.

This mission could change my life and, I hoped, the lives of children around the world. My destiny felt clear.

Once both parents were on the line, I began. "I have exciting news!"

By my tone, they likely anticipated I was either engaged or pregnant. Proud tears welled up. "I've received the official letter from NASA. I'm in the running for the Teacher In Space Program. I could be chosen to go up in the Challenger Space Shuttle next year! I feel it in my bones. This is mine."

"Wow, amazing, honey! Congratulations!" I could hear my dad's pride. "What happens next? How does this work? When will you know?" As his questions spilled over the phone line, there was a deafening silence from my mother. I braced myself.

"No! You can't do this, Molly. You *know* you're an accident waiting to happen. Go into space? Are you crazy? It's dangerous!"

There it was. I hadn't heard that painful line since moving to Colorado three years earlier. And, just like that, the wound reopened—I felt the criticism course through my veins, echoing: *You're an accident waiting to happen.*

I mostly received those words in childhood from my kind, loving, and worry-obsessed mother. Never to be mean or criticize, only to warn and protect. Granted, I was too often sick, usually at the worst times. We could count on a raging ear infection or bronchitis on any vacation, making packing antibiotics a standard vacation procedure. In the 1960s, we had no awareness my frequent infections were tied to dairy and wheat sensitivity. Death by pizza. Who knew?

But there was more to this label. Certain situations added up to this earned reputation in my mother's eyes. I admit being too adventurous, pushing the boundaries from childhood through college. Funny, I actually saw myself as lucky. Hey, I always *lived* and dodged serious trouble, didn't I? C'mon. The State Police were only at my house once. The truth? I liked risky leanings and the unknown. However, I was unaware of how deeply being "an accident waiting to happen" was embedded in my psyche (or its possible consequences).

Moving to Colorado in 1981, the curse lifted. I kayaked, skied, mountain biked, and hiked with limited casualties. Though still dealing with lingering injuries from a violent assault several years prior, they no longer felt linked to this old belief. I felt free. But in reality, it had only gone dormant. This call home reawakened it, and we faced our biggest showdown yet: my mother's fears versus my biggest dream.

With the next round of NASA good news, my mother cut off Dad's accolades and demanded, "Molly, withdraw your name right now. It's too dangerous!"

I've fulfilled her prophecy for too many years. I'm done. I hung up in tears.

When I didn't make NASA's next cut, I was devastated and sure NASA and God made a colossal mistake. But in time, lessons were learned, and clarity was gained. Once I surrendered, I found it inspiring to watch the chosen teacher, Christa McCauliffe, prepare for flight.

On January 28, 1986, a few teachers, students, and I watched the televised launch. My knees turned to jello when the Challenger exploded. As we tried to understand what we'd witnessed, a PA announcement summoned me to the office for a long-distance call.

Now? Who? Maybe my mother? Yep, an "I told you so" call. Not in any mean-spirited "gotcha" sense, but rather in a pleading one. "*Now,* will you believe me about your foolish ideas? Will you make safer choices *now*?" Her words stung. I slammed down the receiver and slid to the floor, sobbing, oblivious to my surroundings. My mother just won our darkest battle—it scared the shit out of me. *Damn! Her worry-wart negativity feels like I'm hexed for eternity.*

Tears subsiding, the principal kindly called a sub so I could go home. Driving up the mountain pass, "Somewhere" by Barbra Streisand came on the radio—the song I'd once declared the anthem for my Challenger dream. I ached for Christa, the lost shuttle crew, the students and families who witnessed the tragedy *and* simultaneously felt guilty (and defeated) sitting in my own shit, pissed off that mom was right, but overwhelmingly grateful for being alive. With a sigh, I whispered, "Thank you, God, for unanswered prayers."

Teaching the next day, the ever-faithful mantra *I guess I am an accident waiting to happen* took up too much damn real estate in my head. Freezing cold, fierce winds blew, and the snowy blizzard ended school early. Visibility sucked—the storm's accumulation made driving a scary ride, and slick conditions caused a four-car accident ahead. I slowed, then, bam! A truck slammed into the back of me, catapulting me into the first wreck—I became car five in what quickly became a sixty-car pileup.

In the ambulance, I shuddered, thinking how quickly I'd fulfilled my mother's prophecy. *Damn, was she right? Am I an accident waiting to happen?* After the ER released me to friends, I called my spiritual counselor. I was frightened the resurrected belief was coming for me with a vengeance. Do I think *I* caused that accident? No. But when it was happening, I didn't understand my inner power. Now, I *know* we're powerful enough to attract situations with our strong emotions, negative thinking, and outdated beliefs.

Over several years, my comeback from "Hexed for eternity" slowly unfolded. It wasn't my path to go into space. My soul had an even *more* challenging task: to *stay grounded.* Being asked to inspire lives without my feet leaving Earth stirred a new faith, and I began trusting even the most crushing disappointments would work out on my behalf.

There are, of course, times when that faith goes dark.

The mad dash for our Paris flight conveniently distracted me from the *Camino* challenges ahead. Faith would surely be calling on my better angels, and I'd soon discover that some of 'em wear hiking boots.

CHAPTER 2

ON YOUR MARK. GET SET. OH, WAIT a SECOND!

On the Road to Find Out

~ Cat Stevens/Yusuf

ON YOUR MARK...

MAY 11-12, 2019 PARIS—BIARRITZ—ST. JEAN PIED DE PORT

The Paris customs officer peered suspiciously over my shoulder, sounding accusatory as if someone dubiously hid in the shadows. "Are you traveling *alone?*" *Hmmm. Were my two friends who had recently died traveling incognito with me? Hopefully, they packed their celestial compression socks.* Then, looking him in the eyes, "Yes, sir, alone," I replied.

In the Paris sunshine, René and I had three hours. With my Igor leg in tow, we did the obligatory selfies at the Eiffel Tower, The Louvre, and Notre Dame, then boarded our short flight to beautiful Biarritz. After a no-sleep night, we caught the morning train for St. Jean Pied de Port. There, the mountains majestically portrayed just like the guidebooks promised.

ST. JEAN PIED DE PORT: THE MOTHERSHIP

We heard tales that St. Jean Pied de Port initiates pilgrims, often before their feet hit the trail. *Our* initiation—discovering our room was on the third floor. No elevator. Did I mention our heavy packs? Climbing the winding dark stairway, a bit haunted by an old Eagles song, a creepy thought ignited: "Yikes, René, I'm hopin' we can check out anytime we want—*and* leave. She snickered. "Welcome to the Hotel *Camino*, Mol."

That evening in town, the buzz around the Pilgrim's Office was infectious. We stood in line under its stone archway to register, feeling the powerful presence of this mothership. Thoughts ruminated: *Wow, my plan to walk the first week with René sure went south—what a plot twist!* With my hamstring unable to handle the Pyrenees, she'd cross them alone.

I recalled the night I first told René about the *Camino de Santiago* (translation: "The Way of St. James"). My 800-kilometer route—the *Camino Francés*—would cross the French Pyrenees into Spain and continue across northern Spain to Santiago de Compostela. All René retained: I was going for a long walk—something about a *holy* guy named James. She remarked with a smirk, "Hey, who doesn't love a good walk?" Soon she'd figure out what she actually signed up for.

Finally, we were checked-in at the Pilgrim's Office by a kind, elderly, French-speaking gentleman. In somewhat decipherable English, he asked, "Why are you here?" We bumbled through our response, then, he showed René route options over the Pyrenees. Routes to take. Routes to avoid. She only caught about every fifth word, as I remained fixated on his first question: *Why are you here? Excellent question, sir. Why the hell AM I here?* I hushed my anxious mind gremlins while René politely listened for trail advice. Admitting later she didn't catch much of what he said, she laughed. "How's a girl to pay attention *and* fight off mind gremlins—they're deafening!"

Next, he explained the Pilgrim's Passport (*Credentials*). This sturdy accordion-folded mini booklet is presented at each evening's destination to be stamped—each stamp with its own unique design. Ultimately, the chronological stamp collection proves (in Santiago) that you've earned your *Compostela* (certificate of completion). Later, I'd understand how sacred these stamps would be.

My thoughts whirled from doubt to trust, back to doubt. *Am I a player here, or just a spectator? A true pilgrim or fraud?* The gremlins focused on the fraud part. I tried convincing them that this injury didn't delay my *Camino*, but rather, it *was* my *Camino*. Mind gremlins scoff at philosophical crap like that—to them, the limp wasn't a good look. Period.

He handed over our Pilgrim Passports, wishing us a heartfelt *"Buen Camino."* The phrase means Good Way. It's a cross-cultural language that wishes your fellow pilgrims well on their walk. With these final words, we felt catapulted from the mothership.

ABOUT THIS CAN OPENER

We faced the music back at our "Hotel *Camino*" after dinner. Hauling our backpacks up three flights made it clear *something* had to go. Whatever we gave up was tossed in the suitcase and would be shipped to Santiago. After an hour of "But what if *this* happens and I need it?" and doubting the irritating saying "The *Camino* will provide," René donned her packing police hat and pried countless items from my grip. The final interrogation item: my giant can opener. "Molly, my God, what does this monster weigh?"

"Wait! Remember, I can't eat grains or dairy. Canned foods are gonna save me!"

"Yeah, but..."

"René, imagine living with the guilt of a poor-starving-pilgrim-dying-a-grizzly-death-on-the-side-of-the-trail." I won that round. But with a price—added weight.

As René slept, my mind reviewed the revised plan. *In the morning, she'll begin her Pyrenees ascent. I'll figure out how to ship the suitcase to Santiago, then find a ride to our mountaintop hostel in Orisson to meet her (I hope).*

My final thought before sleep was the French gentleman's question, *Why are you here?* Unaware this question would haunt me for the next 500 miles, my only answer at this point: *I'm on the road to find out, sir.*

We slept hard on our final night in the arms of the mothership.

GET SET…

I'll Play the Blues for You
~ Daniel Castro

MAY 13, 2019 – ST. JEAN PIED DE PORT TO ORISSON

Making my way through town in the morning bustle of pilgrims, I scribbled down where to meet the transport van, then found a quiet side street to sit and get grounded. Instead, the mind gremlins kicked in:

How the hell did we get here? We're in a foreign country, don't know the damn language, lugging a heavy backpack, nursing an injury you stupidly did before leaving home. We're doomed.

I reminded them of Plan B: *When my leg heals, I'll walk. Until then, I'll keep up with René via any transport I find. We're fine.*

My explanation didn't satisfy them. They pulled up even more worries:

When you hugged René goodbye this morning, sure, she sounded upbeat, but you know damn well her anxious face said otherwise. That look said, "I could get lost up there! What if we never find each other again?"

Then, twisting the knife, they continued: *When she turned to begin her ascent, and you called, "Buen Camino!" don't think we didn't hear you mutter, "I'm so sorry to desert you, dear friend." Yep. You pretty much suck as a friend!*

Ugh.

Their next biting comment addressed when I returned to "Hotel *Camino*" (after seeing René off) to finish packing:

We watched as you struggled with that still too-heavy, lopsided pack (ya gotta learn to pack that thing!). Then, when you thumped the suitcase destined for Santiago down from the third floor—one treacherous step at a time—you coulda killed us and innocent bystanders! And when you filled out that form to direct the suitcase to Santiago at the shipping office, we heard exactly what you said to yourself as you watched it disappear into the back room.

I did recall *two* thoughts: *I may never see that suitcase again*, and *What if I never see Santiago?*

Their final concern:

About your non-existent French and Spanish. How do you expect to communicate?

The warm noon sun shone down where I sat just as my inner wisdom interrupted the crazy mind banter and advised: *Snap out of this funk! Acknowledge all the good that happened this morning!*

Agreement washed over me as wisdom offered up the morning's first golden nugget (which grew to be four 'cause who wants just one nugget?).

One—*Acknowledge this important Camino truth: Any carefully made plan for your Camino **will** be turned on its head.* Beautiful wisdom, but still irked me.

Two—*Regarding your friend going alone: walking the first week is a big deal. She has Camino lessons to learn in a short time frame. It's final—René walks the Pyrenees alone. Get over it.*

Three—*You completed your "Hotel Camino" check-out with flying colors. And you didn't kill anyone—a big win!*

Four—*You handled Google Translate like a champ! All your questions translated with the touch of a button. And ta-dah! You have a ride to Orisson and your suitcase will be waiting in Santiago. Google Translate will save your ass in Spain, too. Congrats.*

I agreed. It *was* a very productive morning here in the mothership.

SCORE: Wisdom: 1 Gremlins: 0

MY ASCENT

Arriving at the rendezvous spot, the young driver waved me to his van filled with backpacks being transported over the Pyrenees. "Cuts down on pilgrim injuries," he explained. I could barely lift my leg into the passenger seat. Pouting wasn't allowed except for the aching blues song coursing through my veins. It soothed the gremlins.

My driver, José, was delightful. I began sensing the possible order hidden in this seemingly bad B-movie. Hearing about René walking without me, José assured me of its perfection, then taught me about the Pyrenees, the rugged life of sheepherders, and the locals' commitment to the success of every pilgrim. "Expect to meet angels on this journey," he smiled. "Watch for them!" Then, he grinned even wider when I answered, "I'm counting you as my first."

Needing my opinion and encouragement, he shifted the conversation. "Should I risk moving from Spain to Ontario, Canada? A job and a beautiful woman are calling me there."

"Most definitely!" I answered.

The blues song playing in my head faded. I surrendered to my *Camino* beginning in this beaten-up van on this old road, dodging sheep and ruts deep enough to swallow a Volkswagen. However, I wouldn't tolerate more miles in a van than necessary.

We arrived in Orisson, excited to locate René. The ascent kicked her butt, but she was elated. My first Angel, José, hugged me goodbye. "Send me a postcard from Canada," I winked with a smile. I quickly jotted down in the NOTES section of my phone so I wouldn't forget:

JOSÉ—ANGEL NUMBER ONE (YOU NEVER FORGET YOUR FIRST).

 CAMINO MESSAGE #1:
Any carefully made Camino plan __will__ be turned on its head.

CAMINO MESSAGE #2
Watch for angels.

OH, WAIT A SECOND!

Inner Demons
~ Julia Brennan

"Maybe you are searching among the branches
for what only appears in the roots."

~ Rumi

MAY 13, 2019 ORISSON, FRANCE

Carrots, roots, snake venom, patience: the *Camino* words for today. Oh. And angels. We can't forget the angels.

When I was little, my mother had a small vegetable garden. As the carrot greens sprouted, I'd tug to extract each carrot to check its progress (like any five-year-old concerned for her harvest). Too small? No problem. Stick it back in the dirt and wait a few days before another inspection. My mother couldn't understand why her carrots rarely did well, until eventually catching my agricultural procedure. An enlightening lecture followed. "Be patient, Molly. You've gotta stop pushing the river and start trusting nature to take root." That took sixty years to sink in.

That might have been my first lesson in grace. Grace *allows* things to happen rather than forcing them. With grace, we offer inner demons a seat at the table to witness how things work out with patience. "They need not be yanked out," as Mom would say.

Soaking up the late afternoon sun in the hostel front yard, René drifted into her well-earned *siesta* as I kneaded every known muscle in my leg before taking the first walk since injuring it (over a week ago). I tested my hamstrings on an incline with noticeable improvement. Rest and self-treatments paid off. That evening, we dined with pilgrims from five different countries. *They* were pilgrims. *I* still felt like a spectator, but grateful for our shared personal United Nations.

Morning delivered chilly mountain air and a robin-egg-blue sky. We checked off experiencing our first pilgrim dinner and the first night bunking with strangers. These strangers-turned-budding-friendships cheered my "van plan" until I could join them. In awe of René rockin' this challenge alone, I tearfully wished her "*Buen Camino*" as everyone trickled out. Everyone's destination: Roncesvalles. My transport would deliver me there late morning.

ANGELS TWO, THREE, AND FOUR

The café breakfast menu dripped with white flour and cheese. Ugh. Killin' words for *this* pilgrim! Returning outside (still hungry), a spritely bearded gentleman, Roman from Ukraine—embarking on his second *Camino* adventure, invited me to sit at his table. Listening to his intriguing life story as he ate, my crashing blood sugar interjected, "You mind sharing where that soup came from?" He leaned in through the kitchen window, saying something in Spanish. Poof! An enormous bowl of steaming vegetable soup magically appeared—pure bliss. Then, pulling a jar from his pack, Roman poured mystery lotion into a small baggie. My eyebrows raised.

"Here, for your hamstrings. Snake venom and turpentine—heals everything." Sucked into the *Camino* vortex, I accepted his gift without hesitation.

Mark, a laid-back American hostel volunteer, strolled out of the café over to our table and asked, "How's your *Camino* going so far?" I answered with slight resistance, "Technically, mine hasn't begun yet. Injured hamstring—it's a long story." Then, he offered a fresh perspective.

"Molly, what if your *Camino has* begun? Disregard what you've heard. You don't have to do the Pyrenees to be a legit pilgrim, and injuries don't halt your *Camino,* either." Yep! Angel number three was on the scene (they were coming fast).

Roman agreed, "Yes, that thinking's bullshit."

Mark continued. "There's no *one* beginning point for this Francés route. Medieval pilgrims started from their homes, entering the route wherever they could. Intuition tells me this mountain isn't what *your* pilgrimage is about, or it wouldn't have unfolded this way. Good, you listened to your gut." I was stunned at how easily this man could read me. He continued, "I'm pretty sure your physical body is trying to keep up with the demands your soul came to do—until you push it too far."

Wow! He saw right through me. Tears emerged from nowhere. *Who me? Push myself too far?*

Roman jumped in. "This is a marathon, not a sprint. Your lessons will be delivered in the *long* haul, not up here. These mountains could ruin your leg for the rest of the trip. I'm guessing your body's saying, 'I'll have your back, if you have mine.'"

My jaw dropped, wondering how they knew my master plan. I shared the pact made. "I promised my body that *it* calls the shots, not my ego aiming for Santiago." I reached for tissues. The *Camino* reveals the truth when the student is ready.

"Hey, grab your Pilgrim Passport. Follow me," Mark said. I complied. You know, the whole *Camino*-sucking vortex thing and all. Inside, he stamped my booklet. "You've earned this," and he hugged me encouragingly.

Outside, Roman gathered his belongings to continue his climb. Kneeling to adjust his laces, he scooped up a handful of dirt. He looked up at me as it slowly sifted through his fingers, cascading to the ground like a waterfall. "You won't understand this now, but this is holy dirt, Molly. Wrap your whole being in it. Get dirty." I filed his words away. He was right. I didn't understand.

Hugging goodbye, he reminded me, "Use the snake venom," and wished me "*Buen Camino*," then was gone. Gratitude washed over me, and this new reality kicked in—*The Camino provides.*

"Molly, more hot soup for your ride to Roncesvalles?" the cook broadcasted. Leaning out the kitchen window, smiling ear to ear with a twinkle in his eye, he handed me a warm thermos.

"Wow. Gracias!" I responded.

Overwhelmed by the kindness (with leaking eyes), I added to my NOTES section:

ROMAN, MARK, AND THE SMILING COOK—ANGELS TWO, THREE, AND FOUR

 CAMINO MESSAGE #3
The Camino provides

ROOTS

I parked myself on a large rock overlooking the luscious green valleys and snowy peaks to wait for my ride. Warming my cold hands around the soup container, a group of women speaking various languages passed, calling, "*Buen Camino!*" This *was* my *Camino* (for now).

A young girl, maybe twelve years old, walked by with her father. I met them briefly earlier. Her tall, thin frame and long hair parted down the middle barely allowed a glimpse of her sweet face. She reminded me of myself at that awkward age. I thought of my father (twelve years gone). How amazing it would've been to share this experience with him. My mother would've worried and fussed so much had Dad ever considered doing such a crazy thing, he would've bowed out to keep the peace. Had she demonstrated that same angst toward *me* about doing this walk, my inner rebel would have packed faster (and left sooner). Such was our family dynamic.

Roman and Mark's exorcism of my *I'm doing this wrong* thinking, and their grounding presence, dissolved my body tension in record time. The relief even seemed to boost my leg's healing. Then, as if delivered an instant invitation to the "Life Review Hot Seat," memories of some well-rooted life events (the good, the bad, and the ugly) surfaced. A "roots of the matter" internal examination? *Challenge accepted!* I dug deep, thinking it might explain why I ever thought this *Camino* thing could be a good idea.

My first root to review appeared front and center—Michael. As if hearing me whisper his name, I instantly sensed his spirit in the breeze and could hear his sweet Spanish guitar.

PART TWO

THE ROOTS OF THE MATTER

CHAPTER 3

MICHAEL

Bristlecone Pine
~ Michael Johnson

"You know that moment when it's time to end a phone call, but you can't seem to do it gracefully? Hanging up while the other person is speaking would be too obvious, and, rude. Instead, hit the disconnect button while you're the one doing the talking. They never suspect. C'mon. Who would cut off their own sentence right in the middle of making a point? No one. It looks like an unfortunate dropped call. No harm. No foul."

~ Michael Johnson

A typical conversation with Michael Johnson. That's all one word, by the way. MichaelJohnson. Friends for twenty-five years, I couldn't mistake his distinct voice. Yet, anytime he left a message he'd say, "Hey, Molly, MichaelJohnson calling. Give me a call when you want to. I hope you want to today."

Michael never missed an opportunity to cleverly skirt a challenging conversation, so his "just hang up while you're talking" idea didn't surprise me. "I have to hang up now" felt like a conflict to him. He was an honest guy who didn't like to rub people the wrong way. Though he did that anyway with his dysfunctional efforts *not* to. Therapy success—he finally got it. Ahhh…growth.

Michael had weaknesses (hell, don't we all). But I recall his gentle, funny manner, how he loved his friends, how his twisted stories triggered our sarcastic eye rolls, and his willingness (much later in life) to be accountable after any careless action. Mostly, I loved the in-depth conversations we shared about life. I met Michael thirty years prior when my then-partner was his sound engineer. I couldn't have possibly predicted the importance Michael's friendship played in future years.

Hard to fathom the gray matter cooking up "hang up while you're the one talking" cohabitated with the same brilliant brain cells that created the magic flowing from his classically trained fingertips when playing guitar. A 72-year perfectionist, singer/songwriter, still touring and mesmerizing his following on a seemingly endless magic carpet ride. In Nashville, Michael was the "go-to guy" for the secrets to guitar mastery. However, no student could match the spiritual infusion and soul madness only Michael could bring to the strings. In later concert years, he couldn't dodge the frequent requests for his old hits (now heard in grocery store aisles) such as "Bluer Than Blue." His smooth, liquid sound never disappointed—a true master of his craft.

How could one with an expert level of competence and demand for personal excellence in his craft fall so sadly short in his private life's "love fulfillment" column? He had also made an art out of avoidance, criticism, inconsistency, addiction, and too often, breaking hearts. Despite his flaws, I loved him—truly, madly, deeply. And he loved me right back.

Despite our mutual admiration for each other, we discovered early on that being in a romantic entanglement would prove destructive, so we carved out a rare sacred friendship. Knowing his negative habits had broken *my* heart on more than one occasion, Michael learned to intercept any thoughtless moves, fearing losing our bond. He once wrote, "My dear Molly, the wiser, better, more evolved man buried inside wants to meet you in your loving realm—so I can see myself as you see me, and finally exhale." His poetic manner never failed to melt me.

In early 2016, Michael played his last concert performance using oxygen due to advanced emphysema—damn cigarettes. He was depressed and didn't want to talk, so I didn't hear from him much. Talking is tough when you can barely breathe. Reading was challenging, too, because putting his head down restricted his oxygen. One night, on one of our rare calls, he mentioned, "Damn Molly, I wish I could read *The Alchemist* by Coelho just one more time. You know what it means to me." He understood it as *his* story. He gifted me the book ten years prior, and it highlighted our special bond—two *Wanderer* archetypes, forever seeking.

The solution was clear. I'd read it to him over the phone. Over several weeks, I'd read a chapter, and we'd talk about the meaning gleaned from it. One particular chapter (and what Michael said about it) remains etched in my mind. A quick recap: Santiago meets the Alchemist in the desert, and later, as they part, the Alchemist tells Santiago that he must travel the rest of the desert alone to claim his power and Personal Legend.

I uncovered more about Michael's heart in those precious conversations than in all previous years. Many would say he'd fulfilled his purpose, his legend, by following his passion for music. "The truth?" Michael said, "Music was the easy part. Sure, I was diligent and disciplined in my art. It was *part* of my destiny. But it was never 'the desert' my soul was being called to cross. Music and travel came naturally. My 'desert challenge' was to cross the barren land to finally open my heart, and I never accomplished that. I hid from it, lied about it, gave lip service to it. I never had the balls to step up and really love. You know, the hard kind of love. The messy stick-with-it kind of love. Oh, I've had my moments. I'd like to think I've loved my boys. Though they might say differently. But the rest was pseudo-love. I'm sad I'll die without claiming *this* part of my legend. I can be such an asshole. I loved the easy parts. Disappeared for the uncomfortable ones. My heart's like a steel trap, and I never could get past the pain that locked it up."

It killed me to listen as Michael cautioned me *not* to make the same mistake—to not shy from my *own* desert (whatever it might be). It made me wonder. *What is my desert?*

The following summer, Michael died suddenly. It wasn't emphysema, but a sudden heart attack that took him. I felt thankful for his quick, painless exit. Yet, the early loss without saying goodbye took my breath away. He was my soul brother. This would take time to heal. I never had the chance to tell Michael I'd walk the *Camino de Santiago* to face my desert and hopefully meet my own alchemist.

A year later, several months before leaving for Spain, we spread his ashes at the foot of a bristlecone pine in the Colorado mountains, not far from his childhood home. We played his mesmerizing song, "Bristlecone Pine." It whispered through the trees and the surrounding canyon like a final outdoor performance. Before leaving, I found a small, sparkling rock glistening in the sun under his special pine. I tucked it into my jacket pocket.

Driving home, I thought: *My Camino is only months away. I'll soon follow Michael's directive: to answer the call to "cross my desert."* I held the small rock tightly in my pocket. I longed to tell Michael I suspected the *Camino* would tempt countless, risky challenges and how that scared the hell outta me. I like to be in control. In this journey, I'd have little. Fear led me to curse Michael, *The Alchemist,* and Paulo Coelho, for ever planting this metaphorical idea of some crazy desert waiting for me.

Michael's warning tale inspired an adventurous journey I felt compelled to do, yet one I understood very little about. At this point, neither I nor this sparkling rock knew that it'd be going along with me for this wild *Camino* ride.

CHAPTER 4

LIFE'S a BEACH

JULY 2017 ERIE, PENNSYLVANIA

I flew east to visit my sister in Pennsylvania, several weeks before the news of Michael's death. There, the call to walk the *Camino* would unfold, and my personal "desert to cross" would be unveiled.

Sitting on the bow of my brother-in-law's 33-foot sailboat, I held a beer in one hand while the other kept my crutches from sliding off the deck. Left behind in the car: a left knee brace and my right ankle boot. I booked this trip well before the MRI reported two torn ligaments from a snowshoe incident months prior. My sister encouraged, "Come anyway, who cares if you look like the centerfold for *Orthopedic Monthly?*"

Our sailboat glided out into Lake Erie, past a certain beach that held a distinct memory from forty years ago. Beach 10.

On many college summer-school mornings (1976), I'd head for Beach 10 to make sand candles to sell as centerpieces for beach restaurants. Arriving at sunrise with fire and candle-making supplies and extra sunscreen, I never tired of this Zen, all-day process.

At day's end, I'd walk out to Seagull Point and return with a shoulder bag filled with beautiful driftwood for candle-making the next day.

I returned one evening, surprised to find the beach unusually quiet, with only one boat on shore. Two families extinguishing campfires loaded up beach toys and waved hello as I turned down the trail to the parking lot. From a parallel trail, a strange man hurriedly cut through the bushes.

The pounding of his feet running down the trail echoed behind me. Hairs stood up on my arms, and my stomach tightened as the sound got louder and closer. I anxiously moved my wide load of driftwood to the side so he'd pass—he didn't. In a swift attack from behind, he jumped me, sending wood flying—a violent struggle began. We landed hard on sharp, scattered wood. I met his rape attempt with a fierce fight. We rumbled on the ground, rolling over the wood. He tried to control me by pinning me down and stuffing a rough towel in my mouth but failed. My heart pounded out of my chest—I struggled, fighting for my life and praying the families on the beach were still there. My three shrill screams pierced the otherwise calm evening, until a hard blow with a piece of wood silenced me.

"We're coming!" A male voice yelled. Relief mixed with the adrenalin. *My prayer was heard.* The attacker jumped up, and in the heat of the moment, I jumped just as fast. Desperately grabbing a sharp stick, I threatened, "I'll ram it through your fucking gut if you come at me again!" I wondered, *could I actually kill him? Yes. I could.* Panicked by the approaching rescue team, the madman bolted. My heightened awareness then went to the driftwood impaled in the back of my thigh, and my dislocated knee. Adrenaline still coursing, I quickly pulled out the wood, slammed my knee into place and limped toward the approaching two men and their three young boys. These angels saved my life.

They carried me to my car. Still in shock, I expressed deep gratitude. They ensured the car started and the doors locked me in, as I promised, "Yes, I'll report this and get medical help." *First, I've gotta get to my sister's apartment. It's safe there.* My head rushed with haunting thoughts of my mother's warning: *Molly, you're an accident waiting to happen. Be more careful.* Unprepared to deal with the risk of her hearing about this, I drove to a friend's instead.

Grateful the worst-case scenario was dodged, in the months and years that followed, I couldn't deny the free spirit inside me died on the beach that night. It'd be a long time before any sign of resurrection.

Now, forty years later, secure on this sailboat passing the same beach, it troubled me to still be dealing with the same injuries from the incident. Emotional anxiety no longer stirred regarding the incident—I spent many years healing this trauma. My body, however, seemed to be holding onto the insult.

At that moment, I mostly felt relief. My years of work paid off. But forty years of these injuries was enough damn time. I silently vowed *I'll do whatever it takes to heal. I just need some sort of carrot to hold this inspiration.* That's when the inner voice suddenly answered.

The Voice: *I have the perfect solution. You'll walk the Camino de Santiago.*

I was startled by the Voice itself, let alone its crazy suggestion.

Me: *Yeah, right. Thanks, but no thanks. I'm not walking the Camino.*
I ruled out that idea when my friend Patrick mentioned it a year ago.

The Voice: *Well, I think you are going to walk it.*

Me: *I said I need a carrot, not a death march. C'mon, I have two torn ligaments here!*

The Voice: *The way I see it, it's your only chance to blast the old belief you've held onto for way too long. You know what I'm talking about.*

Me: *You mean, I'm an accident waiting to happen? Nah. I've let that go.*

The Voice: *Not true. You've only covered it up, like frosted poop.*

Me: *Are you done?*

The Voice: *For now.*

I eventually came to know this *Voice* as wise input from my soul, my higher-self. Wise or not, the *Camino* idea sounded crazy.

As we sailed farther out, the past now in the rearview mirror, I smiled for having created a rich life, one never imagined in darker days.

However, it seemed *the Voice* had some wild scheme about a rendezvous in Spain for further closure. I think not! *The Voice,* unwilling to be completely silenced, made it clear that it would be a force to be reckoned with once I returned to Colorado.

CHAPTER 5

THE GREAT BLUE HERON

Old Friends/Bookends
~ Simon and Garfunkel

Powder-blue, polyester, wide bell-bottoms, and saddle shoes with blue wool knee socks. That's the visual Linda always shared when describing the first day she met me in our college freshman dorm. I'd always remind her that she omitted the part about my sterling silver charm bracelet jingling with charms collected since third grade. Hard to un-see all that. Linda Marie Simpson and I bonded that day for life. Sadly, her life fell about thirty years short of our intended plan. It'd take walking 500 miles through a tunnel of grace to accept that she had an appointment with The Great Blue Heron.

JULY 2017

Arriving home from Pennsylvania, I tossed my crutches and immediately called my dear friend, Linda. "Hey, bud, ya better crank up your puzzle-solving brilliance. Really bizarre things happened in Pennsylvania. Some strange voice in my head kicked in—promising to heal these ancient injuries." After sharing every detail, Linda offered up her feisty opinion.

"Walk 500 miles across Spain? No, thank you! Ick, I can taste the dust now." I wasn't surprised. She's the Queen. I'm the Bohemian. "But you know me, Mol. Any chance to sort puzzle pieces in one of your weird plots—I'm game!" Thankfully, she was a master at it.

With decades of mutual trust between us, brain probes and poking the bear were fair game. After intently listening, Linda tossed out three thoughts. Hanging up, I took our puzzle data, her questions, and disappeared into my cave. With a journal and pen, I'd determine an action plan to return my body to a healthy state. First step, contemplate Linda's questions.

Question 1: *What if the idea about doing the Camino isn't to be taken literally? You're all about metaphors, right? What if the concept is metaphorical, suggesting some equivalent healing journey? What if walking 500 miles sabotages your healing?*

Linda couldn't grasp why anyone would walk 500 miles. She loved to travel, but not in hiking boots. However, her question was valid.

Question 2: *Would walking the Camino be about proving your body could meet the challenge? If so, isn't that redundant? You've already proven you're a tough cookie to a wicked fault. What's left for you and your body to prove, Mol?*

Ouch. Okay, point taken. I reframed her question. *What would it take to create a plan for my body's needs, not my ego's?*

Question 3: *Are you prepared to ditch the "I'm an accident waiting to happen" story for good? You can't walk with that belief hovering. You've powered through physical challenges just to disprove that belief and never listened to your body's needs. What has it cost you?*

She was right. At some point, I disconnected from my body. *I* and *it* were separate entities. My body seemed, at worst, the enemy. At best, an ally (but only if it cooperated). Let's just say, my body hadn't exactly been on my Christmas card list. I usually skirted knee and back issues, unconsciously fearing the emotions locked in my injuries—emotions I wanted to leave behind.

Highlighting these unproductive habits, the *Camino* idea moved down the list of wise considerations. By day two, my journal filled with confessions, victories, and flashbacks, taking me to my college days when a sleep disorder firmly settled in (after the assault). I lived in a sleepless fog yet somehow completed my Master's, taught for four years, and danced until 4 a.m. in Buffalo discos—functioning on autopilot and rarely feeling present.

Moving to Colorado, it hit me. I'd ignored caring for my body for too long. Intrigued with kayaking, mountain biking, and hiking, I discovered I could play hard with new healing methods. Massage, pilates, healthy eating, Rolfing®, and chiropractic became routine. My efforts rewarded me physically, emotionally, and spiritually. The door to trusting my body opened significantly until old injuries haunted me again, making these recent injuries even more disheartening.

On day three, Linda texted. "How's the puzzle coming, Sherlock?"

Ready to close my journal, one final startling question crawled out of my pen. I tried to dismiss it. Didn't work.

Now that you've finally shown up for your body, what if the injuries are here to stay, and all this damn effort is just too late?

These defeatist words shook me. *Too late to course-correct? No! My body can't forsake me now.* Only one surprising solution pushed to the front. I called Linda.

"Linda, I'm walking the damn *Camino*, and I'm walking it alone."

I prepared for her inevitable rebuttal.

"Wow, okay. But WHY?"

"You know how I've always pushed my body, wanting it to prove something to me? That ends *now*. My 'desert to cross,' as Michael would say, is for me to prove something *to my body*. That I can show up for it. Love it. Listen to it. Lay down my sword against it. No more *I* and *it*. To survive this would require being a *we*. We'll set a wise pace with the guts to pull back when needed. A win can't equal making it to Santiago. A win's gotta be forging an inspired devotion for this body."

Gently blowing her nose, voice cracking, Linda finally spoke. "You've always been the bravest person I know. But that's the *most* courageous thing you've ever said. How can I help?"

"Stick by me. Be my biggest cheerleader. I'm gonna need you." Our sacred pact was sealed. Surprised at my clear reasoning and inspired by it,

I'd call Michael that night to report I understood what "my desert" was. But I never got the chance. His sister called *me* first.

"Oh Molly, it's about Michael. Breaks my heart to tell you, he died today. A heart attack."

Catching my breath after this devastating conversation, I called Linda back.

We always sensed that if she and I weren't who we already were, we'd likely switch and morph into being the other. Most of our forty-year friendship was spent states apart. Yet, so profoundly, we swam in the same beliefs, explored the same spiritual teachers, shared a connection to the Mother Mary archetype, and were both drawn to the magic of the raven totem. We breathed in the same sparkly magic about life as if we woke with glitter in our hair from the other's dream the night before.

We spent hours talking of Michael, life, death, and healing my heart. Linda knew how to lighten things up. She grilled me with *Camino* questions: "What about your back and knee? How's physical therapy going? Will a donkey carry your pack? *Really, Linda, a donkey?* Will you find no-grain, no-dairy food in Spain?"

Late one night, she texted a funny, rambling message.

> I know it's still two years away, but will you be able to call me from the *Camino* if there's a problem? You know, Mol, I think you'll have fun. I just wish you weren't going alone. Are you packing your sexy knee braces? They'll surely drive the French men wild!" 😆 😆 😆 😆 😆

These late-night texts had become tradition, but little did I know this would be our last.

Linda's husband, John, called. "Mol, Linda's gone." A brain aneurysm took her in twenty minutes. Like a deer in headlights, I could barely breathe. Ravens surrounded my deck for the next two days, their magic lost on me.

I took her spirit on a hike with me before traveling to her celebration of life service in Buffalo, where I'd speak. *What do I say to your family and friends? Are you even with me? Linda, are you listening?*

Tell The Great Blue Heron story suddenly popped into my head. We discussed this story's profound message about abrupt life changes only a few weeks prior. The irony was overwhelming. I recognized the idea as being Linda's (given the sparkles circling it). *Okay, the Heron story it will be.*

Feeling Linda's strong presence, I talked to her. *I have to say the ravens were a nice touch after you died. And, ya know, if I still had them in my closet, I'd proudly wear powder-blue bell-bottoms and saddle shoes for your service.*

I'm pretty sure I saw five laughing emojis in the clouds.

Walking home, it hit me—the sting shifted to anger. *My two soul friends woven into the very fabric of who I am—are gone. Linda, what about our sacred pact? And damn it, Michael, you leaving so abruptly feels like you hung up on me while you were doing the talking.* Any former *Camino* inspiration lost its fire.

I think Linda reminded me of *The Great Blue Heron* story to emphasize our poignant conversation regarding its meaning. I understood what she wanted me to consider, but I needed time to figure out the rules of this messy game of life. At the moment, it felt like a reckless, betraying house of cards.

THE CYCLIST

BY MARK NEPO
(AKA: "THE GREAT BLUE HERON STORY")

On the day of the world-class race, he waited at the start with the others and felt that life was waiting for him in those hills. Was this the day his dream would come true? He couldn't quite say why, but he sensed a blessing was about to happen. As the starting gun went off, he could hear the rush of all the racers breathing—like young horses in the morning.

He had trained for months, up and down the sloping hills, cutting off seconds by wearing less and leaning into curves. His legs were shanks of muscle. He often said, "It's the closest thing to flying I know." On the second hill, the other racers thinned, and he neared the front. They were slipping through the land like arcs of light riding through the veins of the world. By now, he was in the lead.

As he swept toward the wetlands, he was well ahead of the pack and gaining time, when out of nowhere a Great Blue Heron took off and swooped right in front of him; its massive, timeless wings opening just in front of his handlebars and brushing his fingers. Its shadow covered him and seemed to open something in his soul he'd been chasing. The others were pumping closer, but he just stopped and stood there, straddling his bike, staring at what the Great Blue Heron had opened in him cutting through the sky.

In years to come, others would sometimes stop him and ask, "What cost you the race?" Wherever he was, he'd always look south, and he'd say, "I didn't lose the race—I left it."

PART THREE

THE PILGRIM PREPARES

CHAPTER 6

TAKING THE "HELL" OUT of GUIDEBOOK HELP

Still perched on the hardest seat in the house in this Pyrenees theater, I reflected back to that challenging period after losing Linda. I was positive she yanked me from my grief and placed me back on track to prepare for my *Camino* two years ago.

OCTOBER 2017

Several months after Linda died, *Camino* inspiration slowly reignited. Immediately, the anxiety gremlins set up camp, gleefully disclosing my insecurities. Ear plugs helped.

In *The Pilgrim's Guide to the Camino de Santiago* (2019), author John Brierley states:

> "It's always advisable to put in some physical training before you go. I would be surprised if more than 10% of pilgrims actually act on this advice."

I refused to be one of the foolish pilgrims in the 90 percent. I excitedly informed my friends, Patrick and Bill, about my *Camino* decision. Patrick initially introduced the idea a year before. Both completed the pilgrimage separately in recent years and knew what lay ahead for me. Without skipping a beat, Bill tossed guidebooks and trail apps my way. Both promised they'd have my back in preparing to confidently walk the Pyrenees and beyond.

The plan: I'd depart for Spain in May 2019, leaving me eighteen months to rehab and train. Given my past assault history, the idea of walking alone raised eyebrows in my inner circle. However, Bill and Patrick assured me that my plan was safe. The gremlins shuddered.

TRAINING

My mind raced. *I really shouldn't be alive. After all, I'd once been beaten by a madman trying to kill me. I'd aimed to go up in the ill-fated Challenger space shuttle. And, once in sixth grade I talked back to Sister Vianney. Any of these could have taken me out. So, why the hell am I feeling this sense of danger? I'm just walking into the gym with my 500-mile goal. Maybe it's the decades of poor habits and beliefs to undo. Or past attempts at weight training causing further back and knee injuries.*

So, I opted to train my legs for a 500-mile walk—by walking. Brilliant. Living in the Rocky Mountains, I could be on a hiking trail in minutes. However, the rest of my body was sentenced to gym weights to prepare for carrying a twenty-pound backpack. My trainer served as my conscience. Our short-term goal: slow increments, pull back when I'd typically push forward, and build an internal belief that strength can be a dominant force in my life. Psychological strength first, then I'd slowly increase weight levels.

Patrick, Bill, and I were the gym Three Musketeers. My trainer reminded me to put on the brakes, and Bill and Patrick encouraged applying the gas. Pat nudged me to raise the weight when he sensed I was ready. I'd register my body's internal response: it was either *Yep, I am being a weenie, Pat's right* (one always hesitates to say those words to Pat), or, *Nope, no deal, Pat. I'm keeping the weight as is.* At the latter, he'd just shake his head. My intuitive listening skills sharpened quickly.

Bill's ongoing *Camino* tales were a much-needed motivational carrot that reminded me this was more than a torture trek. Without Pat and Bill's encouragement, I would've progressed too slowly. The gremlins were losing ground.

In the final five months of training, the Three Musketeers parted ways. Patrick moved to the East Coast, and Bill's job schedule shifted. I was on my own. Before departing, however, they shared surprising news. "We've decided to return to walk the *Camino* together, in the same time frame as you. Don't worry. We'll start several days behind you so you can walk alone. But now you'll have friends in the country with you."

An ear-to-ear smile surfaced. "A perfect plan!"

I felt Linda's protective hand in this. My cheerleader was with me after all. Was high-fiving dead people standard *Camino* training protocol? It wasn't mentioned in the guidebook.

BOOTS, CAN OPENERS, AND MORE STUFF

I love REI. And REI loves me. I rolled out of bed into their aisles and smiling faces almost daily. I needed stuff—lots of stuff. Listen, my friends (and the guidebooks) said so. But you can't just buy things and call it good. Nope. You haul all the shit home just so experienced *Camino* friends can tell you, "You don't need that," "You freakin' need a bigger one," "A lighter one," or "You need three more."

In The Pilgrim's Guide, John Brierly addressed "what to bring," stressing how pilgrims always bring too much and that knees and feet will buckle if you carry more than essentials. He stressed this point regarding socks:

> *"Bring several pairs of socks as it is a good idea to change socks a couple times and massage your feet halfway through the day (even if you don't think they need it)."*

If only this tip had been in a LARGE neon font. Missing it cost me dearly.

The gold stars definitely go to the brave men and women of the REI shoe department.

We're family now. They smiled as I returned the tenth hiking shoe they'd given me to try. For the record, don't even *hope* you'll end up with that attractive boot you love with the adorable colors. Ain't gonna happen. I guarantee the ugly gray and shit-brown ones will fit you best. Sorry.

The shoe gods had mercy, and I *finally* landed the proper boot. Next stop: Valentine Shoe Store for orthotics. Result: boots that fit right for the first time ever, and a walking shoe that perfectly cradled my high arch (aka my "magic shoes"). Footwear was checked off the list.

Karen, a friend of thirty-five years and a *Camino* veteran, was my go-to for tips. Like me, she faces food challenges and advised, "Scope out *mercados* (markets) for fresh and canned foods when everything else is dripping with melted cheese on white bread. Pack a small can opener—it's a must!" Little did I know, the packing police would be coming for me.

RENÉ

Some friends thought accompanying me to Spain might be interesting. I kindly declined—this was mine to do alone. Then, five months before leaving, René said, "I'd love to walk the first week with you." No one was more surprised than I when, without hesitation, "Yes! Great!" fell out of my mouth. It felt right and sounded ridiculously fun.

René made this fire-aim-ready decision, knowing little about the *Camino*. Most curious was her comment, "It's strange. Walking this crazy thing was never on my radar. I just sense I'm to go with you." This, too, had Linda's sparkles all over it. We decided we'd fly together and walk seven days from St. Jean Pied de Porte to Logrono. From there, she'd return to the US, and I'd continue solo.

René has a knack for calling things as she sees them, while being easily amused by life's absurdities. We figured the first week could be tough. We also knew our tendency to view screwups with a ridiculous lens—a twisted one that would save our sanity. Together, we spelled trouble. There could be no better friend with whom to take the "hell" out of guidebook help.

7 A.M. MARGARITAS

One night, Bill and I watched *The Way* (the movie where most pilgrims first fall under the vortex spell). I'd already decided to go (with or without the movie), but one scene sealed the deal in my mind. *I must make it at least as far as The Cruz de Ferro (the Iron Cross)*. Since the eleventh century, this mountain of rocks marks where pilgrims leave a stone representing something to be released or honored. It seemed an easy goal, right? That impression was abruptly marred later by Brierley's guidebook:

> *"This day is a peak experience for many. While the ascent to the Iron Cross is steep in places, and will require determination, remember that far more injuries (sprains and strains) are experienced in the treacherous downhill that has an extremely sharp rocky descent."*

My knees squirmed. They'd surely fail this steep descent. Assignment: research treatment options to resolve knee pain.

Following much procrastination due to the terror of long needles with no anesthesia, I finally scheduled prolotherapy for my knees one month apart. The gist: inject hormone nutrients into the injured, over-stretched ligaments, intentionally inflaming the tissue to cause the body to build new stronger tissue. Genius. Except that meant no painkillers, no anti-inflammatories—before, during, or after treatment.

The doctor suggested a tranquilizer to withstand the eight to ten painful injections. Then she asked, "Hey, do you like margaritas?" An unexpected but easy question. "I don't encourage making a habit of this, but consider mixing yourself a strong margarita (maybe two) on top of the tranquilizer. You'll feel pain, but you won't care." Things were getting stranger by the minute. This plan wasn't in the guidebook! "Oh," she added, "Have a designated driver."

The night before my appointment, I did what any responsible patient did before a medical procedure. I laid out my Valium, a shot glass, margarita mix, a bottle of tequila, and a cutting board. Oh, don't forget the limes. My brave friend Sallyanne arrived to pick me up. I was smashed, with a third margarita ready for the road. Hey, if two were good, three would be better, right? Not being a big drinker (and definitely not a tranquilizer consumer), Sallyanne was amused by the unlikely drunk occupying the passenger seat with ice clinking in her glass. She laughed at me with compassion, providing a perfect balance of friendship.

When the procedure began, I squeezed her fingers as the pain escalated. The doctor quickly graduated me from hand holding. "Here, use this tennis ball." If I'd been sober, I would have noted Sallyanne's relief.

I survived the injections with a slight recollection of asking, "Hey, what about another shot of alcohol over here." The doctor reached for the bottle amidst her medical supplies, making me *simpatico* with cowboys in old westerns requesting another shot of whiskey when removing a bullet from their leg.

With drugs and alcohol in full swing, I don't recall the rest of the procedure, the ride home, or Sallyanne tucking me in to sleep it off.

One knee down. The way I saw it, this put me halfway to the Iron Cross.

CHAPTER 7

WHAT COULD GO WRONG?

This Is It
~ Kenny Loggins

Reality check. The soup warming my cold hands affirmed actually being on this mountaintop. I needed confirmation because the way things went south just a week before coming, I almost didn't make it here.

MAY 3 – MAY 10, 2019

WEEKEND WARRIORS

The mind gremlins returned for a final convention a week before leaving for Spain. They were holding court for our lack of training. In my defense, the knee injections caused training delays, and René had a work crunch. But hey, we had a plan. We scheduled a fifteen-mile walk the Saturday before leaving to prove we could survive it. The day before, I planned another ten-mile hike with other friends. Ugh.

René and I set out for our trial walk. At the ten-mile mark, we were spent, though my knee ligaments were noticeably more stable likely thanks to the third margarita. The last five miles kicked our ass. Sweat-drenched and ragged, we laughed—this would be an *average* day on the *Camino*. What had we gotten ourselves into? Regardless, we were jazzed to do this crazy thing.

Getting out of bed Sunday morning, a searing pain in my right hamstring dropped me to the floor. *How dare this renegade body part rebel now. Damn. Is it torn? Pulled?* I inched down the steps on my butt, crawling to the kitchen for ice. The gremlin chatter was deafening. *Really, girls? A fifteen-mile walk with no prep? Brilliant.*

Friday was departure day, so I invested a fortune in bodywork for the next 48 hours. There was little improvement by Tuesday, and pain now in both hamstrings. Barely able to climb my stairs, I cringed, gripping the railing and envisioning the Pyrenees. Reluctantly, I called René to report my status. Her patience was a gift. Close friends understood the old "accident waiting to happen" saga. Rene encouraged, "Continue therapy, and whatever happens, we'll deal."

Calling upon my new mindset, it took everything I had to fight the reruns playing in my head. *New rule: Crossing my desert starts now. I'm on my body's side—not its opponent. Wow, where'd that come from?*

SABOTAGE

Wednesday's slight improvement wasn't enough. I dreaded calling Patrick because I'd listened at length about his *Camino* three years before. For months, he cheered me on to experience my own. He likely thought my call was to ask another "important" packing question like: "How many almond butter packets should I take—four? Twenty?" But not *this* call.

"Hey, Pat, I'll just get to the point," I sighed. "It's crazy. I seriously screwed up my hamstrings and can barely walk up my stairs. It kills me to say this, but I think I've gotta wait and do this *next* spring."

He didn't skip a beat. "Sorry, but you've mistaken me for someone who'd buy this story. Not going is *not* an option. You might not walk right away, but you're going. Think about it, Molly. Your reason for going is to work through injuries, not hide from them. I think the *Camino* is testing you."

I weighed his words with the inner voice he wasn't aware of. *I promised my body veto power.* Big dilemma. *Which voice belongs to my wise self, which to the doubting voice of my past?*

Patrick hesitated, "I have another question, but I don't want to hurt your feelings."

"Go ahead, ask."

"Could you be sabotaging yourself so you don't have to go?"

He knew me well. I wanted to fight him on this, but my teary response spilled out. "I hope not. But if that's true, it's deeply unconscious. I've worked so hard for this."

Pat's next words pushed me to my final decision. "You choose, Molly. You can get on the plane in two days and start walking when it heals (and it *will* because you're meant to do this). In the meantime, find rides to keep up with René. Or, stay home pouting in your kitchen, and in a week when your hamstrings heal, kick yourself knowing you should be in Spain. I'll be so disappointed if you don't go."

My perspective flipped quickly. I checked in with my body. We both knew Patrick was right. Again, hard words to admit to Pat. Decision: I'd be on Friday's flight. My challenge: be ready in thirty-six hours.

ABOUT THIS CAN OPENER

Twenty-four hours before departure, Karen, scanning every potential item going, noticed the different backpack in the corner. "Hell, did your pack grow larger?"

"My doc recommended taking my knee braces. So, I borrowed this bigger pack." I could hear her mind calculating the added weight.

My packing police (experienced in this 500-mile game) gave a firm "no go" on many items, including my heavy journal. Brutal. Then came the anticipated reprimand: "Really, Molly, you couldn't find a smaller can opener? This is a flippin' monster!"

Begging for mercy, "I'll die a grizzly death of starvation without it!" We laughed, and it was granted a reprieve. Despite paring down, the pack still felt uncomfortably heavy—because it was.

DO THE VOICES IN MY HEAD BOTHER YOU?

Surprisingly calm, I collapsed into bed that night, though the gremlins scratched at the door. In these quiet moments, it seemed wise to call a mind committee meeting. The committee consisted of: 1. *The Voice*—my soul's highest intuitive voice. 2. The general commentators—sometimes wise, often neurotic and ask a lot of questions. 3. The gremlins—these suckers are negative little bastards who can't wait to criticize and point out every mistake and predict doom around every corner. This invitation was for general commentators only. No gremlins allowed.

As if turning the pages of a faded photo album, I reviewed the decades that rolled out the red carpet to this moment. *Our Camino actually began long ago, and starting tomorrow, we'll add one more day, then another, and another, as we've always done. Simple.*

One nasty gremlin squeezed under the door. *Don't give me this one-day-at-a-time bullshit. Look at you! You're freakin' limping! We've never relied on a stupid can opener for survival before, and no one here speaks Spanish! We're all gonna die!* I smothered him with a pillow.

The committee seemed surprised I had no lofty *Camino* goals. Sure, I had "crossing the desert" guidelines for honoring my body's needs, but I had no burning questions to answer. The *Camino* could paint my experience as it saw fit. If I had any plan, it was simply to have fun—with a healthy leg.

Some members shuddered at walking this proverbial cliff's edge without guardrails. I assured them, *I'll have my AAA membership road service card,* and *we can be helicoptered off any mountaintop with one easy call if necessary.* With my sarcasm alive and well, they figured I must be in my right mind and quieted.

One more brief conversation before sleep. This one with *the Voice*. After all, it started this escapade. First, a request. I asked *the Voice, can you reserve time on our flight tomorrow to discuss something important?* It agreed. Second, a question. *Something feels unsettled, as if some big shift is brewing. Is this an ending of sorts?*

The Voice answered, *just the end of what's familiar.*

THE MAD DASH

Friday morning brought nervous tears. *What the hell am I doing?* I finished packing with Karen and Peggy's help. Patrick's phone call to rally my spirit also helped the cause. Our noon deadline to leave for the airport hovered. "What am I forgetting?"

"Nothing! You're forgetting nothing!" Karen and Peggy claimed while I hobbled back upstairs. "Nope, I'm forgetting something."

On my dresser lay my sparkling "Michael rock." I grabbed it for the Iron Cross. Next, I slid Linda's wooden beaded bracelets onto my wrist. I'd wear them until I returned. *The Voice* caught me by surprise with an unexpected directive. *Choose several songs. Store them on your phone.*

I hadn't planned on bringing music, but, obeying, intuition chose the tunes. Loading them, I caught my reflection. My thought: *Who will she be the next time I look in this mirror?*

Downstairs, I zipped the rock into the designated Iron Cross pocket. *Now I have everything.* At the last minute, intuition said to leave out the heavy knee braces. I tossed my pack and trekking poles into an old suitcase to be discarded in France. We hugged Peggy goodbye, piled in Karen's van, and rushed to meet René at the Denver airport. Peggy shook her head as she waved us off, holding back what read boldly on her face—*I swear you're all flippin' nuts!*

CHAPTER 8

SPIRITUAL NEGOTIATIONS
at 36,000 FEET

100,000 Angels
~ Bliss

Walkers passed my rock perch fully caffeinated, calling "*Buen Camino*" as my root memories surfaced. My guess, each passing pilgrim had their own root excavation going on. *My* digging timeline advanced to departure from the Denver airport.

MAY 10, 2019, DENVER AIRPORT

René and I boarded our Denver-NY-Frankfurt flight like bubbling cocktails of curiosity with a twist of humor and a splash of angst. Given my hamstring wild card, I kept thoughts light, sometimes ridiculous, just to deal with everything. I imagined my mind gremlin committee following as stowaways. Scanning the crowd, I curiously looked for signs of Linda. *Hey, Linda, a stuffed blue heron on a sporty hat would be rockin'!* Only self-restraint prevented me from asking the flamboyant woman beside me, "Excuse me, do the voices in my head bother you?"

On our long flight, I walked the aisles to ease my hamstrings. A man stretching his legs asked, "So, where ya headed?" I told him about our *Camino* plans.

"Gee. Sounds like a ridiculous hassle to me. Why not stay in Colorado and hike a bunch of *shorter* trails? Wouldn't that accomplish the same thing?"

My answer was directed not just to him but to anyone who ever misunderstood, judged, or tried to dim my desire to seek the unknown. "No, it *wouldn't* be the same. I'm pursuing a master's degree, not an evening class." With that zinger, he returned to his seat. I applauded my off-the-cuff retort. *Yes, a master's degree—in freedom, risk, and joy.*

Later, the cabin lights dimmed, and *the Voice* spoke.

You mentioned you had something to talk about. I'm all ears.

I'm not religious. Nonetheless, I've got a strong, solid spiritual thread running through my life. And, given *the Voice* has serious connections with the higher-ups, it seemed critical to make my appeal.

My confession poured out:

Look, I kinda kicked God off my spiritual team two years back with the shock of losing Michael and Linda. Sure, I leaned on my spiritual beliefs at first. I recall saying to whomever was listening in the ethers, losing Michael has been rough, but I'm getting through it, and I'll be okay. I shouldn't have claimed I'd be okay as life lessons kicked in, proving otherwise—I never saw Linda's death coming. That happening felt like Spirit responded, "Oh yeah, Molly? Ya think that was tough? Hold my beer."

The Voice softly interjected. *Spirit is never snarky like that. You weren't being punished. You know that, right?*

My confession continued.

I know that now. But back then, I felt like a stunned bird hitting the window. I mean, damn! Hit with losing Linda, on top of losing

Michael, was too much. And, ya know what surprised me most? I stopped meditating—my usual go-to for feeling safe. That disconnected me from you, Spirit, Mother Mary, and my angels. I was avoiding cruel betrayal from beyond the veil. I stopped connecting. I told the Universe: I'll figure it out myself. Screw. You.

Fast forward two years. In the air at 36,000 feet, descending into the biggest challenge of my life, deep down, I realized an actual disconnection from Spirit could never occur. *I'd* turned away—entering the dark night of the soul. I wondered where I stood (with myself and *the Voice*). Hearing rumors of miracles occurring on the *Camino* (and wanting that for myself), I worried I'd ostracized myself from this "Miracle Club." Now, it seemed wise to reconnect with anything holy. Hell, if circumstances on the trail called for an SOS, I wanted direct access to help, peace of mind, and guidance, which only this kind of connection brings.

I concluded my confession to *the Voice: I miss that peace and want miracles to find me. How do I get back into the mystical game?*

Just hearing this neurotic stream of thoughts and questions bottled up for two years, I laughed at myself. *The Voice* laughed even harder. It hit me! *Reinstating my God membership card isn't necessary—it was never revoked. Nothing was broken. What a relief! I still have access to the club's secret handshake, my angels are still in the game, and my work here is done (for now).*

Ah, I sensed 100,000 angels by my side.

With no directions other than a few guidebooks, I surrendered. Not unlike that precarious heart-skipping-a-beat-nano-second when your boots skid on loose gravel, I realized the disorienting new rules of the game: *Forget all the rules.* Let the holy games begin.

WHEN ROOTS MEET SKY

MAY 13, 2019, ORISSON, FRANCE

Lively chatter caught my attention as five passing Polish men popped the cork on a bottle of champagne walking out of Orisson. Their spirited exclamations of joy and laughter yanked me back into the present (and my rock perch).

Pulling up roots is an informative dirty job. My intermingled roots of saddle shoes, sand candles, soul friends, morning margaritas, deserts, and a space shuttle led me to a game without clear rules.

Holding my soup gone cold, I sensed old weight melting away from my mind, but none from my backpack, unfortunately. It triggered a flashback to my dreaded fourth-grade math teacher towering over my desk, warning me the correct answer only counted if I "showed my work." Like long division problems, I've poured my heart into writing forty-plus years "of my work" in all its foolish and worthy risks for you. What can I say? I'm a good student.

The van pulled up, squeaking as it rolled in. Gazing, I took a last look at this kind mountain reprieve. I released all regret about not beginning my walk in St. Jean Pied de Port and thought: *Miracles needed to unfold exactly as they had here. Tomorrow, I'm walking.*

Now, if you'll excuse me, I have sheep to dodge, cold angel soup to consume, friends, and a can opener to engage at the bottom of what has already felt like a very long, arduous road. The *Camino* laughed. *You ain't seen nothin' yet.*

PART FOUR

BOOTS ON THE GROUND

CHAPTER 9

RONCESVALLES, KIDNAPPERS, and AUSSIES

My text seemed innocent enough. René's panicked response said otherwise. Her alarm spiraled to: *"Molly's been kidnapped. Shit! Has she tangled with the likes of Hannibal Lecter?"* The string of events leading to this confusing text exchange is worth reviewing to understand her logic for launching a criminal investigation.

My van adventure offered stunning vistas and backpacks bouncing in the back with an occasional renegade hitting me in the head. Arriving in Roncesvalles, my assignment was to scope out the process of reserving our beds in the large monastery.

Knowing René's angst about the confusing Pyrenees route directions, I sent her good ju-ju all day. She replied with photos showing breathtaking views (until cell service dropped). She unintentionally took the route she was warned against, walking the steep rocky descent without another pilgrim in sight. Given her unexpected isolation, understandably, her mind gremlins dredged up the true and tragic story of a woman who had once been killed on the *Camino* after the yellow arrows were manipulated. Alone in the woods, René became suspicious of every arrow. Perhaps that's where the suspicion took root for our confusing exchange later.

FROM THE LAND DOWN UNDER

Our original baptism-by-fire plan was to stay at the large monastery for our first 110-bed group sleeping (or not) experience. But it shifted quickly. In Roncesvalles, an exhausted, pleasant Australian couple climbed into our van. They walked the ascent out of St. Jean Pied de Port and descended into Roncesvalles *all in one day.* My hamstrings bowed in awe.

Following quick introductions with Gabby and Pablo, I exited the van preparing to locate our accommodations, until I heard Gabby's comment. Discovering a mix-up with their hotel reservation, they were informed there were no beds left in the large monastery, nor in their hotel, due to the record numbers on the trail. Ugh. This surprising news called for Plan B.

Pablo suggested riding with them to the next town of Burguete, where they just reserved an Airbnb. "Maybe there'll be room for two more." My gut said *yes.* Sure enough, the owner confirmed she had room—René and I lucked out. Even the hair dryer gods smiled upon us.

In one hour, I'd gone from no room at the inn to sitting in a peaceful kitchen with the aroma of fresh oranges and cinnamon tea, conversing with new Australian friends. Being the first Aussies I'd ever met, and given I can't help myself, the tune "Down Under" playfully rooted itself in my brain cells as an earworm for hours. Gabby explained, "We're originally from Argentina, where we met and got married, then we moved to Australia." Their first language was Spanish, their second, English. "Your friend will be relieved to stay here instead of that crowded monastery. She'll need a good night's sleep," Gabby kindly commented. Our synchronistic meeting already felt like destiny.

KIDNAPPED!

Knowing René would soon be off the mountain, I texted her about the monastery issue and the great solution. When her exhausted self arrived in town, she sent a thumbs-up on the new plan but *had* to find something to eat and drink first.

Grabbing some food, a conversation with a local official informed her I had erroneous information. There were indeed *plenty* of beds available at the monastery and hotel. This conflicting information confused and troubled her with worries of foul play.

In her defense, she just came off the most physical day of her life, exhausted, hungry, in pain, disoriented, and a lot changed from our original plan. A series of anxious texts frantically rolled in:

> Molly, I think you've been tricked! There IS room at the monastery!

> Who's with you? Where ARE you?

> I'm so confused. Why would they lie and say there wasn't room here?

> I'm concerned because what they told you is false! I'm afraid you're in danger!

Now, *I* was confused. *There was room at the monastery?*

I knew, from my end, the Hannibal threat was unfounded. But in her weary state, I understood why she might suspect something sinister.

Pablo and Gabby expressed, "No wonder she's worried, I wish we could do something," as her anxious texts rolled in. We determined that, although they speak fluent Spanish, many words are interpreted differently in Spain than in Argentina, and they obviously scrambled information.

Eventually, I calmed René's fears of being kidnapped. When she finally met Pablo and Gabby, we all laughed as she declared, "Criminal case closed."

We attended the mass dedicated to blessing pilgrims that evening at the ancient Royal Collegiate Church of St. Mary, in existence since 1219. In crowded pews among walkers from all nations, each person held a sacred reason for answering the call to be here.

"Wow. The warmth in here almost glows, doesn't it? I didn't expect this feeling," René whispered.

"No kidding, I feel it too."

The priests' multicultural loving outpouring showered us with blessings in almost every language of those present, sending shivers up my spine. I wasn't reading about it in a book anymore. I was here. Here, where we bit our lips on the verge of tears, knowing everyone's gut ached with the same fears, our hearts pounded with similar excitement—we were all connected. Feeling our common bond, we'd each step onto the road tomorrow following the different reasons that drove us here.

After Mass, René and I ran into warm, familiar faces who cheered my readiness to walk the next day. No longer a fraud or spectator.

In the morning, René's body could surprisingly move. We found a heartfelt note that Pablo and Gabby left before slipping out at sunrise, signed, "*Buen Camino*! Keep in touch!" We arranged to transport our packs to Zubiri to lighten my hamstring load. With 21.9 km (13.6 mi) ahead, I couldn't wipe the smile off my face as we prepared to set out together. The sun shone, and a buzz of excitement filled the morning air.

I looked up, sending a private thought to Michael. *Hey guy, this is it. My desert begins now.*

With that, my boots finally touched down on the *Camino de Santiago*.

CHAPTER 10

THE SHITTY FIRST DRAFT

BURGUETE, TO ZUBIRI, TO PAMPLONA

Don't be fooled by any guidebook's dramatic silhouette pictures of pilgrims walking into town as the sun sets romantically behind them. If the sun is setting, they probably had a rough day, took a wrong turn somewhere, are now late for dinner, and may not find a place to sleep.

In retrospect, these sometimes-cynical early days unfolded with humorous, great perfection. They're not unlike the process of being a writer, wisely explained by one of my favorite authors, Anne Lamott (*Bird By Bird*, 1994):

> *"...shitty first draft. All good writers write them. This is how they end up with good second drafts, and terrific third drafts. The right words and sentences just do not come pouring out like ticker-tape most of the time. In fact, the only way I can get anything written is to write a really, really shitty first draft."*

The way I see it, René and I were living the required shitty first draft of our *Camino*. We analyzed more than we felt. Map reading took precedence over beautiful views. No angels whispered in my ear as advertised. As for grand insights, no lightning strikes. René's hip pain set in, and my monkey mind took up too much real estate in my head.

Don't get me wrong. We had great moments too. Walking from Burguete toward Zubiri initially inspired a novel high. Emotional candy. The terrain flowed from easy trails along meandering creeks, through a magical old forest, to hills climbing into the countryside. Walking through one small village, the air filled with mystical Gregorian chanting transporting us into an ancient world.

Stretching my hamstrings on a forest floor amidst decaying logs, insects, and fungi, I was ecstatic seeing Roman, my "holy dirt angel," appear. Jazzed to see me, he approached, "How's the hamstring?"

"Hangin' in there. And wow, your snake venom and turpentine worked magic on René's hip pain." Thrilled, he smiled and gave us the best hug. Pointing at his map, he warned of rough terrain ahead. Eyeing the map ourselves, our respective responses fell out.

"Holy shit."

"Holy crap."

Roman laughed and challenged both remarks. "No ladies. It's holy *dirt.*" And he was off again. I'd never see Roman from Ukraine again. Such is the way of this trail. *Buen Camino, Roman.*

My hamstrings signaled potential malfunction upon hitting hour five on a desolate hilltop. Holding to my firm agreement (my body calls the shots), I limped into the café and called a taxi with a sigh of relief. René forged on alone.

She later arrived in Zubiri ranting, "Holy crap, that was hellish." Exhausted and beaten by the rugged trail, she reported, "The steep, last section was a bear; good thing you weren't on it. Shit! I've got one hell of a blister." My hamstring thanked me for stopping when I did.

On the upside, we joined a fun, youthful group from various countries for dinner. For openers, we exhausted the standard early-on pilgrim complaint of "Why does Spain close down from 1-5 p.m.?" and "Why don't they serve dinner until 8 p.m.?" These hardy young ones even shared a few hamstring woes—international *simpatico.* Our whiney drivel shifted to trail talk. Things got real. We learned these spry young ones' packs weighed half of what ours did, and they practically sprinted through the day, referring to it as "easy as pie."

Quick, sharp glances and furrowed brows exchanged between René and me were devoid of any *Camino* love that previously flowed. We had no choice but to now resent these young traitors and make mental notes of any (and all) of their flaws.

In keeping with our not-yet-surrendered-still-in-our-heads irritated, sarcasm-filled shitty first draft, we fell into bed for our usual late-night-talk-in-the-dark.

René initiated. "I can't believe I have a damn blister. Pisses me off! And we have to fucking walk *again* tomorrow! Is that all we do here—just walk?" Laughing, I changed the subject. "I felt ready to start carrying my pack until I weighed it today. René, the damn thing is six and a half pounds EMPTY! I had no idea when I borrowed it."

"Yikes! Mine's only *three* pounds. Can't believe we're fucking walking again tomorrow."

René's usual upbeat, *do whatever it takes* attitude had temporarily given way to this uncharacteristic negativity, often said tongue-in-cheek, that I found amusing.

"Yep, walking is the point here. Says so in the guidebook. Hey, I've decided to buy a lighter, smaller pack in Pamplona tomorrow—time to lighten up and send more shit to Santiago. I don't want to search for a new one when we're tired and hungry, so I've gotta get to Pamplona early. I'll catch a ride at some point into the city."

Her supportive response killed any need for my prepared defense strategy.

"Great idea! Will the monster can opener be going with it to Santiago?"

Amused, she shared her dreamy plan. "Let's get a massage in Pamplona. I'm springing for a nice hotel. With a spa. I already booked it."

"No argument here—sounds like heaven. Thanks, Blister Sister." As we drifted off, I heard her grumbling under her breath. "All we do here is fucking walk…."

A friends' rendezvous in the magic forest.
Roman (of Ukraine), René, Gabby, and Pablo

PAMPLONA

Dropped off at the edge of Pamplona, I navigated the old city section with a trail companion's help. Victory! I found my new lightweight Osprey pack. Once René arrived, our agenda: shower, massage, laundromat, dinner, and a whirlwind exploration of Pamplona.

On a mission to find herbs to soak her blister, we landed one that required boiling. René continued exploring, I returned to boil the herbs and transfer stuff into my new pack. I predicted another weight-dumping showdown. I chalked it all up to being our shitty first draft.

Fortunately, a bored, good-natured front desk manager greeted me. Using Google Translate, I explained that I had to boil herbs for my friend's blister and held up the bag. His eyes widened. The look on his face said, "Another crazy American." He gave me access to the lounge, previously closed for the night, with strict instructions, "No turn on light, others think we open for business." Using my phone flashlight and feeling our way to the bar, he pointed out a hot plate, water faucet, and a small pot. He lingered, sneaking a glimpse of my mysterious bag of witch's herbs, then glanced again with eyes slightly squinted, showing a hint of confusion while walking away.

With limited boiling time, and feeling like Sandra Bullock from a scene in *Practical Magic*, I tossed in a few magic spells for good measure: "Caldron of herbs, boil and brew. With the power to heal René's blisters by the morning dew." Steam whacked me in the face with the pungent, bitter smell, and the fun turned to thoughts of *this shit better work*. The sloshy dark brown potion was complete at last and it smelled like crap. Conducting alchemy experiments in an empty dark restaurant in the middle of Pamplona, boiling blister stew, I pondered, *was this part of my shitty first draft or the start of an exciting, better chapter?*

I carried the hot, gross-smelling, swampy brown concoction to the lobby. The manager kept a safe distance from my magic potion.

In the room, I studied my three piles: keepers, Santiago-bound, and what-if-this-happens-and-I need-it pile. Just then, René burst on the scene.

"Sista, I'm about to make your day!" She whipped out several pictures she took of canned goods from the *mercado*.

"Cans? I don't get it, Rene."

"Look closely. See those tabs on top? Spain now sells cans with pop-lids!" She rummaged through my "keeper" pile and pulled out the can opener.

"*This* baby is going to Santiago!"

No one else would understand why canned food could cause two grown women to fall to the floor laughing 'til they cried—a Tony Robbins breakthrough moment. The laughter subsided, and to repay her kind deed, I handed her the smelly, herbal brown sludge.

"You want me to stick my foot in *that*?"

"You damn well better after what I just went through." While soaking, she laughed at being implicated in "The Witches of the Fifth Floor" and further tarnishing the reputation of Americans.

Morning came quickly with René's first mumblings from under the covers: "Oh God. Do we really have to fucking walk *again*?"

I opened the curtains to our view overlooking City Hall Square—and pouring rain. Ugh. René doctored her blister (I failed Witchcraft 101). I squeezed my magic shoes into my smaller pack—no way *they* were going in the Santiago bag. We'd bonded like Tom Hanks and Wilson (his soccer ball).

The hotel helped arrange for my original pack, holding more relinquished items, to be shipped to Santiago. With *two* bags waiting there, now I *had* to make it.

Wearing ridiculously monster-sized ponchos draped over our packs (not our best fashion moment), we walked in the rain to breakfast, did a cathedral tour, and followed the arrows out of the city into the countryside. With my lightened load, our shitty first draft made way for a bright second chapter. We disappeared into the fog looking like two wet hunchbacks of Notre Dame.

CHAPTER 11

I NEED the EGGS

PAMPLONA TO OBANOS

The Wind

~ Cat Stevens/Yusuf

Outside Pamplona, the silhouette of steep hills hung in the misty distance. Walking silently in the drizzle, a sudden Eureka moment. *My world feels large, but my belongings are limited, close, and trimmed. Like a turtle, everything I need is on my back. Shockingly, my life's been reduced to what's tucked conveniently in its rightful place.* I considered sharing these realizations with René, but silence remained, allowing this satisfying sense of order to take hold. Curious, if not hopeful, this epiphany would follow me home.

Connecting on the trail with Erin, a young woman from the Pacific Northwest, we all fell in muddy step, as did our conversation. The *Camino* has built-in permission for pilgrims to cut to the chase.

Erin came to sort, think, and journal to heal her broken heart. Her words dripped with sadness and confusion from a relationship gone south, still hoping they'd work things out. After hearing the painful story of ugly betrayal, René and I exchanged judgmental glances that asked, *Really? Who would want a cheating creep like that back?* Erin was too raw for such logic. We just listened.

Our chatter shifted to laughing about the saying "the *Camino* provides." *We* were the only ones laughing. That line irritated the hell out of Erin. A newcomer to the trail, she didn't appreciate her heartache watered down with, "Don't worry, the *Camino* will provide."

Sister Blister and I concealed our guilty smirks. We couldn't say exactly when we'd gone from eye rolls to nodding in agreement like a dashboard bobblehead when this *Camino* mantra was uttered. Good chance our attitude change came when miracles emerged out of the blue when things looked most bleak: a bowl of steaming vegetable soup for breakfast or, better yet, a peaceful private room when all possibilities seemed exhausted. Then, the *Camino* tossed a hair dryer into the deal. Yep! We became believers. However, wise believers learn not to speak the mantra to an irritated pilgrim when within stabbing distance of their trekking poles.

We assured Erin that something would happen to shift her perspective. Rene joked, "We'll turn you into Pollyanna yet." With a sigh, Erin rolled her eyes. "Don't count on it."

The subject returned to heartache. Erin hanging onto her dysfunctional relationship made me think of the classic movie *Annie Hall*. In the last scene, the male character, Alvy, vividly sums up this common, often dysfunctional, relationship phenomenon of someone "needing the eggs." *That's it—Erin "needed the eggs."* Alvy explained this with an old joke:

"This guy goes to his psychiatrist and says, Doc, my brother's crazy. He thinks he's a chicken!' The doctor says, "Well, that's nutty, why don't you turn him in and get him some help? "The guy responds," I would, but I need the eggs."

Alvy explained that's pretty much how he viewed relationships—totally irrational, frustrating, crazy, and sometimes unfathomable, yet he couldn't deny the human need to still engage in them—we keep putting ourselves through them because we *need the eggs.*

True. We'll tolerate crazy frustration, equivalent to the metaphor of putting up with a crazy guy believing he's a chicken, because of the return (the eggs) we get from it: companionship, sex, intimacy, joy, care, and, above all, love.

I get it. Eggy payoffs are often worthwhile, but will bite us in the butt if we sell out what's most important.

The sun disappeared, and the wind kicked up. Egg-ish thoughts resumed after we paused to pull up our hoods. I've been lured by eggs in other arenas, like draining jobs I've held well past their expiration date. I needed their eggs—of security, the benefits package, or a responsible-looking hiding place until finding the guts to leave.

My contemplation was abruptly interrupted. "Holy shit, what the hell?" Four male pilgrims passed at racing speed, splattering mud everywhere. René's jaw dropped. "Seriously?" One called back, "We're determined to finish the 800 kilometers in record time, *Buen Camino!*"

Harsh, inner judgment drowned out the runners' flight of fancy. Then, like in the cartoons, a shoulder angel appeared on my left, and the devil (pitchfork in hand) on the right, swinging their little, skinny legs off my pack, ready to spar.

Devil: *Idiots! What a rude, ridiculous pace. Wasting time on competitive nonsense—such stupid eggs! Off with their heads!*

Angel: *Molly, unexpected people show up on this walk. Whether they whiz by or hang out for the afternoon. LISTEN. They might deliver a life-serving message.*

Me: *Like Erin? Her musings have definitely made me think, though her focus feels exhausting. But the mud-splashing, flying-like-bats-out-of-hell assholes—I think my message there is 'what screwballs!' Right?*

Devil: *Yeah, what helpful message could those jerks possibly offer?*

Angel: *Here's a clue: it's unlikely that your spiritual lesson there is "Oh, you're so right, Molly, they are doing it totally wrong!" Comprende?*

Me. *Super. Now my angels are speaking in Spanish. But okay. I comprende.*

And POOF! The angels dissolved. I wiped the splashed mud from my wet, wind-beaten face, and a bit wiser, returned to my final egg thoughts.

Which eggs in my life have been worth gathering? Which ones sucked time and energy? When the latter, did I find the courage to walk away? I'm still learning.

Geez, my brain's scrambled (yeah, like eggs), and now I'm hungry. We gotta pick up the pace.

The wind nipped at the heels of the fog, revealing wind turbines lining the distant mountain ridge. Our plan for the next village: lunch (*please be a hot one*), then—that ridge.

Erin planned to stop for the night in this next village, *if* she could find accommodations. The familiar sound of ringing bells echoed across the landscape. Every town has a centrally located church, and bells *always* ushered us in. Truthfully, they tolled like that regardless of who was or wasn't entering, but let me have my fantasy. They tolled for me.

We weren't fooled by deserted-looking towns, and neither should you. Life and good food are often found behind large, unmarked doors. Intuition led our wind-weary selves down the cobblestone street to open a heavy, hand-carved wooden door.

Magic was afoot. We were escorted in by the sound of Cat Steven's *The Wind*. "Unbelievable, René! I put this favorite song on my phone before leaving home. Freaky magic!" Wide-eyed, we drank in the cafe's artful walls—the vibrant textures and colors lured me to touch them. It all blended with the smell of soup steaming on an antique stove.

Devoid of any life force energy, I fumbled with Google Translate but couldn't formulate intelligent communication (low blood sugar) as I approached the Indian-looking gentleman at the counter. Pointing to the gigantic pot on the stove, "*Hola*! That smells heavenly!" Then came his sweet words in clear English. "That's my homemade vegetable soup!" My "foreign" chef hailed from downtown Chicago. The *Camino* provides—*and* entertains.

Melting into hot soup and french fries, always french fries, Cat Stevens triggered a touch of homesickness and a sense of awe. *What's the chance of a favorite song playing in a tucked-away café on a mountaintop in Spain?* The "soundtrack of my *Camino*" began taking shape. With each song, I sensed my angels nodding with *atta girl— keep going.*

When arriving, Erin immediately connected with a French woman who'd just reserved a room. "Erin, there's an extra bed. Want to share the room?" With an ecstatic "Yes!" she accepted.

René couldn't resist. "The *Camino* provides, Erin!" I choked on my tea. Erin rolled her eyes—this time with a slight twinkle of belief.

We hugged goodbye and wished her safe travels, knowing everyone's *Camino* is different. We hoped hers would serve her tangled web of heartache well.

Leaving the café, I thought about Erin and the racing pilgrims. We can't say how another person's *Camino* should look. Still, I was tempted to take Erin aside to tell her the eggs she desperately sought from her doomed relationship weren't worth it. I didn't, of course. I convinced myself *she'll reach the conclusion in divine time. Her Camino will be perfect, even if she walks 500 miles and still doesn't figure it out.*

René broke the silence. "Mol, have you noticed I haven't complained about fucking walking for hours? Time's up. My blister and hip need a break. You're on your own tomorrow. *I'll* be the one catching a ride." Naturally, I supported her plan, but my stomach momentarily flipped. *Yikes. My first time walking alone.*

With many days still ahead, I admitted, "I'm already tired, and my body aches in places I didn't know existed." I reflected, *Shit, can I stay out of my own way? I don't wanna make the same pushy mistakes with my body that, in the past, were for the wrong reasons—the eggs.* Cat Steven's message about never making the same mistake again played in my head. *No, never, never, never...Buen Camino, Erin. Thank you.*

CAMINO MESSAGE #4

Each pilgrim's Camino is as it should be.

CHAPTER 12

GIVE ME a SIGN

OBANOS TO ESTELLA

"And when I think about it, I guess it is true. That people always arrive at the right moment at the place where someone awaits them."

~ Paulo Coelho

Looking out the window for a sign of dawn, my eyeballs hardly hurt—the *only* body parts that didn't. René, sound asleep, reveled in her healing day. I silently spoke to Linda in the pitch-black room. *You said walking 500 miles across Spain would be fun. Yeah, right.* No response. *You also promised to be my cheerleader for this crazy-ass idea, and then you go and die. I at least deserve a book to fly off the shelf or something—anything but silence.*

Forcing my stiff legs to move, I slowly stood. Ouch. The day before took its toll. The cold bathroom floor felt good on my burning, aching feet, giving relief as I dressed.

I'm starving, Linda. I foresee two tortilla de patatas in the near future. I can actually eat everything in it! I'll grab a third for the road, you know, to avoid the starving-pilgrim-dying-a-grizzly-death-on-the-side-of-the-trail scenario. Damnit, Linda, do you hear me?

The whistling wind outside warned me to grab another layer. My hamstring cringed, lifting the heavy pack onto my shoulders. Its lightness wore off. Opening the door, I looked back, offering one final thought to the spirit world. *Okay, Linda. I'm outta here. Hey, do me a favor. Today, show me a sign that you're here, okay? And make it ridiculously obvious, so I have no doubt it's you.*

Silence.

Alone, I stepped outside into the cold without seeing anyone for miles. The first few hours brought uneasiness. Scanning the area behind me and eyeing trees ahead, hyper-vigilance remained a by-product of the beach incident forty years ago. Monitoring my safety never occurred while walking with René, and I didn't like it ruining the moment now. Regretful thoughts of the Mother Mary earrings that René gifted me in St. Jean entered my mind. *Damn, why did I send them in the suitcase to Santiago?*

Mother Mary became a protective talisman for me, long before I embraced her archetypal meaning. I shook my head. *Seriously? We really decided earrings were too heavy to keep? We're nutty.* With the earrings miles away, I hoped my telepathic SOS sent to Mother Mary-Who-Art-Buried-In-A-Suitcase wouldn't overshoot the target and land in the stinky pain cream beside her. *Mary, really sorry for deserting you. I need you! I refuse to waste this solo day doing neurotic reconnaissance. Hopefully, your spiritual Wi-Fi signal and protection work from the suitcase.*

Yikes. I immediately felt her protective presence engulfing me *and* forgiveness for abandoning her. *You don't need the earrings to summon my help, silly girl.*

I knew that, but was relieved to be reminded. *Sure appreciate your quick SOS response time, Mary. You're fast—have you considered a job with AAA road service? Cool, now that you're on duty, if you don't mind, I'll be handing over all these neurotic worries to you, and put my attention on poppy fields, spotting yellow arrows, and giving my nervous system a freakin' break. We good? Hey, Mary, I'm curious, can you breathe okay in there?*

Though I sensed she always rolled her eyes at my flip comments, she was happily in this with me for the long haul. Wrapped in a cocoon of new-level trust, I walked.

Stopping for a water refill, a German woman lamented to her friend, "My allergies are making it hard to find enough food to keep me going." I empathized and shared, "I so get it. I'm really craving hard-boiled eggs myself. Take care. *Buen Camino.*" Outside, I claimed a patch of grass to "do my balls." A Chinese man watched, curiously eyeing my rolling pin. His wife giggled when I gestured to give it a try. He dropped to the ground, rolling his calves with oohs and ahhs until I departed.

Two hours later, climbing a steep, rutted mountainside, I caught up to two strangers, Gloria and Evan, from Long Island, New York—a cool aunt and nephew team.

Breathing hard, Gloria asked if I'd ever been to Long Island. I smiled. "Once, with my good friend, Linda, and her husband, John. Linda died two years ago." I twisted her wooden beads on my wrist.

"Almost twenty years ago, I went with them to a 4th of July celebration at Linda's aunt and uncle's home on Long Island Sound. It was also their fiftieth wedding anniversary. This outdoor lawn extravaganza stretched from their veranda to the water's edge—the tables covered with gourmet food and margarita fountains. It was amazing! Another famous musician, TV personality, or politician appeared every time we turned around. As the sun set on the Sound, we were entertained by the Rockettes, and later, Whitney Houston! Pinch me!" I continued.

"Uncle Jim is an extraordinary man. He's gone from a hard-working blue-collar laborer to great riches in the media industry, and now, very wealthy, remains the same kind, humble, generous man he's always been."

Gloria stopped. Staring at me strangely, she interjected, "And after Whitney Houston, you watched the fireworks over Long Island Sound, right?" I froze. *How did she know?* She continued. "I know Linda's wonderful uncle! And, I watched the same fireworks that night, not far from where you were. Every 4th of July, we take our boat and anchor it in the Sound with other boaters to enjoy the fireworks her uncle provides every year! He's a good man."

It's been years since I've thought about our Long Island time together. Wow, Linda, when you give a sign, you do it big!

There I was—on a muddy mountaintop in Spain, traveling with thousands of pilgrims. The *one* person I connected with not only knows my best friend's favorite uncle but had been in our midst watching the same concert and fireworks twenty years ago! Our arm hairs stood at attention. My new friends were thrilled to have played starring roles in this synchronicity of Linda's first appearance on my *Camino*. It wouldn't be her last.

Walking in awe-like silence, I let it sink in. *Thanks, pal. You sent the sign I needed.* The Great Blue Heron story crept unexpectedly into my thoughts from the ethers. Unprepared, I resisted and confessed, *Linda, I'm still not ready.* She understood, and the heron faded.

As fatigue and hunger gripped me, a fruit stand appeared at the top of a long hill under a rickety canopy. *A mirage?* The generous host even set up a library among the ancient olive trees, complete with stocked bookshelves and chairs for weary pilgrims.

Sitting in the whimsical vineyard library, inhaling a peach, I contemplated what to do about my right foot, which was becoming numb. I reconfigured my boot lacing, praying to the *Camino* library gods it'd relieve the pressure. I figured they were the closest gods at the moment. A mile later, I felt darn smug—the numbness was gone. My resume now includes a "Master's in Shoelace Management."

After meandering small villages and rocky descents, the Long Islanders and I parted. René, waiting in Estella, would soon get an earful about "Molly's most excellent solo day." My Mother Mary-Who-Art-Buried-In-A-Suitcase connection led to some big-time magical eggs. My basket runneth over.

GLORIA AND EVAN – ANGEL TEAM NUMBER FIVE.

Journal Notes

May 18, 2019
Late night in Estella

Asking for a sign this morning, I questioned if anyone in the unseen would do my bidding. I didn't see today's miracles coming. Maybe connecting with Linda was Spirit's reward for my negotiations at 36,000 feet and its way of punching my God membership card. Tomorrow, first thing, I'll quiz René on today's important lesson:

"René, do you know what happens in the Camino time continuum just before a really HUGE request you've made comes true? Do you have any idea, René?"

Next I'll inform her:

"Nothing. Absolutely nothing. At least nothing we can see brewing with our limited perspective. You swear nothing's happening. Until BAM! The miracle appears."

Then tell her (so I remember it myself):

"So, from now on, when we feel absolutely sure nothing is happening, We'll consider it a sign and be on the lookout for a Long Island surprise or a library in an olive grove." Well, Camino, we'll walk again tomorrow. Could I be starting to like this?

G'nite from your miracle egg gatherer

CHAPTER 13

I HAVE BALLS

TO LOS ARCOS

Meandering out of Estella, stopping in a *mercado,* I noticed the Chinese couple from the day before. He smiled, motioning to my pack pocket, which held the rolling pin. Patting the pocket, I smiled back.

Essential items tucked in my mesh pack pocket weren't exactly lightweight. Yet, the packing police wisely knew to look the other way. Let me tell ya, the beating my body withstood day after day could only be explained with this—my balls.

Every morning, while on the trail, and again in the evening, I pulled out my small mesh bag of tricks. The drawstring loosened, and its priceless contents rolled out: a lacrosse ball, a softer rubber ball, and a tiny, spiny ball. Each item was a welcome pressure-point tool for strained muscles. But there's more!

Before leaving Colorado, I knew a do-it-yourself torture kit would be necessary to keep my leg and back muscles functioning, and my balls could handle most of the job. I also used a long roller on my legs at home while training. I dreaded being without its magic on the trail, but it was too big to carry. Rejoice! The *Camino* provides long before one arrives in Spain. I just didn't expect it to happen in the utensil aisle at Walmart.

Two weeks before my trip, there it was, hanging next to the spatulas—a mini eight-inch rolling pin intended for campsite baking. It spoke to me. Despite the strange looks from shoppers, I put it to the test by rolling my shins and quads. Eureka! It exceeded my expectations. I splurged, paid its whopping sale price of 89 cents, and walked out of the store giddy with the final addition for my massage kit.

In our first several days on the *Camino*, pilgrims passing by understandably showed concern seeing me flat on my back trailside, unaware I was just treating tight muscles. I stopped frequently, or be in big trouble later. The best technique: lay flat with the hard lacrosse ball sinking into my tight hamstrings and lower back. "Just workin' out the knots," we'd reassure anyone inquiring about my well-being.

After demonstrating the balls' purpose, many asked to try 'em out. Most were won over and became disciples. Yep! I was loved for my balls, and that didn't bother me a bit. The mini-rolling pin, however, really brought curious laughs. That's until they tried it. Who was laughing now, huh? Laughs turned to envy. They wanted one.

The Chinese gentleman and I discovered that "Ooohs" and "Ahhhs" are the same in every language. Seeing his big smile again with his pantomime rolling pin gesture brought home how we're living inside a shared Universe bubble, the likes I'd never known before.

After a few weeks, familiar pilgrims passed by as I stretched out trailside, greeting it as a normal occurrence. They'd call a jovial *"Buen Camino!"* Often stealing a quick roll of the rolling pin and continuing forward. We weren't in Kansas anymore.

This survival kit made the difference for my body continuing each day, or not. In the coming weeks it was coveted and shared with walkers of many nations. If given the chance, I believe my balls could've brought peace to the Middle East. The demand for the rolling pin alone proved worthy of a Nobel Peace Prize.

I would've humbly declined this honor, however. How would I ever break it to the world that, after all these centuries of turmoil, world peace costs only 89 cents, plus tax, at Walmart?

The Camino clearly requires balls.

NO SOUP FOR YOU!

Wounded Bird
~ Graham Nash

Question of the day: Had René and I run head-on into an actual Soup Nazi, or was he only *acting* like one? We wished there was a direct hotline to Jerry Seinfeld for his input on this issue—the distinction matters. The true certified kind are rude and clueless. And, given the right attitude, entertaining. If one is only *acting* like a Soup Nazi due to a temporary bad day, they're negotiable, so not as much fun. Discerning the difference is critical, especially if you're suffering from low blood sugar, ready to eat your own arm.

Our conclusion—the albergue host in Los Arcos was definitely the certified kind. Google: *Seinfeld episode, "No Soup For You,"* to understand this *déjà vu* Soup Nazi moment. I'll rewind to earlier that morning so you can get the full scope of the situation, which likely started on the drizzly outskirts of Estella.

Filling our cups for the road at the long-anticipated *Fuente del Vino* (the wine fountain) is where it began. Trailside, this drink-what-you-want-for-free-you-foolish-pilgrims opportunity greeted us at 9:30 a.m. It certainly didn't help our pace when the wine decided it'd be hilarious to take pictures doing our best Dorothy-laying-in-a-poppy-field-trance impersonation. Perhaps it was our buzzed filter, but *we* were amused.

Finishing our Oz photoshoot, we continued through rolling farmland and vineyards. The rain left behind endless rich shades of green, like fresh, wet paint on an artist's palette. Our morning happy hour and poppy field photoshoot, followed by our afternoon dawdling to take pictures of the jaw-dropping landscapes, caused us to hit the wall way too soon. The last 12 km (8 mi) of our 21.5 km day had no towns or water stops. Certain our destination of Los Arcos would be around the next bend—it wasn't. Instead, more rolling hills, still no water, warranted a call to our reserved hostel to report its lost lambs would wander in later than expected.

After more endless landscapes, we decided we weren't lost lambs at all. Nope! More like someone's ant farm, serving as their lab experiment. Our feet burned. My hamstrings threatened to take me down (and almost did), and René's searing hip pain wanted AAA road service to send a helicopter. Even my bag o' balls couldn't touch our bone-deep aches and pains.

We dredged up old funny stories about our lives to pass the time, juicy and embellishing, of course. Sitting in the middle of the trail, trading boots for my magic shoes, dirt cascaded like a waterfall into my jacket pocket, dumping onto my half-eaten protein bar. Ugh. I flashed back to Roman's Pyrenees comment, thinking, *holy dirt, my foot.*

Light as air, my magic shoes felt like floating on clouds. Our exaggerated storytelling eventually delivered us to the elusive town of Los Arcos. Enter Soup Nazi: stage left.

Looking forward to a reserved private room and the camaraderie of our pilgrim dinner is what inspired and kept us going throughout the long day. Relieved, we entered the albergue. Met by a tall man at the podium peering over the glasses at the end of his nose without ever making eye contact, he chastised, "You're late! Too late for the dinner list!"

Rene diplomatically replied, "We *did* call you about being late."

"I said you're too late for dinner! Late always means too much wine."

I glanced at René, *well, there is that.*

Without skipping a beat, René, channeling her favorite Seinfeld Soup Nazi episode, turned to me and broke the bad news. "NO soup for YOU!"

We cackled with laughter up the narrow, steep steps, dragging our packs to the room. My swinging boots clunked the wall with every step. It was satisfying to know that it likely irritated the Soup Nazi below. Disclaimer: trail fatigue and low blood sugar can regress one to third-grade humor.

After showering, we descended wearing our scarlet letters and passed the *good* pilgrims enjoying delicious-looking soup. We slipped out to find dinner.

Ah, *Camino* magic, walking into an Italian restaurant, there sat Pablo and Gabby (a.k.a. The Roncesvalles Kidnappers). This unforeseen evening of laughs about our personal "No Soup For You" episode ended with making plans to meet in Logrono the next night for René's send-off dinner.

In our late-night-talk-in-the-dark, René mentioned what we'd avoided all day.

"Tomorrow is my last day on the trail. Mol. I can't believe I'm leaving. No more fucking walking!" she said with honesty and regret.

"We're just getting warmed up, Sister Blister. Postpone your flight. Keep walking with me." But to no avail. From the beginning, the plan was for one week only. And what a week! She knew it held hidden gems, most to be uncovered once she returned home.

"Molly, promise me, if you ever figure it out, you'll let me know what all this is *really* about. It's gotta be more than just fucking walking."

Drifting off to fuzzy visions of my solo adventure ahead (and the two bags waiting in Santiago) René's request lingered in my head. *Hopefully by the time I retrieve them, I'll have the answer to her question.*

Graham Nash's sweet tune "Wounded Bird" played in my head, reminding me to just breathe, and calmly wait, when seeking an answer. Its message so penetrating, it landed as the next *Camino* message.

Enjoy Nash's song at the chapter's opening.

CAMINO MESSAGE #5

When haunting questions hang in the balance, muster patience and grace until the "answer hat" is here.

CHAPTER 14

ESSENTIAL RULE: DON'T FALL

LOGRONO

Maybe the ant farm conspiracy, or possibly intuition, planted the stellar idea of arriving in Logrono early to enjoy tapas, Spanish wine, and explore the city before René's departure. In retrospect, our bus ride into Logrono inspired yet another destiny meet-up—its significance to be revealed down the road.

As if being moved on a chess board, we were guided toward the open seats across the aisle from a young woman. Then *it* happened. I tripped. Over, well, nothing, triggering another laughing jag. Once recovered, we situated our butts in the seat, noting the woman across the aisle looked equally amused. A telltale sign someone is "your people."

This woman, Gina, frustrated and teary, shared her predicament. Listening with compassion, we determined humor would be her best medicine: even *our* humor.

Warm, determined, and typically an upbeat pilgrim from the UK, she was sidelined by a knee injury crossing the Pyrenees. "You guys, I never pictured my *Camino* looking like this. I kiss my husband, Brad, goodbye every morning and he walks—without me! And it sucks to catch a bus—alone—then wait at the hostel for him—and for my knee to heal. Am I pitiful or what?"

I understood her angst. "Hardly, Gina. Been there."

Call it spontaneous intuition, but René and I knew our mission: create a ridiculous diversion. Our off-the-cuff remedy—reveal our undercover, known-by-few, *Camino* areas of expertise, including my Master's in Shoelace Management and Pressure Balls; Sister Blister's counseling degree in Master Level Blister Care and Packing Police Priorities. Elaborating on the minute details of our significant talents triggered a breakthrough. Gina's tears turned to laughter, then, to curiosity.

"Okay, I gotta ask. When you got on the bus, what was that laugh frenzy about?"

"That's easy. I tripped."

"And that's *funny?*" I glanced at René with a look that asked: *do we dare tell all?* Already laughing, she answered, "You start. I'll jump in wherever."

"Well, Gina, answering that question will take filling ya in on some history. It's sort of a *three*-part story—we call it 'The Curse of Karen Club.' You might not wanna know us once we're done."

Gina laughed, "You can't get any weirder than you already seem."

"Okay, you asked for it. It started before leaving for Spain. One night, talkin' *Camino* on the phone, all I did was tell René about the warning from my good friend, Karen, a *Camino* veteran. She told me something along the lines of this: Whatever you do, don't fall on the *Camino*. You've gotta watch every step, Molly. If there's a view, stop walking. *Then* look. One slight stumble, you're goin' over from the weight of your pack. Trust me. *I know.* I learned the hard way. Remember my black eye? I tripped over tree roots and face-planted. Listen to me. Watch your feet."

Gina cringed. René and I took turns spilling parts of our story.

René: "I cringed too, Gina—just picturing her nasty face-plant. So, I told Molly, 'Crap, you never should've told me this! Now, falling is *permanently* burned into my brain!'"

Me: "Because of that, falling has haunted us all week. The topic's become a Kodak moment fixation—just waiting for a fall."

René: "Saying 'don't trip and fall' normally sounds like caring, right? But with us, it's more of a *dare*. If one of us skids on gravel or just stumbles, it's a disappointing blooper."

Gina: "You two are so sick. Keep going."

René: "Our rule—if it looks like one of us is goin' down, the first instinct isn't to break the fall. Nope. Go for the camera and capture the landing. Friends don't let friends miss an embarrassing photo op."

Me: "Hey, we never claimed to be sane."

René: "Or compassionate."

Gina, now officially inducted into "Curse of Karen Club," couldn't shake this haunting possibility. It's all a trade-off. At least, we, the Angels-of-Doom, lifted her spirits.

Our ride of twisted, ridiculous, sadistic joy finally arrived in Logrono. Gina and I exchanged numbers before parting, still laughing, promising to connect again.

Let the adventure begin! After settling into the plush hotel worthy of René's send-off, duties called: laundry, and replenishing shampoos and lotions. First stop, lunch and wine, not in that order.

I lifted my glass. "A toast to a wild week, Sister Blister!"

"Cheers! And a toast to neither of us taking the dreaded 'big drop.'"

"Uh-oh, don't jinx it. The day is young." I thought I was joking.

Later, walking Logrono streets, René, the tech wizard of our twosome, wanted assurance that I'd mastered Google Maps in "walk mode" before leaving. Her insistence saved the day in the coming weeks.

"Okay Mol, you're navigating for the rest of the day. You're gonna get this!"

I fixed my gaze on the arrow, and still made the wrong turn. "Crap, this damn blue arrow is out to get me, René."

Lugging our packs with clean laundry, she stayed patiently amused by my navigation learning curve. Finally, an A+ when I successfully guided us to our store destination. Excited, I stepped toward the door to enter, not seeing the four-inch cement doorstep. My boot hit the obscured hazard, jerking me forward. The pack's weight, as Karen predicted, knocked me off balance. I reached with both arms to break my fall into the store's large glass-paned door. Allow me to offer a slow-motion, play by play:

Visualize me stretched at a 45-degree angle with toes barely anchored on the sidewalk. Both hands are flat against the glass door, bearing most of my weight. As gravity would have it, my hands slowly squeak down the glass door, with the grace of a gazelle, until landing flat on the cement stoop.

Hanging at forty-five degrees, calculating the softest landing possible, is when I registered René's laughter. Infectious—my own laughter started on the descent, mimicking a slo-mo scene from a Road Runner cartoon.

I sincerely regretted blocking people inside the store who needed out and those outside wanting in. I never should've glanced behind me. Spotting René sitting on the sidewalk in the kind of hysterics that includes occasional gasps and wheezing snorts, made the threat of peeing my pants real. Future eye contact was now forbidden.

With as much grace as I could muster—a little stiff, definitely humbled, I slowly rolled my stranded turtle-self upright, allowing customers to pass. Some locals chuckled at the pilgrims gone mad, others pretended nothing happened. But something *had* happened. We knew the truth. I'd delivered *big* in the eleventh hour. Our only regret—no photo. But we were witnesses.

That evening, in our chatty dinner with the Aussies, no one wanted to face the inevitable goodbye. But finally, after Pablo, Gabby, and I made plans to walk out of Logrono together in the morning, farewells were sadly said.

Heading to our room, a final "dump more weight" session awaited. Given this one last chance to lighten my load, the Packing Police's final questioning was brutal:

René: "What about these packets of almond butter?"

Me: "A girl could starve on the trail."

René: "Why reading glasses?"

Me: "Well, what if my prescription pair breaks?"

René: "About your magic shoes. You're talking two flippin' pounds, girl!"

Me: "Too far, Sister Blister. Non-negotiable."

Whatever I handed over, she'd take home. My goal: drop two pounds. By midnight, I knew what I needed to do. René's eyes widened as I handed over my magic shoes. My boots were serving me well, I convinced myself. No blisters. No pain. They'd do fine.

"Just take the damn things before I change my mind," I told her as my brain monkeys slung turd pies at my shocking decision. I finally understood how Tom Hanks's *Cast Away* movie character felt watching Wilson hopelessly drift away from his life raft.

Only in hindsight do I know how this one rushed decision and Elvis' song "Fools Rush In Where Angels Fear To Tread" would shadow me for all remaining miles.

Our final late-night-talk-in-the-dark was brief and melancholy. Sometimes, only silence can transition you through a scene change on your Hero's Journey.

At daybreak, we scrambled. René's train to Barcelona would leave soon. She walked me to the elevator. At this point, there was nothing left to say other than a teary, "I love you to pieces, and I miss you already." She called, "*Buen Camino*!" as the elevator door closed. My heart sank. I exited the hotel—truly on my own for the first time—and off to meet the kidnappers of Roncesvalles.

GODSPEED, DEAR RENÉ, MY HIGHEST CAMINO ANGEL OF ALL.

WHATEVER YOU DO, DON'T FALL (WITHOUT ME THERE).

PART FIVE

STEPPING OUT SOLO

CHAPTER 15

GREMLINS, KINGS, and FLYING UNDERWEAR

LOGRONO TO NÁJERA

Perhaps because I faced the next 29 km on my own, or maybe it was overhearing the pitiful attempt to book a hostel for that night (in my version of Spanish), whatever it was, the gremlins were restless.

Outside of Logrono, the Aussies forged on as I paused trailside, putting my balls to work. A surprise text from Mike, my friend back home, popped up.

> Did René leave? Are you on your own? How does it feel? You'll rock this!

The gremlins, now fully activated, blasted their retort.

How do we FEEL, Mike? You know that instant when you've rocked too far back on the rear legs of your chair, and you're about to fall? THAT'S how we feel!

They'd been pushed to the edge and demanded the floor to air their grievances:

1. *Three years of high school French pretty much sucks as support right now. Is that all ya got?*

2. *René's gone. Who'll laugh with us when things go south? We foresee ugly meltdowns (ours).*

3. *You're a woman walking alone on long stretches of isolated trail. Easy for Bill and Patrick to say, "Oh, it's fine. You'll be safe." Hellooo! They're guys!*

4. *Thanks to you, we're minus a damn can opener and magic shoes. We're toast!*

Getting the gist of the charges against me, I interrupted their banter by returning my feet to the trail. A dependable plan of action: when gremlins grumble, find your feet. Note to self: buy a journal to record such lessons.

My attention was pulled by Patrick's text:

> You're leggy. You take long strides. Slow down. Shorten your steps. Give those hamstrings a break.

Adjusting my stride *did* help. *Ugh. Pat's right again.*

Reconnecting with the Aussies, we shared a great time until we each turned toward our destinations. Crossing a footbridge over the River Nájerilla into the charming old-town section of Nájera with welcoming church bells, I wondered if the massive sigh of relief that accompanied arriving each day would ever stop happening. *Nope—never.*

Sandwiched between the river and a dramatic high rock face, I made several circles around a myriad of narrow side streets, looking for my hostel. Each loop, I passed the same building with a life-size mural of a king dressed in red robes resting on a bench.

Four pilgrims stood beside the mural. I hadn't noticed them on my first pass of the king. On the second, we exchanged waves. By the third, they laughed as one called over, "Third time's a charm! Are you the king's lost queen?" Our funny exchange that followed made it tempting to hang around, but I continued my search. As I left, the funny Brazilian led the others in a send-off gesture forever deemed "The King's Salute." The four lined up in honor of my obvious repeated loyalty to the king, in unison saluted, declaring, "Hail the Queen!" I countered, "That makes you The Kingsmen, yes?" That one silly shared moment would create a rare bond for the remainder of our *Camino.*

Intuition led me down an alley to the elusive Stork Nest Hostel. My private, peaceful room seemed a lucky find given my non-existent Spanish-speaking skills. But I couldn't rely on luck for long. I messaged Patrick and Bill, who were three days behind me. We exchanged a few "How ya doin'?" texts in the past week, but this one was of a critical educational nature:

> Hi guys, I'm in Nájera. René left this morning, so my days of plush accommodations are over. I need coaching. What's the difference between a hostel and an *albergue*? The guidebook symbols are confusing. Will I be sleeping with 50 other pilgrims in one room? Help!
>
> Signed, Now-solo *Pellegrino*

Their responses rolled in, making future bookings easier. It felt good to touch base with someone familiar. I revisited my choice to walk alone. The fun and security built into the camaraderie Bill, Pat, and their friend, Kaz would experience had advantages. But my reasons for doing this alone remained solid. How else could the gremlins tap into every dark fear, then emerge on the other side with the magic elixir? Yep, this was *my* Way. I never questioned it again.

Every day here is Groundhog Day: Alarm sounds. Walking begins often in a mystical fog. Keep walking. Miss yellow arrows, go back, find your way. Change socks, don't learn this the hard way. Complain your feet ache. Be in awe of beauty. Swear the destination town is close. Nope! It's only a mirage. Keep walking. Now it's really close. Just kidding. Keep walking. Finally arrive. Receive a well-earned stamp. Find a room likely on the highest floor. Peel off boots. Shower. Do laundry. Hang to dry. Laugh through dinner with strangers, now friends. Journal. Sleep. Repeat.

This was my first day hand-washing my clothes and hanging them on the window ledge to dry in the sun. A sudden gust of wind blew my T-shirt, bra, and panties down three stories to the alley below. Yikes. Saved! By two male pilgrims! They wadded them up, and pitched them back up with perfect precision, laughing, *"Buen Camino, Senorita!"*

Observation: What would typically feel awkward was becoming normal, including airborne underwear.

Tolling bells signaled—time for *real* food! I couldn't eat one more french fry. Meandering the maze, acknowledging the king as I passed, a woman inside a café by the window feasted on green beans, fish, and a green salad. Yay, green things! One lone chair at the same table led to finding a new Australian friend, Kim. "I'll have what she's having."

Bright and easygoing, Kim had slowed her pace, staying extra nights in towns, so finishing in Santiago coincided with her daughters arriving in early July. She traded familiar community for a relaxed journey and a grand family reunion in Cathedral Square—another interesting approach to this wild ride.

Later, leaving the café, there stood Gina, our Logrono bus comrade. Our jubilant reunion changed to frustration as she reported her knee remained rebellious. At the end of her rope, she considered returning home to the UK until receiving timely angel messages from fellow pilgrim, Bill of NYC. Gina forwarded his WhatsApp message to me to save for future inspiration.

Knees are complicated. I'm glad you are listening to your body and not ignoring it and pushing yourself too much.

I look forward to being in the same city again, hopefully soon

I hope you are getting stamps in every city, you are an injured Pilgrim on The Camino who is not turning around and flying home and even if you take the bus from every city from here to Santiago de Compostela you still are completing The Camino and you deserve your Certificate even more than all those who are not injured.

Decision: she'd give her knee more time. We joked about the well-meaning, but annoying strangers who analyzed her injury. "If one more person fucking tells me the *Camino* has some deep lesson buried in all this, I'll kill 'em!"

This called for another ridiculous intervention. "Gina, I've got it! We'll start a *Camino* transport service for injured pilgrims! Picture it. The side of the bus is marked, "Another Fucking Life Lesson *Camino* Transport." I took the spewing of her mouthful of water as approval of the genius plan. When able to breathe again, she expanded the idea. "Yes! I'm seein' it. A full-service bus with counselors in the back working through the emotional cause of injury, or better yet, they'll just make one up for you—no extra charge!"

Maybe it was fatigue, maybe pure brilliance, but our ribs ached from laughing. Gina resumed, "It's gotta have staff skilled in blister management, knee braces, compression socks 101, and…" I interjected, "a margarita bar!"

Concluding our ridiculous plan, we parted, faces frozen in laugh mode, vowing to remain in touch.

It was almost dark. Seeing the king's mural signaled my turn was near. I nodded, thanking His Royal Highness for his navigational wisdom.

Muscles unwound as I lay in the dark, curtains billowing in the warm breeze. My mother used to clip a clothespin to the hem of her curtains on breezy days. Not I. There's something whimsically freeing about billowing curtains. As if some message rides the breeze to remind me of something important. Not surprising, the whimsical tune, "Summer Breeze," filled my mind on this dark night, in the middle of Spain.

Pilgrims passed below my window, singing in German. I thought about the king, Gina, and our bus business venture and laughed again. Absorbing these emotions and sounds, I vowed not to forget one detail.

The day had begun with gremlins touting the crimes I'd committed against them, and closed with some vague message whispering in the breeze, something I couldn't quite hear (I prayed when I could, it wouldn't be in Spanish). Cramming thoughts into my phone wasn't working. I'd find a real journal or risk having freaked gremlins, guiding kings, and flying underwear memories fade.

Presenting: The King and My Kingsmen

BLISTERING HEAT

Nájera To Santo Domingo

Is it bad form to salute the King with the same hand holding a half-eaten breakfast tortilla? Given our close, albeit brief, relationship, it seemed only proper to pay my respects on my way out of town. Wiping my greasy hands on my shorts (don't judge me), I texted René, about to catch her flight out of Barcelona.

> G'morning, Sista! Breaking news. I'm fucking walking! Again. Missing you.

Hitting SEND, a presence brushed my face. I sensed Linda's entrance. I never felt her so viscerally as when her energy fell into step next to mine. Was this her plan all along—René out, Linda in? What *was* clear: the "you-will-never-catch-me-walking-the-*Camino*" Queen had laced up her celestial hiking boots.

Good to know you're here, buddy. Wanna protein bar? We've got 13 miles ahead. My ghost chat amusement was interrupted by spotting small spiral notebooks through a shop window—a miracle. I nodded to both the king and Linda, not knowing to whom the credit should go.

Tucking away my new journal, I found a steady pace alongside my unexpected walking companion. I stopped to take a quick picture of laundry hanging outside a second-story window. I sensed Linda's sarcastic reaction. *Yes. Nothing says 'I did the Camino' like a shot of that guy's underwear.*

For me, it was a reminder that life goes on. People who live along the *Camino* aren't actors. They live a responsible day-to-day existence. Jobs, families, bills, hobbies—and laundry. Pilgrims temporarily opt out of that reality to live a string of groundhog days searching for *something*. Something meaningful we hope follows us home. The clothesline reminded me of the Zen story framed in my office:

"The novice says to the master, "What does one do before enlightenment?"

"Chop wood. Carry water," replies the master.

The novice asks, "What, then, does one do after enlightenment?"

"Chop wood. Carry water."

In this strange new world—a world of befriending painted kings—these hanging clothes and the Zen story remind me *if I can master my mind, I'll find the extraordinary in the mundane.*

Was I the only one moved by hanging long underwear and dishtowels? I doubted, however, I was the only pilgrim moved by another thought: *when we return home to our same old exterior routines of chop wood/carry water, we all privately hope much will have changed on the inside.* I (we) walked on.

Shortly, we came upon a large, extended Chinese family. The best communication mustered was, *"Buen Camino!"* as I accepted to join their picnic lunch. An astounding feast spilled from their packs like twenty clowns pouring from a tiny Volkswagen. I graciously reached for what was recognizable. Two apricots. However, one thing spoke both languages—my rolling pin passed from one giggling person to the next. Linda's voice whispered, *this is my first Chinese picnic and massage party.*

On this pleasantly hot day along asphalt back roads, I ran into Kim, my Australian dinner companion. Her casual pace provided patience with my frequent stops to find the small thorn or pebble in my sock, stabbing the base of my toes. Never found it.

The three charming Irishmen we joined, joked, told grand Irish tales, and sang for two hours. Santo Domingo finally in sight, the Irish lads—envisioning a cold beer, hugged us goodbye and set out at a fast clip toward the city. Kim went on ahead, I chose a slower, more patient pace wondering what the hell was up with my foot. That patience was rewarded by Gabby's incoming text invitation:

Hey, wanna share the great apartment we just scored?

YES! Saved from the 100-bed *albergue!*

Whew! I'm feeling like a grateful rescue dog.

Once settled in town, after doctoring her own toes, Gabby studied my foot. "Geez, girl, there's a long blister brewing along the base of all your toes!" My tight hamstring couldn't bend to see it for myself.

"Crap. My boots weren't rubbing it. It must've been rubbed raw by my hot, sweaty socks bunching up." This journey would now forever be categorized as "pre-blister, blister, post-blister."

Finally, sliding into fresh sheets with my journal and freshly bandaged foot, a text from Patrick came in:

> Trust me on this. Reserve a bed at Refusio Acacio & Orietta in Villoria del Roja for <u>tomorrow night</u>. It's owned by close friends of the guy who *wrote The Alchemist*. Town's like a hobbit shire. It's magic, Molly.

Sleepy thoughts: *Too late to reserve it now. I hope a bed will save until morning.*

Linda's reassurance engulfed me. *I'll handle that—get some sleep.*

 ### *CAMINO MESSAGE #6*
If I can master my mind, I'll find the extraordinary in the mundane. Chop wood. Carry water.

Journal Notes

May 22, 2019
Santa Domingo

   Today's poppy fields, the Aussies' kindness, and Linda's steps by my side are etched in my mind. Hey, Linda, running into Gina and the crazy rendezvous at the king's mural tonight had your sparkles all over it. Nicely done. Good to have you near, friend. I'm curious. Do ghosts wear compression socks?

HELPFUL CAMINO TIPS

1. When buying laundry detergent, double-check the label in Google Translate. It could be toilet bowl cleaner. (It was.)

2. After using pain cream containing camphor—do NOT rub your eyes. They'll water. Other pilgrims assume you're crying and wanna help. It's challenging to explain what you've foolishly done when they don't speak English.

3. Act cool when undies you laid on the windowsill fall three stories to the street below. Some guy WILL confidently, wad them up, and throw 'em back up. It's all good.

4. Befriend your neighborhood king. He comes bearing guidance (and attracts twisted friends).

5. Don't change blister bandages at lunch when others are eating. Just don't.

6. Save analyzing "chop wood, carry water" for later. Just walk. (Oh. Do carry water.)

7. When gremlins interrupt possible answers, find your feet. Just walk.

8. Don't dismiss curtains billowing in the breeze. They hint at magical things to come.

CHAPTER 16

ROAD to the SHIRE

VILORIA-BOUND

Hey, Bilbo Baggins, we gotta talk! You and your little hobbit friends sucked me into this whole Hero's Journey club. How do I cancel my membership?

Rumors that my destination of Viloria would resemble a magical shire (as in the movie *The Hobbit)*, might explain why its key character, Bilbo Baggins, appeared in my head. Unfortunately for him, as my emotional punching bag.

My stinging-bee blister pain reached its limit. Only Blister Sisters know how this irritation (if pushed too far) will escape the foot, travel a pathway up the leg, past the stomach, aiming to connect with the voice box. Once the voice box is hijacked, we aren't responsible for what's unleashed.

In the first rant, I cursed Paulo Coelho and the Alchemist's stupid desert idea. Then cried foul on Dorothy's three enabling companions who continually bailed her out going to Oz. And God help anyone who dared to wish me "*Buen Camino*" right now. Nothin' *buen* about it.

My voice box continued railing on poor Bilbo. "Tell me, how do you justify your damn blockbuster Hero's Journey hobbit story on the big screen, Baggins? You know—the staged, well-crafted, we-all-know-this-will-have-a-happy-ending crap. That's not real life. I teach this stuff remember? You set us up—what with the popcorn, cushy theater seats, and the movie trailer that (spoiler alert) reveals you're still alive in the end. This ain't Hollywood. It's Spain.

Since I don't get a film trailer that hints at the outcome, tell me, am I killed off in the end—death by blister?"

Limping into a tiny town, ranting subsided, I decided to try dripping self-pity on for size.

A familiar Scottish voice spoke behind me. "I know a little place with fresh-out-of-the-oven almond cake. That'll cheer any gimp right up."

It was Bren, my intriguing, handsome Scottish acquaintance. Our paths frequently crossed since Logrono. Several hours of walking together on various days sparked something more interesting with every encounter. However, his rugged prince handsomeness lumped him into the same resented fairytale category as Dorothy and Bilbo. I wasn't having it.

"I'm pissed off, Bren, but don't know who to be mad at. If anyone tells me 'the *Camino* will provide,' I may kill them." Regardless of my threats, the prince invited me to breakfast. I buckled under pressure. Did I mention he was handsome?

Admittedly, Bren was a gentleman. He intuitively "got me" and showed genuine interest in my *Camino*. Sensing my grouchy state to be out of character, he welcomed my unloading.

"This journey took a wrong turn, Bren. This can't be my *Camino*. My knee and hamstring pain have my complete empathy, but this blister shit is an outlier. I'm tellin' you; it's like bee aliens meet the wicked witch who never fucking melts!" Bren laughed, shooting orange juice through his nose.

He summed it up: "So, it's the devil you know versus the aliens you don't know? And you sure didn't sign up for any fucking aliens! I get it. You think this isn't your script. But it is. Your Hero's Journey hasn't gone wrong. And I know a Hero when I meet one." He fed me his last bite of almond cake as his sister Kylie stormed in.

"I can't find *one* Compeed bandage in this whole poor excuse for a town! Either I find some, or I'm hitch-hiking to Santiago! I'm serious, Bren!"

I easily recognized blister-speak. He reassured her and called a number scribbled on the café wall. Within minutes, we piled into a taxi, and headed to a pharmacy three miles away. The drama progressed from pity party to solution mode. Maybe I was a little hard on Mr. Baggins.

My gallant Scotsman's generous piggyback ride from the taxi into the pharmacy was followed by, "Okay. Take it all off, my Lord! Let me see everything ya got!"

Thinking it sounded a bit forward and inaccurate, I corrected "my Lord" to "my Lady" until I realized he was referring to my last name and was only asking me to take off my footwear. Disappointing.

I peeled off my boot, socks, and bandages, exposing a fiery blister. The full rack of Compeed patches had Kylie in seventh heaven. She handed me one.

"Here. For your specific flavor of victimhood." Smart-ass. I liked her, regardless of her calling the victim kettle black. I watched with a touch of jealousy as she changed into kinder shoes to give her blister a rest. I grieved the vision of my cushy, long-gone magic shoes. Note to self: *forgive yourself for letting the magic go.*

Kylie announced she booked a hostel right there in Redecilla del *Camino.* Bren wisely agreed to cut their day short. Never re-aggravate a voice box that's been nicely de-escalated.

The pharmacist checked out my foot, nodded, and loaded me up with blister essentials.

Peering over his glasses, he inquired, "You have backup shoes, si? Walk in those, so you heal." I was silent. Bren repeated the question, "You *do* have back-up shoes, right?" Crickets.

I patched my foot and eased it into my boot. I had many miles until the Shire, so once more, the Scotsman and I parted. He took a stab at his best *Casablanca* (with his sexy Scottish accent). "Here's looking at you, Kid. We'll always have Redecilla." It melted me a bit.

Back on the trail, I sensed Linda's crooked, suspicious smile. *Yeah, yeah, I know, Linda. He's handsome and pretty special. But I'm not here for a complicated romance. I came for something else.* The Great Blue Heron story flashed in my mind, then faded. I spoke out loud to firmly change the subject. "Let's get to Viloria, Linda, it looks like rain."

The trail veered toward a lush green countryside that glistened in the drizzle, much like a shire. I thought of Bilbo Baggins and having accused his farce Hollywood movie set of not being real life. I viewed things differently now.

What if my journey, all of our journeys, actually are sort of a show? Projected up on some mystical big screen, complete with popcorn and cushy seats. This last scene featured two warring halves: one wanting the predictable comfort zone versus no assurance of outcome. What if all this is a movie featured on Field of Stars Netflix? And on the couch sit the Camino gods, holding my magic shoes for safekeeping, munching Milk Duds, watching, nudging, cheering, and conspiring—on my behalf. What if?

 ### CAMINO MESSAGE #7

When magic finds you, hold it loosely and dear.

BUTTERSCOTCH

"The Shire" of Viloria

The good news and bad news about the *Camino*—you have endless time to contemplate.

I paused to greet a woman approaching from the opposite direction, triggering a peculiar conversation. Usually, anyone walking upstream on the trail had forgotten their walking poles, credit card, or their kid in the last town. But this older Croatian woman was intentionally walking from Santiago to St. Jean Pied de Port (to each their own).

She described the area she'd just passed through as "intoxicating!" Then, glancing over the surreal landscape, she added, "A better word—butterscotch!" As her arm swept the view, she reinforced it (as though I understood it the first time): "Like I said—butterscotch! All of it! *Buen Camino*, dear!" And she was off.

Squinting at the hills, I wondered what I missed. *Butterscotch? How the hell is this place butterscotch?* I sensed Linda's confusion as well, but then lifted my hand. *Wait a second, Linda. It's déjà vu.*

What I'm about to share has no logical place in this book. That is, until "butterscotch" forced my hand. I flashed back to a past Christmas and opening a gift from a friend, a white, scented candle in a glass jar. The scent's name was printed on the front: "Sleigh Bell." I tilted my head, squinted, and re-read the label, hoping my imagination would interpret what the name tried to convey. I sniffed it. Nothing recognizable. Did the candle-makers *intend* to mess with my head, sending me down a rabbit hole in search of logic? "Sleigh Bell" didn't compute.

This candle lesson stuck with me. Back then, a possible explanation surfaced. It might speak to the limitations that words alone can put on our five-sense experience. At times, I've dismissed a new perspective simply because it violates *my* rules of logic. It humbled me to realize what I judged as an illogical Christmas scent, actually paralleled my current life's work—decoding what happens when music crawls inside our heads. To sum up what I've heard from thousands of workshop participants is this:

"I love this song! Sure, the melody is beautiful, the tempo is catchy, and the lyrics touch me. But it's more than that. I can't quite put my finger on exactly why it moves me. It's beyond words. It just does."

In matters of the heart, the whole is greater than the sum of its parts. Like music, sleigh bells and butterscotch stumble over inadequate words to express the heart's emotions. Had I met my own "Word Alchemist" today?

Music performs alchemy. Emotion and sound transform us beyond the gates of sensibility. We somehow accept this mystical occurrence with music. We somehow have permission to temporarily suspend logic, and allow our nervous system freedom to breathe it in. Strangely and on cue, after being temporarily suspended, our judgment and strict rules return when the music stops. We return to a world where obscure lyrics as in "MacArthur Park" and Leonard Cohen's "Hallelujah," only make sense when we, once again, push play.

The Croatian woman was long gone. I wondered: *would she hold onto the butterscotch high?* Therein lies my earlier stinging-bee challenge—to hold onto the butterscotch.

Walking farther into the mint-green valley, stucco structures with orange tile roofs dotted the landscape. The Shire neared.

I asked, *Hey Linda, what's your take on my strange butterscotch ponderings?* My thoughts continued without interruption, which I took as her agreement.

A candle smelling like a sleigh bell or a butterscotch view can either settle well with one's soul or summon a demon from the ninth circle of grammar hell. When one can't decide their holiday favorite scent—eggnog, pine, or sugar cookie—why not lump 'em all together, name it Sleigh Bell, and call it a day?

I soon found my night's resting place: Refugio Acacio & Orietta. I was greeted warmly by Acacio, the husband in the owner team, along with the scent of sandalwood, a trickling fountain, and native flute music exuding the essence of Carlos Nakai. Being the first to arrive, I sat for a moment in peace. I texted Patrick:

Arrived in Viloria. I think angels live here.

The quiet blended with the flute song. I viewed the wall of photos and quotes of the owners' friend, Paulo Coelho, author of *The Pilgrimage* and *The Alchemist*. I felt the warmth of Michael's presence. He understood why I was here.

I chose the bed by the window, showered, finished blister maintenance, then headed out to roam the quaint shire. When I returned, greeted by Acacio's wife, Orietta, I met seven others from various countries. Two wood-burning stoves crackled—one in the living room, the second in our sleeping room. Heaven. Whatever dragons took hold of my voice box earlier, now purred.

Summoned for dinner, my days of wishing for healthy lentils and a green salad were granted. A delightful twenty-two-year-old French woman patiently interpreted the different languages spoken at the table: French, English, German, and Swedish.

As wine was passed and delicious food consumed, Orietta asked what inspired us to come to their *albergue*. The French woman interpreted as each shared their answer. Inhaling a deep breath, I told Michael's story.

"My dear friend, Michael felt a deep connection with the character Santiago in *The Alchemist*. We both were born with the heart of the Wanderer archetype. Michael and I shared the often-tiring tendency to "always be seeking." The group laughed and nodded. I was clearly surrounded by fellow seekers. I continued.

"Two years ago, Michael was dying. He mentioned looking down to read interfered with his oxygen flow and regretted not being able to read *The Alchemist* one final time. He lived several states away, so I agreed to read it to him over the phone. Then, chapter by chapter, we shared our thoughts. It stirred deep conversations we'd have never had otherwise. Michael died soon after."

Looking across the table, Acacio and Orietta's eyes brimmed with tears. She asked, "May we share this story with Paulo?"

A rush of emotion swept through me, being the steward of Michael's story here in this sweet Spanish hamlet hideaway. I knew how he'd answer Orietta's question.

My eyes welled with tears. "Michael would *love* that!"

Pretty cool, huh, Michael? Paulo might actually hear how much he inspired you before you died. I'm feelin' your smile, friend.

A light rain fell outside. Wine glasses were topped off while the wood stove warmed a deeper connection between people who, hours before, were strangers on the trail. My Colorado friend, Bill, mentioned how he counted group dinners as the *Camino's* highest blessing. I understood.

House rule: lights out at 9:30. Crawling under the cozy blanket, the rain tapped on the windowpane while the wood-burning stove radiated soothing warmth. I doubted there'd be a day like this again. Given the thoughts drifting through my mind, Linda agreed.

Way to go, Mol! We sure perked on some pretty wild theories today—music and human emotion (I kinda miss those things). And, I love what happens when we're at a loss for words.

Yeah, wild alright! But Linda, I've gotta be open to other theories on all of this.

Hearing this challenge, she answered: *Even a theory that suggests butterscotch has no significance at all, Molly Ann?*

Unfortunately, even that one, Linda Marie. And what if "sleigh bell" was only a last-minute idea thrown on a candle by someone whose shift ended, and he just wanted to get to the bar to meet the guys?

I sensed her laugh before she signed off with one more insight: *About the Croatian woman…what if she's just batshit crazy and does everything backward?*

Ha! I think the whole point is that when meaning is placed on something, I must remember I'm the one who put it there. G'nite, dear friend.

Before fading, I thanked Paulo Coelho for the sweet peace he brought to my friend, Michael. I drifted off, here in the place where angels watch over dragons, bees, and pilgrims as they sleep.

CHAPTER 17

TRUE NORTH

VILORIA DE LA RIOJA TO SAN JUAN

The connection of the prior evening's group dinner had given way to disconnection from my True North. My mind committee, Department of Body Parts, and Personal Power Programs all crashed at once that morning. Cause: my blistered foot hitting the hard bathroom floor. Turning the power button off and back on did nothing. Angels left the building, and the fire-breathing dragon returned.

I chalked up my nausea to it being day four of the blister's folding-in-half trick—gross! I froze on the bathroom bench, thinking, *if I budge one inch on this foot, I'll puke. I'm stuck here. Maybe forever* (insert violins here). I envisioned the headline:

Immobilized pilgrim dies grisly decaying death in albergue bathroom.

I heard other pilgrims finishing breakfast and heading out the door for our 29 km day. No one was coming to save me. Distracting myself, I recalled a favorite TV commercial that resembled my pitiful stuck self.

> Two executives are on an escalator when the power shuts down with a loud thumping jolt. Having no cell phones, they panic. Their desperate SOS calls echo through the halls to no avail. Demoralized, sitting on the escalator steps, they surrender to their inevitable fate: "We're stuck here until help arrives," as their stationary stairs (that extend in both directions) beg to be noticed as a path to freedom.

My inner victim rolled its eyes, thinking, *all right, fine, I get it.*

Cringing, I rebooted enough to brush my teeth and return to the bench to bandage my foot. "Do your magic, Compeed."

Orietta greeted me in the dining room as I spread my maps on the table. The general *albergue* rule: be out by eight o'clock. I had fifteen minutes.

"I'll be out as soon as I figure out the closest town to catch a bus."

Without judgment, she kindly viewed my maps.

"Don't worry about the time, I can help." She pointed. "*This* town. Get a bus there." My relief was short-lived, seeing the nine-mile walk to get there. My foot shrieked as if stuck on the escalator with no hope of survival. It had to be done.

Studying the map, printed in Spanish, I noticed the bus route veered *away* from the general direction of San Juan, my destination for that night. I thought out loud.

"I'll need to negotiate with the bus driver, using my stellar Spanish skills, to drop me off somewhere along the highway. That should go well, huh?" Orietta picked up on my sarcasm and chuckled as I continued. "I'll figure out how to reconnect with the *Camino* trail from there."

As I put on my poncho, Orietta offered her best blister care advice, "Use vinegar and salt." I added the remedy idea to the long list. Hearing me sigh, she advised, "Don't be discouraged. It'll heal."

"It's not the blister. It's about taking a bus," I explained. "I accepted the whole transport thing for my hamstring injury, but for a blister? A bus feels like cheating." Her hand came down hard on the table. In her Brazilian accent, she delivered my much-needed talkin' to.

"You STOP that right now! It's NOT cheating. Too many pilgrims think the only point here is walking. Nonsense. The *Camino* is more than that. It's a state of mind. Your Way is whatever the *Camino tells* you is *your Way*. I promise, it's not about suffering on your foot. There're many tools here other than feet. Taxis, buses, *farmacias*, water stations, all of them are tools. There's a reason we're called to any one of them. So, you get on that bus, you trust the Way put you there for a reason, and you hold your head high. *That* is your *Camino!*"

Sacred Angel Number Seven had spoken. Tears welled up. "I needed to hear that, Orietta. Thank you. You just shifted *everything* for me!" We hugged, she warmly wished me *"Buen Camino,"* and I left this special place where angels dwell.

A few (painful) strides down the trail, I felt Linda fall in step. I swear I could hear her boots crunching in the gravel. *Just get me to the bus, Linda. Something's not right with this foot.*

Her voice, clear as day, filled my head. *Sure. I can do that. Hey, high points for walking off the escalator back there.*

A Canadian couple soon caught up with me. Pals within minutes, I mentioned where I'd catch the bus with no apologetic tone. Progress. The guy asked if I heard the semi-trucks in the distance. I had.

He firmly advised, "Don't walk nine miles on that foot! My first *Camino* ended with an infected blister. My guess is those trucks were less than a kilometer from here—beyond those buildings and through those trees. I bet you could find a petrol station or a café on the highway to call a taxi."

His girlfriend balked at the risky idea. As did my chattering gremlins. Their worries flooded my head.

That's the stupidest idea ever. What if we get there, walk a few miles on the highway, find nothing, and have to turn around and try to find this trail again? It could add over five miserable miles on this foot!

Linda's response interrupted, silencing them all (my head was a busy place). *Hey, Mol, you asked me to get you to the bus, right? I just did! Listen to this guy. That was my idea!*

Taking a leap of faith, I informed my trail companions that I'd head for the highway. I was tempted to add, "My dead friend here told me you were right," but decided to keep Canada and US relations kosher.

Following their worried-sounding *"Buen Caminos,"* I cut across the field. Sure enough, on the other side of the trees was the highway. Looking a quarter mile down the road my heart leaped seeing a flashing neon café sign; I was giddy. Giddy for trusting the voice I knew was Linda's. But mostly jazzed that she delivered.

Entering the café, the smell of every food imaginable greeted me. Linda proudly whispered, *Who's yer buddy, huh?* If only I could high-five her for real. I ordered almost every item that wafted in the air. When the waitress brought my plates (yes, plural, don't judge me), I asked if she spoke English.

"A bit," she replied. I spoke slowly (and louder) because, of course, it'd help her understand better. Ugh.

"I'm-a-pilgrim." She eyed my pack, poles, and boots with a look of, *duh.*

"I have a blister. I can't walk the whole distance today. Do any buses come through here?"

"Bus? Si. How far can you walk?"

Sigh. I figured she'd direct me to the same town Orietta had suggested. *Darn. I doubt taxis come this far into the boonies.* The waitress continued, pointing to the front door.

"To get a bus, go out door. Go ten steps. Stand there. Bus comes in one hour."

"Whaaat?" We burst into laughter. She'd taken me for a ride, and I loved her!

Given she spoke better English than she let on, I explained my optimistic plan of asking the bus driver to drop me off at some point along the highway. She looked doubtful.

"Pilgrims don't ride this route. He might not like stopping. It's not on his schedule. But, sure, ask."

She handed me a small map (in Spanish, of course) that included the highway route. I studied it as I finished breakfast. Miracles were piling up in my favor. I only needed one more. Well, one more for the next hour.

Later, as my miracle bus rolled down the highway, the driver grumbled (in Spanish) when I approached his driver's compartment. I pointed (in English) to a sign— "Santovenia 3 km"— a town on the map whose back road, I'd determined, *should* lead me to San Juan.

I don't think Mr. Grouch Driver ever came to a complete stop as I jumped out with my pack and poles. I called, "Gracias!" but he was already gone. Alone in the deafening silence of nowhere, I prayed I'd made the right call.

Some emotions aren't easily explained here. I sat down crying in the weeds by the side of the road that appeared to lead nowhere. A good kind of cry. I cried for being in a foreign country whose language I didn't know, on an isolated back road far from the *Camino* trail. Yet, one I blindly trusted was the Way. Tear drops fell, wishing Linda were here in human form, but grateful for her bizarre companionship. Tears rolled down my face for having negotiated with an irritable bus driver in the only other language I knew—one of fiery determination—and got what I asked for. Finally, I cried in celebration for reading the Spanish map, trusting that San Juan and the room to be shared with Pablo and Gabby, were over-that-way *somewhere*.

Tears turned to laughter for the crazy courage I never knew was in me. Orietta's words circled back. The *Camino* had me take the bus for a reason. This appointment with destiny, in the weeds, was to connect with my True North.

I wandered into Santovenia, where passing cyclists called *"Buen Camino!"* I followed their lead toward a country road. The earthy smell of damp fields caused a flashback to my childhood hometown. I paid little attention except to how content I felt. Then it hit. I hadn't noticed any yellow arrows since town. I assumed the cyclists I followed were heading to San Juan. Doubt set in.

Walking a bit farther, a faded painted arrow appeared on the road. Unfortunately, it pointed back toward town. Though this route felt right, I caved to the gremlins' pressure to turn around. I walked three long miles back and checked in with a café bartender.

He and the guy at the bar laughed. "I apologize. We're not laughing at you. We're laughing at the absurd fact that you were going in the right direction the whole time. That arrow you saw—it's for pilgrim bikers only. If you had gone another half-kilometer, you would've connected with the *Camino* trail!" *Ugh. So much for my True North.*

He generously loaded me up with free water and a sausage sandwich. I walked out the café door, apologized to my blister, and headed up the same damn road—again.

So much landed in the miracle column that day. I hadn't planned to dwell on this mistake. But including it here might remind me (and you) to trust intuition—always.

Once safe and warm in my bunk in San Juan, laughing with Pablo and Gabby, my double trips out of Santovenia saga now seemed funny and enlightening.

Pablo snickered, "My guess, there's a new notch on that cafe wall in town inducting you into their club."

"Oh yeah? What club?"

"You know, Another Hopeless Pilgrim."

ORIETTA—ANGEL NUMBER SEVEN

CAMINO MESSAGE #8

Trust your True North. It's always there.

Journal Notes

In life, we all miss a turn here or there. I'll probably miss more in the days ahead. I trust, when feeling lost, my slowly emerging True North will save me.

Good night, dear Linda. Get some sleep, little gremlins.

Thank you for your wisdom, Orietta, my Angel Number Seven.

MORE HELPFUL CAMINO TIPS

1. Advil is a food group.

2. Chocolate or honey protein bars in your backpack pocket on a hot day will stack all your loose coins nicely in the corner. Forever.

3. You will trim your hair using dull bandage scissors somewhere along the trail. (It looks good. No, really.)

4. If you find yourself on the proverbial stopped escalator of life, before screaming for help, please note: there are exit stairs in both directions.

5. Adding butterscotch and sleigh bell to your vocabulary weeds out the riffraff. Anyone who doesn't get it, who needs 'em?

6. Keep life easy. Watch for the arrows. They're always there.

7. Everything in life has the meaning WE attach to it. May as well keep it fun.

8. Take my advice. I'm obviously not using it.

CHAPTER 18

LISTENING

SAN JUAN DE ORTEGA TO BURGOS

Tired of blister talk? Sorry. You can't force the credits to run on this bad B-movie before its time. Gabby's blisters showed healing, Pablo suffered from a fever and sinus infection. And I was a work in process—texts from Bren, then Patrick, offered more blister advice.

Despite body breakdowns, in the bustle of breakfast and arranging to transport our packs to Burgos, our spirits were optimistic heading out for our 26 km (16 mi).

Now, at the two-week mark, entering the foggy forest on a red dirt trail, the lone sound of footsteps crunching gravel became a morning prayer. Heeding strong advice to skip the long industrial entrance into Burgos later that day, we'd call a taxi from the last small town before the Burgos city limits. After determining our afternoon meeting point, we each found our pace.

Noticing my blister area going numb, I declared: "Spot the beauty day" to stay in the moment. The many simple yet beautiful details along the trail, whether created by Mother Nature or art-minded generous humans somehow made the walk that much sweeter. Phone camera in hand, I set out to tell the day's story through nature, architecture, and rich texture. The mesmerizing old structures revealed peeling layers of their thousand-year history of brick, stucco, stone, and wood. Each holding secrets to an ancient story.

Miles in, a "situation" called for a pressing question:

If Molly trips and falls in a field filled with sheep shit, and no one's there to take a picture, is the fall still valid?

On rocky terrain in ranch country, the ground suddenly rumbled under my feet. Ruling out only the Budweiser Clydesdales, the escalating clanging and hoof-pounding alerted me that some unknown species was headed right for me. They trickled in until the raucous herd of sheep spilled into a space ten times as wide as the path, the sheep herder and his dog bringing up the rear.

Scrambling for my camera while backing into a rutted field hyper-focused on this Kodak moment, I stepped backward too quickly and tripped over a rock. I went one direction, my poles another. My phone flew—just missing a pile of sheep shit.

René missed this perfect 10.0 landing. A bit scraped up, I gathered my belongings. The ruggedly handsome sheep herder passed the *peregrina* amidst the sheep doo. Tipping his cap with a smirk, wishing me, "*Buen Camino!*" his dog rolled its eyes, I swear.

The herd drifted out of sight as I humbly followed faint weathered arrows. My hard-learned lesson from yesterday: direction is provided *if* one pays attention. I fantasized, *what if arrows existed back home, pointing us in our life's best direction? Wouldn't that be grand?*

Some yellow arrows, usually accompanied by the ancient Camino shell symbol, are prominently placed, most are subtle—on the side of a barn, a curb, or hidden in tall grasses. They demand staying alert as the route takes unexpected turns.

"Awesome shot," a young Alaskan woman, Kiki commented, as I took a picture of a weathered arrow on an old barn. "Lotsa juicy visuals here!"

I glanced at the picture I'd taken and laughed. "Photography isn't exactly my bag, but this makes me look *good.*"

Kiki added, "Ya know, beauty's easy to spot, but there's a whole lotta listening needed, too." Ahhh, A kindred spirit! My brain immediately conjured echoes of clanging cowbells and pilgrims laughing. It was true.

We walked together, Kiki kicking off our list of examples proving that listening is as important here as seeing.

"First off, you gotta listen to your inner compass or pay dearly."

"Agreed! There's listening to rich tones of different languages, and to unexpected tunes that show up and speak right to your soul. And can't forget the sound of clicking walking poles rattling our brains!"

"True that! And how 'bout listening to the wisdom of other walkers, and what *really* kills me—birdsong on quiet foggy mornings." *Sigh.*

"Speaking of songs—picture-taking also requires listening. Photos capture the space between the notes. I believe they sing a story that, if left to words alone, might roll out as "butterscotch" or "sleigh bell." *That* brought a blank look.

Entering a bustling village, Kiki rejoined her *Camino* family. Hugging farewell, we knew we'd tapped an idea worth holding onto.

I then noticed a woman approaching, waving wildly to get my attention, the same German woman from days back. She smiled and handed me a hard-boiled egg. She remembered my longing for one! We both knew this represented the *Camino* love we came to drink in. You might say, we both *needed the egg*. Tearfully, I walked on with a grateful heart and an unexpected snack.

Meandering a country road, a distant melancholy bell drew my attention. Listening, I sat on the stone wall. Vast wheat fields stood between me and its wistful sound. The whistling breeze made the tall grains dance like billowing curtains in a window, making me wonder what message it might be delivering. Feeling total peace, I realized I'd already received it: *Rest a bit, listen. Take in this moment.*

The mesmerizing meditation faded, and the weathered arrow on the ancient wall reminded me to move on. With alternating foot numbness and stinging-bee pain, I was relieved to spot Pablo and Gabby's brightly colored coats a short distance ahead. Together, we walked miles of asphalt toward Burgos. Entering a small town, the bells of every church clanged so loudly our brains throbbed. In the next town, we'd summon our taxi.

Oops. How did we misread the map, thinking there was another town before Burgos? Our first hint of error: the Burgos city limit sign. Ugh. That last town with the clanging bells was it. Botching our "call a taxi" scheme to avoid the hot, blister-eating cement stretch with chain-link fences and old warehouses made it open season for whining until we found a reliable business address for taxi pickup. Relief.

The taxi dropped me off for my first stay at a sizeable 75-pilgrims-to-a-floor *albergue*. My wise friends continued to their plush accommodations. Standing at the curb, I stared at the monster four-story city *albergue*. I promised myself I'd try one of these at least once. Somewhere inside my backpack waited with hundreds of others. I took a deep breath. Given my stellar mediation skills from years with the District Attorney's Office, and Google Translate, I'd negotiate its release.

I opened the tall, heavy door and entered the opening scene for "The Night From Hell—Burgos style."

BURGOS

The scene reminded me of unruly children in the care of a pushover substitute teacher. *Am I missing some method to this madness?* My nervous system, having just served as steward of calm and beauty for seven hours, felt unsteady. Confident that Linda (never the fool) followed the Aussies to their hotel Jacuzzi, I vented to my only remaining support. *Hey, Mother Mary-Who-Art-Buried-In-A-Suitcase, WTF? Amen.*

Rumor had it Burgos was the bees-knees, a fun city many pilgrims make into a two-night rest stop. *Really?* I can't say exactly which incident pushed me over the edge, souring my whole experience. It started with recoiling at the thought of my naked, blistered foot touching the dirty floor (hardly *holy* dirt). Next, the *albergue* records showed my pack as being "delivered," but there was no sign of it. Negotiations fell short. *No backpack, no shower. Breathe, Molly.*

While they searched for it, my dirty, sweaty socks and blister limped the city streets, seeking vinegar and salt. *Why not try it?* A fruitless endeavor. Businesses were closed until 5 p.m, of course. Returning to the *albergue,* my pack was found. Hooray! Escorted to the fourth floor that slept seventy-five pilgrims, I was assigned a lower bunk. *Lucky me. I get to sleep next to four farting Finnish guys, their smelly socks wafting in my face. Even better, my bed is right next to the large bathroom. Great! All seventy-five will probably be passing by several times tonight. Super. Can't wait to meet them—all.*

The details of the Burgos train wreck are hard to relay without triggering old trauma. Given the impersonal, unemotional nature of bullet points, it's best I use them to lay out all that unfolded. We'll begin here.

- My blister foot stands in ankle-deep, filthy water due to a backed-up shower drain.
- Exiting the shower, my towel and dry clothes fall off the hook onto the wet floor, flooded from backed-up drain. I don my soaked clothes. *Gee, this is fun.*
- I sanitize the sink before cleaning and bandaging my blister. A pilgrim brushing his teeth spits into my clean sink. No, seriously, he did.

Venturing into the Saturday night Burgos party crowds for dinner, I first aimed to score vinegar and salt. Unfortunately, both were only sold in giant sizes. *What the hell? I'll just pretend I'm at Costco.*

During the evening's only high point—a great dinner with two fascinating Israeli brothers, a thoughtful text chimed from Bill.

How are things going?

To answer calmly would require ordering another bottle of wine. I'd respond later.

Leaving the café, I noticed people staring and pointing at my bag. Ugh. The salt bag had snagged on a chair and ripped, streaming a line of salt in its wake. *Breathe, Molly. Time to change the channel on this shit show, go back, do laundry, and soak my blister.*

Doing laundry with seventy other pilgrims is a real joy. Especially when some guy throws his soaking wet clothes into my dryer when mine are almost dry. Yep, he did.

Waiting for the dryer cycle to run a *second* time, and laughing with some Swedes who'd witnessed the incident, I noticed my phone only had three percent charge left, given its day of photographing. Easy fix. I connected my Euro adapter and plugged it into the wall.

CRACKLE! POP!!! Everyone jumped. White sparks flew, and yellow flames shot from the outlet, followed by a dramatic wisp of black smoke.

Eeek! Gingerly, I unplugged what was left of my blackened, melted adapter—the fate of my phone was unknown.

Freaked bystanders advised, "Let your phone cool before trying to use it," as they scrambled to unplug their phones from other outlets, fearing bad ju-ju in the walls. *I'm the dark angel of doom.*

Gathering my laundry, I returned to the community kitchen. The vinegar and what was left of the salt had vanished. Damn pirates! I was too worn out to fight for it.

Back upstairs, decompressing on my bunk, I looked for the humor in it all. None in sight. Too much had piled up. If I dug deeply enough, under the frustration, irritation, and loneliness—was fear. Yep, truth. *Maybe some women walking the Camino solo don't care if they have a phone. I do.*

Once cooled, my phone screen lit up, showing two percent battery. A text to Bill and Patrick went through. *Phew, the phone works! I just need a new adapter.* The next day (Sunday), media stores would be closed. Shit! *Do I hang out here until Monday? I'd prefer bamboo jammed under my fingernails.*

Initially, negotiations with the front desk guy to partially charge my phone failed. Then, a plan took shape thanks to Google Translate:

Guy: "Sorry, I can't start a precedence with the others."

Me: "I promise, I won't tell a soul. Guilt might work, ya know, it was your outlet that blew up my adapter. I really need your help." His hesitant look turned to agreement.

Guy: "Okay, I'll charge it part way." SCORE: Kind request: 0, Guilt: 1

Me: "You're the best!"

He blushes and types: "*Okay.* I'll charge it *completely.*" *Appreciation wins the day.*

Late evening, I finally answered Bill's text, explaining the adapter drama. Sensitive to my tough evening and knowing I needed support, he kindly empathized. I appreciated that. Pat, on the other hand, in a pissy mood, claimed the explosion was the *Camino* telling me I didn't need a damn phone and I should do without. My thinking: *stick it, Pat,* then, turned the phone off to save it for the next day's long walk.

Anticipating the joy of sinking into a deep sleep, I put in earplugs. But sleep never came. A raucous outdoor concert, that couldn't even carry a decent tune, blared until 3 a.m.

The Finns rose before sunrise, and with their butts in my face as they dressed, wrestled their packs and departed. Ahhh, finally, peace. Well, except for the seventy people snoring like freight trains, including one poor guy—sick as a dog, coughing up a lung.

Not giving a damn about my own rustling, I packed in the dark. *This place is history!*

The golden sunrise glistening on the magnificent Burgos cathedral as I passed made me regret missing the tour the evening before, but my foot had refused to go one more block.

A familiar chant wafted from a patio café. "Hail the Queen!" Followed by the Kingsmen's quick scramble into formation, with glasses of orange juice in one hand and a salute from the other. *Silly? Yes. And somehow sacred—of the highest order.* Sitting with my Kingsmen, eating a welcomed tortilla de patata, they answered my probing questions on their seemingly odd union—from very young to quite old, with a combination of German, Portuguese, and (maybe) Brazilian accents.

Markus from Germany, who spoke the clearest English, and seemed the jokester of the group, explained with a twisted smile: "We're from four different countries. You nailed our nationalities. Except for Stan. We're pretty sure he's an alien. We all met in the Pyrenees. Naturally, we clicked, discovering we'd each coincidentally escaped from prison and joined the International Prison-to-Pilgrim Program. Yep, bought the guards off with cigarettes to pull it off. We've been a happy, dysfunctional *Camino* family ever since."

His crazy comic relief was much needed. After farewell hugs, still laughing, I walked the long distance out of the city. Wanting bad ju-ju behind me, I didn't rest until the "leaving Burgos" sign. One day, this grand city and I will make peace. Until then, sitting on a park bench, I exhaled, reflecting on the past twelve hours, and asked whoever was listening: "What the hell was all THAT about?!?"

CHAPTER 19

THE *MESETA*: A GOOD DAY to DIE

Looking at the songs in the soundtrack of my life, you'd be puzzled to see "Braham's Lullaby" included around my 45-year-old mark rather than in my infant years. But *I'm* clear why it earned that position.

Years ago, during a twenty-five-year sleep disorder—part of the fallout from the assault in college, I was invited to South Dakota for a private, authentic, healing sweat lodge with a Native American shaman. Nervously, I accepted the offer while optimistically believing it was my ticket to healing sleepless nights.

Arriving on lodge day, the Lakota medicine man (and husband of my dear friend, Diane) welcomed me and declared, "It's a good day to die!" Seeing my wide-eyed reaction, Diane explained: "He's referring to the wise practice of clearing our minds and hearts of burdens. To face each new day refreshed, we must "die" to the problems and distractions that cloud our connection with Spirit." I understood. It was *indeed* a good day to die in the sweat lodge. And die I did, to the fear of surrendering, which denied me sleep for years. The *Camino* now called me to another kind of death.

I heard the *Camino* provided three phases: life—death—rebirth. The story goes: we arrive at this pilgrimage carrying the heavy details of life, i.e., our things, beliefs, emotional and physical weight. Next, during the long *meseta* (central Spain's large, expansive, flat plains) with its days of mind-messing monotony providing an endless thinking trap—all the unproductive ways we've clung to in life begin to surface. On the *meseta*, we surrender and are invited to die to these old ways. Following the *meseta* comes rebirth. Our cloudy connection with Spirit clears, and we're renewed. It all rang a familiar bell. What would I choose to die to this time?

LOVE IT OR HATE IT

I heard rumors about the *meseta*. Not always encouraging ones. They projected love/hate opinions from experienced pilgrims:

"Each mile I felt more connected to the land, fell in love with walking, and myself."

"I loved the endless reflective time. Mentally, it's the Camino's most trying stretch. And my favorite."

"I hated the meseta! No stops for miles! I'll take a bus around it next time."

"Hotter than hell, that meseta. Got sunburned through my hat in that God-forsaken place."

"Here, I came face to face with who I really am. I knew something had to change. Me."

OF WHAT IS IT THEY SPEAK?

The *meseta* landscape begins after Burgos and ends in Astorga. This 219 km (136-mi) stretch is renowned for its endless, pancake-flat landscape and big skies.

Once free of the Burgos web, sitting in a café, a South African seasoned Camino groupie joyfully spilled his past meseta experiences: "In summer, it's a scorcher. In winter, freezing cold. Spring and fall—hell, anything is possible: sun, torrential rain, killer winds. Most days are long and alotta of nothin' with hardly any shade or rest stops."

"Gee, all that, and for *free*, huh? And you keep coming back?"

He looked in the *meseta's* direction with a knowing smile and continued.

"The *meseta* messes with you. Your perception of time and distance gets all screwy. That's where the magic sneaks in."

"So, which is the magical part, the nasty winds or the brain probe?"

He smiled, tipped his hat, wished me *"Buen Camino,"* and left.

Some pilgrims shared that it's a monotonous, crazy-making six days. For others, it's the portion of the *Camino* that gets under their skin the most—becoming the soul of their whole journey. One woman summed it up. "Molly, it tests your mind, confronts your heart, makes you ponder your deep connection to this Earth."

When facing unknown territory, I appreciate insight into what's to come. Here, I still felt I knew nothing. The Great Blue Heron knows what should die, and what unexpected turns we must take. Eyeing the long road ahead, I put a question out to Roman. *Is this where things get down and dirty?*

At that, the *Camino* laughed. Knowing *nothing* was about to make this mysterious experience *everything*.

THE MESETA – DAY ONE

To Hontanas

Bachianas Brasilerias No. 5
~ Laurindo Almeida / Salli Terri

Eyeing miles of serpentine trail as far as I could see, the gremlins calculated how many times my blister foot would touch down. This called for a *Camino* knock upside the head. *Molly, stop it! Look around, girl. You're in flippin' Spain! Burn this beauty in your memory.*

Midday, leaving the medieval-like village of Hornillos del *Camino*, I had eight miles to go on that day's wide open *meseta*. Feeling both excited and uneasy, I tuned in, and requested my angels to stay close. A mile in, a spontaneous music piece began playing in my head. This hauntingly beautiful *aria* "Bachianas Brasileiras No. 5" was triggered by the heart-melting, poppy-filled landscape and breathtaking fields of waving grain that appeared before me. Jaw-dropping. Having intuitively added this same music piece to my phone weeks ago, I put in earbuds, and pushed play to listen.

Michael Johnson (years before) introduced me to this *aria*—an elaborate opera melody sung solo. We listened on his living room floor in Nashville through individual headsets, bringing us both to tears. Its surprise emergence here brought me to my knees in tears once again.

In this mesmerizing moment, my heart declared being 100 percent in the game. Santiago, now my destiny, I faced a part of myself I'd never met. I understood I hadn't come to get good at walking, but to seal the deal on loving and trusting myself—truly, madly, deeply.

Many exhausting hours later, I collapsed on my bed in Hontanas, boots hanging off the end covered in holy dirt, staring at the ceiling. It's true. The expansive *meseta* messes with your head. Having my big aha in the poppy field didn't mean I couldn't sadly regress to thinking, *Oh c'mon, are you fucking kidding me?*" (when the map's promise of arrival felt like a scam). Yet, this registered as a favorite day.

I made an unexpected promise to my feet during the afternoon's endless walking—*this'll be your last day in boots for a while.* Yikes. Now, I had to somehow deliver sandal relief. The Aussies, who arrived soon after me, kindly agreed to help with my footwear search the next day. In the moment, I needed to budge from my frozen state on the bed.

Walking to dinner, a fellow pilgrim offered his stark take on his first day of the *meseta* experience: "It's nothing, really." That's all he could say.

THE MESETA – DAY TWO

It's nothing? The pilgrim's words stuck in my head. They again tripped the memory of Jerry Seinfeld's humorous TV show, forever reorganizing my *meseta* perspective.

A show about nothing. That was the premise for Seinfeld's sitcom when pitching it to NBC producers. A show about nondescript happenings in its characters' lives, with episodes that go no deeper than "No soup for you!" In its nutty simplicity, this idea of nothing won over the producers, and millions of viewers.

Similarly, the words monotony and *meseta* are often spoken in the same breath. However, this extensive nothingness is rumored to create space for soul searching and facing what we've been running from. Like my healing sweat lodge experience, this void slowly peeled back the layers and revealed what must die.

It was Day Two here, and until some monumental revelation from the holy dirt permeated the soles of my boots, my screenwriter's mind entertained itself by chewing on a weird idea. *What if we're all just actors in a show called "Seinfeld's Meseta: The Show About Nothing?"*

If this show's producers requested samples of this *meseta* existence, I'd have gladly volunteered the Aussie's and my experiences, play by play, in a non-spectacular fashion (*meseta* style). Take this morning's non-eventful recap for example:

- Preparing to leave Hontanas, the Spanish hostel owner draws a detailed map on a napkin directing us to the promised Tevas in a tiny mercantile in nearby Castrojeriz. Eureka!

- At the outset, the gritty blowing dirt, on top of blister fatigue, our previous *meseta* perception shifted from jaw-dropping beauty to a seeming vast wasteland.

- Arriving in Castrojeriz, Pablo and I locate the small hole-in-the-wall mercantile in search of Tevas. Our thought upon entering: *this can't possibly be the right place!* It resembles disorganized hoarder's junk. The owner only speaks German. *Uh-oh. This doesn't look promising.*

- However, SCORE! With a little magic, good pantomime, and Google Translate, I exit with Tevas two sizes larger than normal— allowing space to avoid rock bruising. *Clown-size sandals with chic socks? Bring on the sexy!*

- Pablo's sinus infection and fever worsen. Time for medical intervention.

- Sitting on the curb, I battle with my online bank account for two hours, attempting an international funds transfer. Patience dwindles.

By this point, I'm wondering: *Does anything exciting ever happen in this show?*

The answer unfolded much later: *No. Not really. But that's exactly what makes it intriguing.*

The afternoon slipped away. With Pablo feeling like hell, and my need to wash and dry my new socks while the sun's still hot, we taxied to Fromista for sanity and a decent night's sleep. Things turned on a dime.

In a sunny *albergue* backyard, I laughed with two hilarious sisters from British Columbia, Myrna and Sylvia, as I flipped my new wet socks every fifteen minutes in the hot sun like juicy hamburgers on a grill. *Does it get any better?*

Hope surged through my bandaged foot when a text chimed from Gina:

> Hey Molly! Good news! I'm walking full days with Brad! My knee is healed and rockin' it!

Big kudos to you, my "Another-Fucking-Camino-Lesson-Bus-Buddy!"

Taking my dry socks off the grill, a kind German woman offered to check my blister status. Her report: "It's healing! There's new pink skin covering the area." *If only it felt that way.*

Evening fell. Lights out at ten. The Canadian sisters and I vowed, "We'll meet again!"

This typical day would surely lure any *Seineld's Meseta: The Show About Nothing* producer and provide a lotta *nada* to chew on. It's a wrap!

THE MESETA – DAY THREE

Morning light streamed in the *albergue* kitchen window. A man from Amsterdam sipped steaming black coffee, watching me assemble my breakfast masterpiece: avocado mashed in a bowl with two hard-boiled eggs, then globbed on top of a *tortilla de patata*. Final touch: tabasco. Breakfast of champions—I'd be good until lunch. This international sensation became known as "Molly's morning mash." Staring at my concoction, the man grunted and walked out. *Was he hurt I didn't share?*

I appreciated these reduced-to-nothing days. Walking through town, grass sparkling with morning dew, I sported my stylin' new socks with Tevas, boots dangling off my pack. What I lack in navigation skills, I make up for in fashion. Three texts chimed:

1. Aussies took the longer river route. We'll meet in Carrion tonight.
2. Bill, Patrick, and Kaz are only one day behind after several high-mile days.
3. An old love's name surprisingly appears, wishing me safe travels.
Already a great day, and it's only 7:30 a.m.

"*Buen Camino*" called the elderly Spanish man sitting peacefully in front of the *mercado*. Sensing he was an old-world treasure, I approached. A curious Argentinian woman joined us, kindly translating my questions and his proud responses. "There's ancient history surrounding these buildings..." His enthusiastic, detailed chronicling of this ancient town wound down with, "No more than 800 locals are left in this town." With a wistful sadness, he added, "Most young ones disappeared to see the world. Rightfully so, I suppose."

Hearing his stories firsthand placed us in the midst of living history. Wars, destruction, rebuilding, growing their own food, learning as a child how to make wine. So many victories, so much suffering, and deep pride for the tenacity of generations before him. His final share: "After the Spanish Civil War, most farmers gave up growing grapes and making wine to grow wheat instead. We sacrificed to rebuild our war-torn community."

This 79-year-old man was James. Some might say "much ado about nothing." For me, he completed my day. Stepping onto the day's 19 km (12 mi) trail, the crumbling architecture and old, overgrown gardens spoke to me of something. Something worth including in this simple, yet complex, nothing show.

Miles later after a light rain, I removed my poncho and changed into dry socks (a necessary Teva ritual). Noting the beautiful, wooded area along the quiet road, my vote was in: *I love the meseta.*

Finally, a café stop. I reached for my prescription glasses to order, usually hanging from my neck. They were gone. I searched everything. Nothing. Damn. Calculating where they'd flown off when removing my poncho, I recalled the nearby woods and their approximate distance back. Two miles? I retraced my steps, eyes and nose to the ground like a bloodhound. The lost glasses would be easy to spot—bright purple.

Reaching the familiar woods, I scoured the ground. If the producers were looking for an exciting plot twist, this had great potential. But alas nothing. I returned to the café, left my contact information in case they were found, and allowed myself fifteen minutes of self-beat up, then surrendered. *I'll survive using my readers and prescription sunglasses. Not cool purple, but they'll do.*

Carrion De Los Condes came more easily than Hontanas. *Tevas, you served me well. As did the meseta. How's it possible I walked miles—with (almost) no thoughts rattling inside my brain?* Some greater knowing was taking hold without any need for thinking.

Entering Carrion, the many church bells competed for endurance and loudness. The tolling persisted as I checked in and showered. *Surely, they'll stop by bedtime, yes?*

We roamed the town's medieval atmosphere, with its ancient history of brutal battles and, per the guidebook, evil vengeful acts of retribution. *Sorry, Seinfeld producers. The only exciting, aggressive act we can stir up for you is this mad rush on the sports store when it opens at 5 p.m.* I scored purple toe socks and a sky-blue lightweight jacket. It's the little things.

Crashing for the night, the bells rarely stopped. Someone, somewhere, decided it's a good idea to remind pilgrims of the time—Every. Fifteen. Minutes.

I can't say if it was the likes of some strange morning mash, 79-year-old James, or maybe the tolling bells that did it. But, even if the Seinfeld producers would never understand, at some point, once upon a time, the *Camino* gods *did*. They honored the *meseta* as an ancient, worthy portion of this pilgrimage. And thousands claim, somewhere in this void, they've been set free.

With several days of the *meseta* still ahead—half-expecting to run into Seinfeld and Kramer in some café—what I knew for sure: its nothingness became *something,* making it a very good day to die indeed.

CAMINO MESSAGE #9

The spectacular is buried in the slow, gentle nothing.

CHAPTER 20

THE *MESETA* – DAY FOUR

CARRION DE LOS CONDES TO TERRADILLOS DE LOS TEMPLARIOS

Walking this sunny, birdsong-filled morning, the judgment from the guy on our Frankfurt flight who had regarded my *Camino* plan as "foolish," flashed in my mind. Recalling his idea that walking a bunch of shorter walks in Colorado would offer the same experience, I replayed my sassy retort: *No, walking in Colorado wouldn't be the same. I'm looking for a master's degree, not an evening class.*

I now stared that master's thesis in the eye. Academia defines a thesis as "a synthesis of discoveries about a topic, and your evaluation of those discoveries." Boring jargon. In my own words, a thesis simply asks: "So what? Now what?"

More nauseated with each step, I sensed I was in trouble. My gremlins did the math—21 km (13 mi) ahead on this foot. Or was it my wise *Voice* calculating and reporting *enough is enough?* Nausea and chills on a warm day wasn't rocket science. Likely an infection. *So what? Now what?*

That's when I heard whistling. A gentleman approached from behind in a cowboy hat, earbuds feeding some upbeat tune into his spirited steps. He caught my smile and stopped. This was Andrea, from Milan, Italy, and my unexpected "let's keep Molly's mind anywhere but on her foot" walking buddy for the day. With his decipherable English-speaking skills, we walked and talked about music, how whistling and humming boosts immunity, our homelands, family, and how much he related to my thesis definition. When I tried to let him off the hook from hanging back at my slow blister pace, he confessed, "I strained my hamstring and would rather appear a hero by staying back with you than tell my buddies I can't keep up with them." Win-win.

In his early forties, with a wife and child at home, and one on the way, he explained "Every summer I walk the *Camino* for two weeks with my buddies, then onto Barcelona to meet family for vacation." He shared his dreams, finding the easiest English words to express them. Understanding the Hero's Journey concept, Andrea laughed about my Bilbo Baggin's angry bee episode. His love of *The Hobbit* trilogy provided common ground. Ahhh, the magic of the arts speaks every language.

By noon, we'd emptied my sunscreen tube walking the hot, endless, gravel path. My new walking routine: two hours in Tevas, two hours in boots, then back to Tevas. It kept every body part somewhat happy. My Tevas and socks continually collected tiny pebbles. Sitting on the ground shaking holy dirt from my socks, I asked Andrea for the Italian word for the dark-blue flower growing beside me. "*Blu scuro*," he replied. Then, pointing to light-blue in the sky, he instructed, "*azzuro*." I repeated both shades in perfect Italian, launching our several-hour English and Italian game of color words.

Spirits were high. The guidebook warned of the day's "featureless landscape." In reality, there's hidden rich artistry in the *meseta's* nothingness. From the tiniest *gallo* (yellow*)*, *rosso* (red), and *blu* (blue) flowers sprouting from the *marrone* (brown) rutty ground, the varied shades of *verde* (green) in the occasional tree to the number of distinct shades of *blu* in the sky, Italians celebrate each with a word that gracefully flows off the tongue like a song.

Our color game paused when I heard my *Camino* name called. "*Buen Camino*, Ms. Colorado!" The Canadian sister, Sylvia, race-walked past us. She called back, "Later, Mol! I wanna get this awful *meseta* over as fast as possible!"

Andrea pointed to another woman, stating, "Purple." He'd proudly identified the woman's t-shirt color, earning high accolades. I responded, "*Si, viola*!" Our color-word skills reached stellar heights.

Andrea shifted focus again. Mixing Italian and English, he read from the guidebook how our far-off destination of Santiago de Compostella translated to "St. James Under A Field of Stars." Then, read aloud:

"Medieval legend says the *Camino* mystically follows the route of our celestial Milky Way, its stars being magically formed by the dust raised by traveling pilgrims."

He scooped up a handful of dirt, letting it pour to the ground. "It's wild to think we could be creating stars this very second, isn't it?"

His dirt waterfall triggered a flashback to Roman's words in the Pyrenees. Out of the ethers trickled what Roman may have meant when he said, "This is holy dirt. Wrap your whole being in it. Get dirty." *Had Andrea and I been doing that all day? Wrapping ourselves in the simple, present moment—or in Roman's term—in the holy dirt? Maybe "get dirty" means daring to live in "what is?"*

My *Camino* messages began merging into one idea: *Find the extraordinary in the mundane. The spectacular is buried in the slow, gentle nothing. Listen for your True North.*

They all pointed to one theme: be in the moment.

Pablo and Gabby's afternoon text announced they'd arrived at our hostel in Terradillo de los Templarios, with their feet propped at an umbrella table, ready to hand me a beer. *I'm so ready for that.* We entered Andrea's and his friends' small destination town. He brought up the topic avoided for hours. My foot. "It's gone on too long. Your whole foot is scary *rosso* (red). So what, now what, Ms. Colorado?" I promised to get medical attention.

He shared how tough it was to end his short pilgrimage each summer. He suggested meeting the Aussies and me for breakfast in the morning with his friends, before walking his final day. I agreed, understanding plans made on the *Camino* are never promised.

We found Andrea's hostel, sad for the end of our grand day. I asked, "How do you say 'I feel blue' in Italian?" With a pouty lip, he answered. "*Sentirsi blu.*" His warm hug and a heartfelt "*Buen Camino*, Molly-from-Colorado" sent me down the trail with a heavy grateful heart. The surfacing fatigue and foot stabbing, mixed with the day-saving connection with

Andrea (Angel Number Eight), made for a weird emotional cocktail that brought streaming tears I couldn't explain for the next three miles.

Entering the hostel gate, the Aussies cheered, until seeing my tear-streaked face. My meltdown began with a dramatic dropping of the pack to the ground and landing in the chair in tears, spewing my frustrations.

"I could put up with the pain in my hamstrings! I've listened for what my knee and back need. I can handle THAT! But I will NOT be brought down by a fucking blister! I'm telling you—if this is how it will be until Santiago, I'm not playing! I refuse to take another bus, but I can't put up with *this* shit either! So, that means I'm stuck here on the escalator. That reference went over their heads. Just push me off a fucking cliff so the death certificate is respectable and not humiliating like 'death by blister!' I've done everything I know to do. Everyone said this would heal. Wrong! I *love* the *meseta* and resent being distracted with every damn step!"

I was taken aback by a gentle male voice from the next table. "Hi, I'm Gary. Originally from Toronto, have lived in Seville for ten years." He pulled his chair over, extending his hand. He shook Pablo and Gabby's hands. He knew better than to reach for mine, given they were covered in meltdown snot. His heroic efforts began.

"I couldn't help overhearing your problem."

Catching my breath, "Yeah, nervous breakdowns are hard to miss."

"Can I look at your blister? Maybe I can help. I've walked 10,000 km of the *Camino* over the years and have seen my share."

Gabby jumped in, "Are you a doctor?"

"No, but I'm a pro at reading blisters."

I pulled off my boot, socks, bandages, and propped my foot for inspection.

"Hmm, yep" he mumbled, poking around my foot. I jerked in pain. "This isn't just a *little* infected. It's dangerously infected. Do you have a fever?"

"Possibly."

"Yep, the top skin has healed but is hiding a cesspool of infection underneath. Like having a blister under your blister. Do you have a pharmaceutical piercing needle?"

I was relieved to report—NO. But Gabby jumped in. "I do!" Ugh.

He pierced the skin as everyone turned their eyes away. A gross yellow discharge ran down my ankle. "Soak in Betadine tonight. It should be checked tomorrow. I'll walk you the five miles to the Sahagún medical clinic in the morning myself." This wasn't his suggestion, but a directive. That's how you know the *Camino* is talking to you. Angel Nine had appeared.

At dinner, over several bottles of wine, sharing our travels, Gary revealed two *Camino* tips for staying blister-free, aside from wearing shoes at least one size bigger than usual. Gabby and I took copious notes: 1. Carry extra socks. Change them on the trail *at least* twice daily. 2. With every change, douse your feet with rosemary alcohol. It disinfects, dries, and soothes tired, sweaty feet We could purchase it in Sahagún the next day. Peace comes with doing the right thing. Maybe I wouldn't have to be pushed over a cliff after all.

I rose with the roosters to meet Gary. Exiting the lobby, Andrea and his friends entered, but our breakfast idea was regrettably foiled. Before parting, Andrea and I confirmed: I had a standing invitation to Milan, and my Colorado door would always be open to him and his family. Thank you, Andrea, for guiding me in the many hues of blue in the sky and inspiring my first understanding of Roman's holy dirt message. *Buen Camino,* my friend.

Gary and I headed west for my date with the healing gods of Sahagún.

ANDREA – ANGEL NUMBER EIGHT

GARY – ANGEL NUMBER NINE

CAMINO MESSAGE #10

"This is holy dirt. Wrap your whole being in it. Get dirty."- Roman, from Ukraine

CHAPTER 21

SOMETHING WILL HAPPEN

SAHAGÚN, TO BERCIANOS DEL REAL CAMINO, TO LEON

You Say
~ Lauren Daigle

"It'll all be okay," Pablo assured me after the clinic visit as I climbed into the taxi, with the plan we'd meet up that evening. There, I'd toss a dart at the map to identify where I'd go to await healing.

My mind committee stayed surprisingly quiet as the taxi pulled away. It was either relief or their hesitation to scream for help from the escalator. I reviewed the medical report, as if I could read Spanish. I knew basically what it said. The Aussies kindly arrived at the clinic and interpreted the doctor's strict orders after Gary left:

"Stop walking—*now*. The infection has wrapped around your toe. Take these antibiotics and stop walking until it's healed, or you'll be forced to stop permanently. When you can touch your foot to the floor with zero pain, only then begin walking again. If the redness spreads, get to a clinic."

Pablo's kind words, "It'll all be okay," hovered. Before leaving for Spain, I'd read a great book, *What To Do When It's Your Turn* (*And It's Always*

Your Turn), by Seth Godin. His perspective stayed with me. He addressed how the phrase, "It will all be okay," is usually interpreted as "Everything will turn out the way you want it to." Godin's viewpoint: it rarely works to "positive think" your way into a designed future, one that likely won't happen exactly your way. The phrase is better interpreted, as "something will happen." Period. Whatever that something ends up being, figure out what to do with *that.* He suggested that pushing for a particular outcome interferes with the best one already flowing to you. He channeled the *Camino* itself.

Fiddling with the bottle of antibiotics in one coat pocket and rosemary alcohol from the *farmacia* in the other, I resisted slapping a smiley face on the situation. Instead, I surrendered to Godin's approach: *This might work, it might not work. Be okay with everything not being okay.* That would allow something better than imagined. I sound highly evolved, yes? Don't be too impressed. Worry and freaking out were one fretful thought away.

My phone's song list nudged me. I found my earbuds, pushed play, closed my eyes, and directed the song "You Say" to whatever *Camino* power was listening.

WHAT'S IN A NAME?

The upbeat taxi driver, originally from Montreal, noticing I'd removed my earbuds, began the usual questions. "Where did you begin walking? Where ya from? Do you like Spain?" My distant gaze pushed him into real talk.

His kind words gave my discouragement a reprieve. "It's hard to know when a blister has gone south. Unfortunately, you can't tell until *after* it's crossed that line. I've been there. Taking a break is all you can do." I exhaled. "So, what town did you stay in last night?" His question caused my recently devised Spanish pronunciation method to be revealed.

"We stayed in Pterodactyl Temples."

His eyebrows raised. "Where?"

"Oh. Sorry. Hold on." Opening my guidebook, I offered him its true pitiful phonetic breakdown. "Terr-a-di-llos de Los Tem-plar-i-os. It's easier to say—*Pterodactyl Temples.*"

"Ahh, not keen on Spanish pronunciation, eh?" Followed by his Canadian chuckle.

"Obviously not. I've been walking with an Australian couple, originally from Argentina. Spanish rolls so beautifully off their tongues I can't catch the pronunciation. When they reach the final syllable, I'm still stuck on the first two. I'm hopeless. That's probably why I was sentenced to grow up near Buffalo. Easy to sound out."

The driver slowly repeated last night's town pseudo-name. "Ptero-dactyl Temp-ples...I'm kinda liking it!" Followed by his distinct laugh. He inquired how this sophisticated renaming technique began. We had time, so he got the whole story.

"One day, a British woman and I were frustrated by our challenge with Spanish. We really did try. But to ease the pressure of map reading, we'd find a word *close* to the Spanish name that we could easily say. For example, Castrojeriz rolled much better as Castrated. Nájera became No Hair; Carrion de los Condes, which spoke directly to my 60s music passion, was now "Carry On My Wayward Son" (hey, our game, our rules). Then there's Horny."

He took a stab at it. "Hornillos del *Camino*?"

"Yep. The Brit and I parted that day feeling pretty accomplished in our new lingo."

During our odd conversation, I leafed through the guidebook, eyeing upcoming towns, pondering the following day's best healing destination.

My chariot pulled up to our hostel in Bercianos. "So, do you have a plan?" he inquired, pulling my pack from the trunk. Until I said it, I wasn't aware I'd made the decision.

"I do. I'll start antibiotics now, skip tomorrow's stage through Mansilla, and taxi to Leon Russell in the morning. I'll park myself there until, well, until the fat lady sings."

"Leon Russell—good choice. It could be a bad sign I knew you meant Leon. For the record, 'A Song For You' was Leon Russell's best tune." I agreed.

Winking, he high-fived me. "You were fun! *Buen Camino, Señorita*, and good luck. But I doubt you'll need it."

Moment of truth. It'd been seventeen years since swallowing an antibiotic. I lived primarily in the herbal medicine world. Before consuming the first pill, we had an intense stare-down until I made it an ally. By the following day, we made our peace. I blessed it and swallowed it again. Taxiing my way to Leon, the blister and I were almost twenty-four hours into stinging-bee and dragon slaying. Not yet sure "everything would be okay," I went with "something will happen."

LEON HIDEAWAY

Leon, Day One: In my private Leon hideaway, I fell into bed and slept hard. The antibiotic kicked my butt. Three hours later, waking in a fog to two incoming texts, it wasn't until I walked several steps to retrieve my phone that I noticed the first inkling of foot relief.

Oh, happy day!

The first text: Bren and Kylie would enter Leon in two days—both ailing with bronchitis. Not good, given Bren's asthma. Surprised I was already in Leon and the reason, Bren schemed.

> Buy yourself a little black dress. That is, if you'll agree to dine with me. Tevas and Compeeds acceptable.

A dress? What's that? Dinner date? Such an invitation from a true gentleman was also foreign. I recalled the comment Kylie let slip days back—about the challenging dead-end non-relationship Bren was stuck in back home. She could only say, "It's complicated." Complicated is never good. Fortunately, my mind and heart were only in the uncomplicated present moment regarding Bren.

The second text: Bill and Patrick would enter Leon in two days and hoped to meet for dinner. The Leon convergence was in motion.

Pulled from the trail like this, I wasn't sure how to occupy my downtime. Would profound insights come if I opened my journal? Nope. Linda's voice materialized in my head.

No big lessons or insights to uncover here, Mol. You've got this. Given your foot is healing, the next priority is finding that little black dress. Let's go!

Exploring the narrow streets in old town, Leon felt different from other cities. Was it the city itself, or was *I* just lighter, more alive, more grounded? With a purchased feather-light black sun dress for dinner checked off the list, I wandered winding streets with notably diminished limping, spent time with two wonderful Canadian women, and made an unplanned purchase: a stronger-soled walking sandal with better arch support. Day one of healing was more fun than should be allowed.

Leon, Day Two: Soaked my foot in medicinal concoctions all day, applied topicals, and swallowed the prescribed penicillin. Lured into afternoon journaling, all unleashed thoughts, questions, and insights on the surprise topics of belonging and integrity provided insight needed down the road. When the pen stopped, I was ripe for an evening escape.

A taxi dropped me in the main square. Sitting at an outside café gawking in awe at the spotlight-lit thirteenth-century Gothic Santa Maria de Leon Cathedral, I listened to joy-filled celebrations of happy pilgrims cheering their halfway mark to Santiago. The sound of partying locals joined the buzz, clinking glasses with friends and family. Spanish street music served as the perfect backdrop for toasting my own sacred halfway milestone. Oddly, I never felt alone. My team of angels, determination, and I found each other's company to be more than enough.

Leon, Day Three: a significant healing spurt occurred. I hadn't walked barefoot pain-free like that in days. Hanging my new dress on the shower bar (ironing, *Camino* style), I headed to breakfast, then to locate Bren and Kylie's rented apartment near the Cathedral. The "something will happen" theory was about to kick in.

FRIENDSHIP IN DOG YEARS

Kylie called from the Leon hospital. They arrived by taxi due to Bren's breathing struggles. Diagnosis: a severe case of pneumonia. Kylie had bronchitis.

Taxiing to the hospital, my mind rearranged its Rubik's cube squares: Bren's *Camino* future hung by a thread; the new dress would remain on the hanger; my recent journal ramblings were coming into focus.

An intriguing *Camino* phenomenon: human hearts, once tangled in the *Camino* web, connect with a mysterious quickening. Friendships that normally unfold gradually accelerate on the Way. You see into people more deeply, more quickly. You listen, hearing unspoken layers. What once seemed cliché-ish, you feel to your core—we're all connected.

It's alchemy. The best analogy is that connections multiply in dog years here. To loosely apply the dog formula, walking with a stranger for two hours has an equivalent depth to two weeks' time at home. Which explains my connection with Bren. It wasn't really a romance, or a fantasy about the Scottish guy in the kilt. Okay, maybe it crossed my mind. Our hours walking together, in "normal time," seemed brief, but connecting the past five days (including the afternoon of my Bilbo meltdown), in dog years, we'd become soul friends.

I sat with Bren in his hospital room, the rhythm of an oxygen machine in the background. This handsome muscular man looked pale and defeated. Having completed one *Camino* in the past, he assumed we'd have plenty of time to talk about his relationship and legal situation back home. But now was all we had. He spilled the complete story he glossed over before, about his former (initially intended short-term) girlfriend who suffered mounting mental illness problems, and, their unplanned, dearly loved, four-year-old son. The child's old-world maternal grandparents were barring Bren from future involvement in his child's life, forcing an ugly custody battle. This Camino was meant to clear his anger. Instead, the anger settled in his lungs.

I felt such respect and compassion.

Patrick texted in the midst of this. They'd arrived and were in Cathedral Square celebrating "something with someone," and if I hurried, I could join them for tequila shots is all I understood. Bren's situation was priority. I'd meet them later for dinner.

Reality clicked: Bren and Kylie were returning to Scotland in three days. Having passed the ultimate "walking with no pain" test, my right foot left me bursting to leave Leon in the morning. My (mostly ignored until now) *left* foot insisted we return the new sandals before leaving town, given they were rubbing several toes raw. *Ugh.*

Bren requested a final favor. He handed me a prayer card he intended to leave at *Cruz de Ferro* (the Iron Cross). It held a Celtic blessing for his family turmoil. I promised to safely deliver it to the Cross and zipped it securely in my jacket pocket.

Though we had an intriguing friendship, I didn't see his question coming. Bren asked if I'd be open to exploring our connection more seriously after the *Camino*. This good man's thoughtful heart would be tempting in any other situation. But Kylie's comment, "complicated," lingered like nails on a blackboard. I've done complicated. And learned.

"An interesting offer if things were different. You're a special man, Bren. However, I won't sign up for something that's already messy at the start. You've got a tough fight and big responsibilities ahead. There's no room for a long distance 'us.' Your child needs you." He admitted facing an all-consuming road ahead. Closing on a high note, we agreed our *Casablanca* friendship was at least forty in dog years.

Kylie snagged me as I left. She'd eavesdropped (in typical sister style). "Molly, obviously there's magnetism between Bren and you. Reconsider your decision."

"It's tempting, Kylie. But I know my worth. I've done 'complicated' before. I'm not going back to a place I prayed my way out of." My soul exhaled with clarity.

I looked forward to the familiar touchstone when heading for Cathedral Square to meet Bill and Patrick. Locating them, it didn't take long to fall into our old swing of things.

One highlight of this warm Leon evening was the moment Patrick—who's on record repeatedly for "needing to be right," proclaimed: "I've gotta say, I'm really proud of your brave solo feat." Then, his energy shifted, humbly admitting, "Molly, I was wrong. I'm sorry for being so judgmental when your phone charger blew up. Bill made me see what a dick I was."

I repeat: Pat actually said, "*I was wrong.*" We all enjoyed a good laugh, entertained by his satisfying confession. These men were my early cheerleaders for this journey. From the triceps machine at the gym, to dinner in Leon, was an unforeseen merry leap. They planned a layover in Leon; I'd leave in the morning. We parted, I with a warm sense of gratitude.

Late that night, back in the room, my long-forgotten hanging dress greeted me. Instead of a candlelight dinner with Bren, I held his prayer card in my pocket. My heart registered somewhere between melancholy and excitement as I packed for the much-anticipated morning exodus. Mostly, it registered as *determined*.

I scrubbed the sandals to be returned until squeaky clean. The morning plan: be first in the shoe store when it opens, then tap dance out of town.

My mind appraised Godin's "something will happen" theory. Something certainly had. Dismissing the need to always be reassured "everything will be okay," I blessed the penicillin bottle and zipped it into my pack pocket with two pairs of socks and rosemary alcohol.

In the morning, I'd walk through the gates of a fresh, pain-free beginning. Wiser. Ready to immerse myself once again in holy dirt. Trusting *something will happen*.

Journal Notes

June 3, 2019
Late Night in Leon

Dear Camino,

I'm grateful the bones of my own integrity held firm, even with Bren's tempting invitation. For your inspiration to gather my courage to walk away—thank you. I have no time for "complicated" in this too-short, precious life.

And Camino, one more thing. I've made my share of mistakes and wrong turns on this walk. And in life. I'll likely make more. But starting tomorrow, I just want to make NEW damn mistakes, okay? Amen.

MORE HELPFUL CAMINO TIPS

1. ALERT regarding the no alcohol rule while on an antibiotic: if gremlins suggest hiding the pill in your french fries—much like concealing your dog's medicine in peanut butter, so you can drink sangria—don't be fooled. It's still in there. Tough it out.

2. You likely don't remember what town or bed you slept in yesterday. That's okay. Keep walking.

3. Clotheslines tell a story we can never fully know. Carry on (chop wood, carry water).

4. Church Bells Lesson #1: Whether walking into a large city or a small village—feet aching to the bone—at first, when the bells ring, you'll swear, "They toll for me!" Then you humbly get a grip and realize, "Oh yeah, they always ring." There won't be a ticker-tape parade for you, either. Sorry.

5. Church Bells Lesson #2: Never complain (out loud, under your breath, or even in your mind) about the bells. Even if they ring every fifteen minutes or all night long.) Because I swear they hear you, and bell karma will assure your next hostel WILL be located right next to the main church in town.

6. When a foolish pilgrim earns "a notch on the wall" in Spain, it doesn't hold the same meaning as a notch on the wall (or bedpost) back home. Just wanted to clarify that.

7. Not every day feels like a good day. Show up anyway.

8. Breathe. Something will happen.

9. Wabi-sabi. These words, seen stitched into a Japanese woman's pack today, speak to the art of imperfect beauty. Nothing lasts. Nothing is finished. Nothing is perfect. This feels like the truth of one's pilgrimage. And of life.

10. The absence of faith in yourself is akin to losing the sheet music to your life's song. You can buy lots of stuff, and travel lots of places, but no thing and no place can bring your song back into tune or fill the dark hole that comes from not trusting yourself. Listen for the harmony of your True North.

Good night.

CHAPTER 22

BURY the PARAKEET

LEON TO SAN MIGUEL DEL CAMINO

Each annoying pang in my mid-back reminded me I'd forsaken my magic shoes and surrendered them to René. Recalling my reasoning (to reduce weight) upped the crazy factor of my current footwear status. Hanging off my pack were hiking boots, plus my *first* purchased Tevas. Yep, that hints at yet a *second* pair. The ones currently on my feet.

Three hours earlier, I'd departed the Leon shoe store wearing a sturdier, higher-arch, more cushiony Teva. That left the first pair and my boots swinging from behind, taking shots to my ribs. Extra weight and jabs served me right for sacrificing my magic shoes. My only care—I was now pain-free.

I cherished *Camino* surprises like the fruit stand along a bustling highway. Reaching for a pear, I heard the unexpected refrain. "Hail the Queen!" coupled with the scramble to salute in unison. Assuming I'd lost my *Camino* family with the Leon layover, I felt giddy hearing my Kingsmen's refrain. Their sweaty bear hugs and sticky peach kisses were heaven. One had a T-shirt around his bleeding calf (gashed open attempting to clear a fence). Stitches were needed, so a taxi was called. Catching up on our journey tales, a wave of belonging washed over me. I knew few details about these men's lives, but I felt their souls. So it is with belonging on the *Camino*.

Accompanying them to the medical clinic was tempting, but I declined the invitation.

As their taxi departed, the Kingsmen joyfully yelled "Hail the Queen!"

Though loud traffic whizzed by, it was the sudden lonely void that seemed most deafening. Walking the *Camino* alone has its downside.

Juggling eating a pear with changing my socks and re-engineering the angle of swinging footwear, this "normal day back on the *Camino*" felt like coming home. A sudden wind whipped up, making me reach for the jacket tied around my waist. It wasn't there. Ugh. Picturing it hanging on the restroom hook about five miles back, I froze. The inner panic wasn't about the jacket but the precious contents inside its pocket.

Excuses ran rampant through my head. About how hectic things had gotten that day at the hospital, and how I could understandably forget to transfer Bren's prayer card to the Iron Cross pocket of my pack. Bottom line: Damn. I didn't have it. My mind raced with possible solutions:

A. Walk back to get it—ten miles roundtrip.

B. Don't go back, and plead for Bren's forgiveness.

C. Don't go back, and don't tell Bren.

All shitty options.

Weighing inconvenience against guilt, things got weird. A sudden vision of Petey, my childhood pet parakeet, appeared perched front and center in my mind's eye.

What's he doing here? Then, it hit me. *My dad's here too!* I never heard his voice, but I felt his protective warmth and sensed what he came to say about my current predicament.

Dad, I think I know what you're thinking. Dang. And I can guess why you brought Petey along.

Growing up, my father often stressed having integrity and "walking our talk." Not integrity in a moralizing sense, but rather like the bones of a well-built house, the integrity that holds up who I am. To understand why my dad popped in at this particular moment, you first must meet Petey.

As a child, through patient training, this bright-blue feathered friend's five-word vocabulary always tickled my seven-year-old fancy. I loved Petey. Tragically, suffering from pneumonia, one cold January morning, he died.

Heartbroken, I wrapped him in paper towels and placed him in a shoebox, along with some birdseed I sprinkled over his little body. Because, well, you never know.

I asked my father to bury Petey in the woods by the stream. You have to understand. Our New York winter just dumped several feet of fresh snow on top of the month-old ice-encrusted layers, on top of frozen ground. Gallantly, my father bundled up, grabbed a shovel, and bravely disappeared into the blowing snow, the shoebox under his arm. I still recall the bitter cold enveloping me upon his return as I delivered his thank you hug.

That afternoon, lamenting about Petey out there in the cold with little protection, I approached Dad with a red velvet-lined wooden box and soft felt material. I explained my solution. "Could you dig Petey up and put him in this new casket? Please? It's warmer." My young self missed any sign of distress on his face, though I'm sure it was there. Still, my hero agreed.

This time, I accompanied Dad to the woods. He dug through the snow, ice, and dirt layers to reveal the shoebox. I tearfully wrapped Petey's frozen little body in the warm material, repeated the sprinkling of birdseed around him (because, well, you never know), and placed him in the velvet-lined box fit for an Egyptian mummy. Dad buried Petey once again. All was well.

Years later, while visiting me at college, Dad confessed the truth about a short-lived, but real option he had considered on that cold day decades ago.

"During the *first* burial, with all the blowing snow, I thought 'it's absolutely crazy to dig through three feet of ice and snow! I *could* just toss this shoebox in the woods. Who would know?' Then I remembered what I promised and snapped out of my almost lapse of honor. And I buried your bird."

Dad revealed how grateful he was for that wise decision. "With your unexpected *second* burial request, all I could think was, *Oh dear God. What if I had gone through with my lazy Plan B? How could I have ever explained that to you?*" There're many reasons I love my father. This memory remains my most treasured.

Now, over fifty years later, clear on Dad's message, I knew what needed to be done. I tossed my backpack into the taxi I'd summoned. I'd indeed bury the parakeet. Fixated on the three *uncomfortable* options for Bren's prayer card mishap, I'd failed to see the easy one. A taxi.

I typed directions to the driver in Google Translate:

"About 8 km back, I left something important at a café. I'd like to get it, then return to this same spot and continue walking. Gracias."

He nodded, did a U-turn, and drove off. Within thirty minutes, Bren's prayer card was safely zipped in my front backpack pocket and I was back on the trail. On cloud nine, I headed for San Miguel del *Camino*.

That evening at the hostel, I can't say what fixed the smile on my face more—the spectacular pot roast pilgrim dinner celebration, or as synchronicity would have it, Gina and Brad appearing and reserving the room just below mine. Pinch me. Could this reunion be bury-the-parakeet karma?

My grateful, soaring spirit rated this day as one of my *Camino's* finest. Bren, unwittingly gifted the visit from my father (and my parakeet, no less), in the most unlikely setting. Dad's reminder to me: the easiest path to living our integrity often hides in plain sight. It's not about right or wrong, but feeling for what answer aligns with our better angels.

Here in windswept Spain, these better angels reminded me: *always bury the parakeet.* Settling in that night, the sacred words of Rumi ran through my mind.

> "Out beyond ideas of wrong-doing and right-doing, There is a field. I'll meet you there." ~ Rumi

Stay warm, Petey.
I love you for eternity, Dad.

 CAMINO MESSAGE #11

The easiest path to living your integrity often hides in plain sight. Bury the parakeet.

Journal Notes

June 3, 2019
San Martin del Camino

Tonight, the faint sound of cowbells clanging in nearby fields, having Brad and Gina sleeping in the room below, equals bliss. After so many weeks in a twin bed, my king bed at home will feel like an extravagant football field (though my bedroom definitely calls for more cowbell). But home is very far off.

The reminder from Dad today, and the reunion with my dear Kingsmen, placed a particular word— one seemingly simple and benign front and center— belonging. For me, the word used to be loaded. But these days, its meaning seems to boil down to sweet connection.

For some reason, I feel called to sort out my history with belonging. Fine, Camino. It'll be my priority brain bubblegum for the coming days on the trail. Then it can be tied in a nice neat bow before reaching Santiago (at that, the Camino chuckles).

For now, sleep. Tomorrow—23 miles to Astorga with Gina and Brad! No knee wincing. No Igor limp. Funny how life sorts itself out in its own time.

G'night.

CHAPTER 23

CAMIGAS' FREEDOM MARCH

SAN MARTIN TO ASTORGA

(I'm Gonna Be) 500 Miles
~ The Proclaimers

Kudos to the Cowbell Symphony last night and the Rooster Reveille this morning. Gina, Brad, and I—all legs in working order—excitedly headed out into the countless shades of yellow in the sunrise over the cornfields.

We didn't get 50 feet before I entered the café across the street to load up on *tortilla de patata*. Gina, narrating the video she was capturing on her phone, announced to the world, "As you can see, we haven't made it even a block before Molly is eating again." If this was any indication of how these two would be, well, I predicted a hilarious day.

Finally meeting Brad left me adoring him, and their partnership. In dog years, we'd been friends for a lifetime. Taking the long route option, we walked peaceful, surreal landscapes and back rural roads. With no limp in sight, it felt to be our freedom march. Brad, absorbed in his morning audiobook ritual, left Gina and me to our first in-depth conversation—

what mattered to us in life, our families, our beliefs. Often circling back to laugh about our synchronistic Logrono bus connection.

At one point, Brad called, "Hey Molly, ya have anything for a blister?"

Who, me? In seconds he held a supply of Compeeds, rosemary alcohol, and mole skin. Molly provides.

The breathtaking landscape and our connection was nothing short of butterscotch. In our silent stretches, I sensed my spirit finally shake off any residual obligations back home. Feeling fully present, I was finally where my feet were.

At day's end, we spotted Astorga through the trees. Without missing a beat, Brad hit play on the surprise tune they said they played every day when their destination came into view. It was *the* favorite on my playlist brought from home. "Great minds think alike," I winked. "Brad, crank that baby up!" The sing-along to "(I'm Gonna Be) 500 Miles." delivered our dragging legs into town.

Bells welcoming us into the ancient city would've registered as more mystical if we hadn't arrived feeling half-past-dead. I knew better than to complain about the bells' lack of mysticism, or their lack of anything, for that matter. Nope! Complaining about bells is bad ju-ju.

Parting to our respective hostels, I walked a maze of alleys until finally spotting the house number on an unassuming door. No hostel name, no identifying sign to ensure I was in the right place. I rang the bell. Hearing, "Is that you, Miss Molly?" through the intercom was music to my ears.

SPIRITUAL KLEPTOMANIACS

The homeowner led me up three steep flights (naturally) to the charming third-floor attic. The vaulted knotty pine ceilings and eight tightly made twin beds in a straight line made me feel I should be on the lookout for hobbits, or Madeline from my favorite childhood storybook. Instead, three delightful roommates greeted me: Nick from Chicago, a young woman from New Zealand, and her boyfriend from the UK. Our engaging conversation found me stretched out, relaxing on the rug, as though I had all the time in the world. Because I did.

After showers, the subject of the Iron Cross came up. We pulled out our offerings for the cross and shared their significance. I showed them Michael's sparkling rock, read Bren's Celtic prayer card aloud, and shared the beautiful Herkimer crystal I'd lay in honor of my body's perseverance. The Iron Cross felt elusive weeks ago, now it was only two days away.

Each had heartfelt stories, but Nick's touched me most deeply. "This rock represents sadness about my father never showing up for me as a kid. I've been angry for too long. It's time to forgive and lay this burden of resentment down."

There were tears and laughs, until hunger took over. We tucked our Iron Cross items in their rightful places and left for dinner.

Talking late into the night, this threesome's twisted humor fell somewhere between Monty Python and Steve Martin. Just as we'd fade into sleep, one would say something ridiculous, and hysterics erupted again. Warm belonging. This reminded me of the topic that still needed to be examined. *Tomorrow,* I promised myself.

Waking in the morning, *ouch!* I paid dearly for pushing so hard after the Leon break. My aches tempted me to curl up and go back to sleep in this cozy attic, but the others stirred, pushing me to slowly get ready to leave.

I double-checked the secure placement of my passport, *Credentials,* euros, phone, glasses, and Iron Cross items. Odd. Michael's rock wasn't in the assigned pocket. I pulled everything from my pack. Nothing. I checked all pockets. Not there. I noticed Nick urgently searching *his* pack and bed covers for something. He couldn't find his "father-rock" (Insert *Twilight Zone* music here). We all recalled returning our treasures to their assigned spots before leaving for dinner. Everyone searched. Strange.

I had an amused inkling that mine wasn't *lost* but rather *purposely vanished,* and I sensed by whom. Nick, on the other hand, was visibly distraught. Before I said goodbye, I left him with a possible thought, "Trust the important message your rock represents. I betcha it's already been delivered on some level." I sense magic in the air.

Outside, facing the final remnants of the *meseta,* I already felt sluggish at 8 a.m. I told Gina and Brad to go on without me. The Aussies, still one day ahead, messaged they're heading to the Iron Cross in rain and possibly snow. *Snow? Yikes. Godspeed.*

Once alone walking out of Astorga, I confronted the thief. *All right, Michael, where's your rock?* I immediately felt his presence in my bones. Then, words floated through me, like a message banner pulled behind a small plane. Michael's voice accompanied it, as clear as if he stood before me.

I don't WANT to be up on that cold, windy mountain for eternity, silly. I liked it where I was in Colorado. Or I'm happy to just stay with you—anywhere but 'up there.'

Hearing him so clearly startled me and brought a grin only Michael could create.

What a party pooper, Michael. Reaching the Iron Cross is a huge milestone in crossing my desert. Your stone was to witness that. Hey, you started this whole damn desert thing!

His response, again, was crystal clear.

Find something that makes you laugh. Leaving that up there would make me happy. His voice and presence faded. I had one day to find it.

Nick crossed my mind. I hoped he found peace, if not his father-rock. As for me, my permanent grin made my face hurt.

NOODLING ON BELONGING

Somewhere Outside Astorga

Girl Scout badges. Loved them. I loved how they looked (each one unique), the feel of their embroidered design, and the effort required to earn one. But being an actual invested member, I couldn't quite muster the allegiance needed to be a true-blue scout. Something didn't connect for me. I appreciated the girlfriends and the fun parts. Oh. And that new, really cool, "Horse Caretaking" badge I spotted in the handbook. I guess my lack of whole-hearted belonging made me a badge-mongering fly-by-night Girl Scout.

These girlhood memories flooded back in the café outside of Astorga when I noticed four chatty, young Spanish girls, all wearing the same blouse with a colorful embroidered emblem. Curious about the emblem's meaning, the Spanish couple in line behind me explained. It's best compared to our American 4-H program. The girls ran outside with their pastries, near where I'd be sitting. They unknowingly nudged the day's topic—*belonging*. Their giggly conversation took me back to my youth.

I went to Camp Fire Girl summer camp from age seven to nine after being in Girl Scouts during the school year. Camp life included horseback riding, canoeing, lake swimming, pottery making, and everything else "camp." The twist of my being a Girl Scout at a Camp Fire Girl camp brought some curious inquiries, but I always felt welcome. It was the best possible scenario—a foot in both worlds, sworn to fun, loyal to none.

Don't get me wrong. I had nothing against belonging. Or Girl Scouts. My childhood standards and boundaries were simply going through growing pains. Maybe our scout meetings being inside a drab school gymnasium all winter contributed to my resistance. Not to mention reciting some scout creed devoid of sincerity, then singing the same song every week in robot-mode—passing it off as *belonging*. For me, it lacked heart.

Camp Fire Girls, however, sat around a blazing fire eating s'mores and singing fun camp songs. *That's* connection. Oh, did I mention Camp Fire Girls earned really cool colored wooden beads? I would've joined, but my town had no organized group. So, I remained a Camp Fire Girl loyalist by summer and a badge-seeking Girl Scout outlier in the winter.

Looking back, my resistance had something to do with early sprouts of integrity. I didn't like being in with only one foot, nor the insincere lie when mumbling the scout creed. I chalked up my decision to stay with Girl Scouts to liking the idea of *inclusion*. Ahh, a different meaning altogether. In my young mind, inclusion equaled being warmly invited for who I was rather than locked into any specific click or group. Inclusion said: "I accept you, no matter how you dance inside the circle of my invitation." To my vocabulary-limited eight-year-old self, belonging required buying into the whole enchilada, no à la carte options. Belonging had strings attached, and I only wanted strings pulling on something I sincerely bought into. If I could go back, I'd assure my young self she'd grow into the idea of belonging, once she no longer feared losing herself.

Had I spoken Spanish, my curiosity would've asked the girls at the next table about their experience of belonging to their youth group. But I could only watch and surmise.

Years later, as an adult, I'd uncovered psychological/spiritual arenas that capture what makes us tick, and where belonging doesn't mean being owned. For example, the Enneagram, Archetypes, *A Course in Miracles*, and don't forget the Sunday paper's horoscopes (I'm an Aquarian. That explains a lot).

My study of archetypes and the Hero's Journey (joined with my love of music) eventually linked into a career. I felt fascinated by our psyche's combination of archetypal patterns, leaving much of our path to free-will and creative options.

These deeper *internal* types of belonging presented an odd juxtaposition. Though they don't rely on inclusion by others, they do require *others* to reflect back its existence. These "others" provide the mirror. The love of every pilgrim on this trail is a mirror, and we magnify each other's light. That explains the strong sense of belonging here. We beam back to each other the love embedded in this trail of holy dirt.

Mid-pondering, the café owner came outside to sit. Birds flocked around her, landing at her feet as she opened her apron filled with birdseed. She offered me a handful, gesturing to join her. Lowering my hand to the ground, to my delight, two birds landed on my wrist, helping themselves to sunflower seeds. This was *her* sense of belonging. Nature mirrored back to her—her beautiful spirit. Realizing I still had 17 km (10.5 mi) until Rabanal, I thanked the kind woman, slid the remaining birdseed into my shorts pocket, and buttoned it. Because, well, you never know.

Grateful for these girls mirroring my past, I closed this memorable look at my younger self. One who found relief in connecting with "her kind." Who rejoiced at a friend's invitation, "Hi, wanna come to my house, drink root beer, and make prank phone calls?" Having someone to giggle and ask, "Do you have Prince Albert in a can?" or "Is your refrigerator running?" held the best sense of belonging ever.

What I knew for sure: *Every pilgrim mirrors the truth for one another. We all belong to an ancient love, and we still do to this day. Let's live it well. Buen Camino.*

CHAPTER 24

EMMA

The Promise

~ Tracy Chapman

The internal bubbling I'd felt leaving our attic hostel that morning hinted of magic being afoot (more than usual) this day. The disappearance of Michael's rock, my unexpected exchange with him, and the synchronistic meeting of the Spanish girls in the café (for me) satisfied that inkling.

I checked in with *the Voice. I'm thinking these three happenings have satisfied my "magic is afoot" prediction, or is there more to come?*

Don't think. Just do your Camino, the Voice replied. I interpreted its evasiveness as there *was* more to come (exact timing unknown). What ended up coming had been predicted several months earlier, in Las Vegas, Nevada of all places.

JANUARY 2019, LAS VEGAS, NEVADA
FOUR MONTHS BEFORE MY CAMINO

I shouldn't have been startled by the spiritual healer's question. After all, I'd come to this appointment for her to rattle the ghosts of my knee's ancestral DNA. Why not equal time for ghosts in general?

"Tell me about the baby you lost," she asked out of the blue, feeling the energy around my knees. My eyes popped open, surprised but not shocked. She continued. "The energy present tells me that she was never really *lost,* and she never intended to be born. She says you already know this."

A warm, lightheaded rush ran through me. This peculiar feeling often accompanies Emma's appearance, usually with some message she wishes to get through. This sensation always signaled *she* was near, and not Michael, my parents, Linda, or some other celestial drive-by. Was having this method of roll call for dead visitors standard protocol? For me, it was. They each had their own signature sign.

"Yes, that's Emma," I explained to Mary. I gave her that name over thirty years ago, before losing her. Years later, she started showing up after the divorce, seemingly as a spirit guide. You're right. I now understand she never intended to be carried full term. Knowing she's here now confirms that."

I made this trip to Las Vegas to visit my friend, Regina, several months before the *Camino.* Knowing my injury history, Regina set up this session with her friend Mary, a profound intuitive healer. I'm not one for psychic hopping, but I've experienced credible, gifted readers through the years. Regina explained "Spirit guides Mary's hands and intuition in a way each person needs." I trusted Regina's hunch that this experience might open yet another door of physical ease for my *Camino* ahead.

As I lay on Mary's table, she scanned my physical and ethereal bodies, clearing any energy blocks. I admitted some skepticism. However, I couldn't deny the fascinating sensation of resistance melting from my body. But, I hadn't foreseen Emma showing up.

Though regrets of never being a mother still surface at times, especially on Emma's projected birth date of December 25, I'd come to accept her true purpose. Years ago, I hesitated believing when the first spiritual reader told me "Emma's time here was temporary, only to establish the necessary bond with you, and for your husband and you to learn necessary lessons through loss." She continued, "Emma's essence always intended to return to the spirit realm. From there, which isn't very far away at all she'll serve as one of your guides." By the time the second and third spiritual readers shared the same information, I trusted its accuracy.

With this knowledge well-anchored, Emma's distinguishable presence became more frequent and pronounced. I cherished our uncommon connection. Mary's words deepened my trust in Emma's purpose. Perhaps that is why I came—to secure that trust.

Emma has an unconventional way of getting a message through. She never offers direct answers though I tell her it would make life so much easier. Instead, she presents a puzzle. She claims the puzzle pieces are easy, chunky, pre-school-type pieces, but to me, they resemble a 1,000-piece jigsaw puzzle of a solid blue ocean. Once a few pieces click, Emma gives divine hints through some synchronistic happening, ensuring I'm getting warm and on the right track. Basically, my guide is an evasive, ethereal smart-ass.

Mary continued. "Emma says she'll be with you on the *Camino*." This surprised me. She didn't seem the hiking boot or sangria type.

"And she encourages getting those knee injections you're considering before the *Camino*. Do you know what she's referring to?"

"Unfortunately, I do." Ugh. Nothing like a celestial conspiracy promoting dreaded eight-inch needles. It creeped me out for a second. Emma knowing about my research on that particular medical procedure made her that much more real. Maybe deep down, I preferred to keep her in the fantasy category, like *Casper the Friendly Ghost*.

"Emma is relaying something else. She won't be obvious on the *Camino*, but she'll support you and make her presence known."

This would be interesting.

Now, weeks into walking the *Camino*, I felt grateful for the unmistakable contact I'd made with my dead-friend-entourage of Linda, Michael, my father, Petey the parakeet, and Mother Mary-Who-Art-Buried-In-A-Suitcase. I wondered if Emma would ever join them in crowding my trail to Santiago.

That morning, I received a timely text from Regina in Las Vegas:

Any sign of Emma?

Not yet, but darn that Michael, he stole his rock!

She replied with a baffled question mark. I'd fill her in later.

Regina's inquiry triggered the first thoughts of Emma while here. Busy with shoelace management, finding enough calories to consume, not to mention the other members of my Dead-Friend-*Camino*-Support-Army vying for my attention, kept me occupied. Emma said she wouldn't be obvious, but I trusted she'd respond to an SOS if needed. Close enough.

Several miles out of Astorga, my lack of energy surprised me. Likely dehydration from pushing myself the day before. I chugged my whole water bottle.

A group of women trailing me soon caught up, and we fell in step. It lifted my wilting energy to see these familiar faces I'd met in the Pyrenees in Orisson. Wishing me *Buen Camino* as they passed my rock that day seemed a lifetime ago.

I lit up when I spotted the young shy girl in the back of the pack, who'd passed that first day in Orisson with her father. She now walked tall with confidence, her hair pulled back from her face in a ponytail, chatting freely with the women. I dropped back to join their group conversation and was pleased she remembered me. "Where's your father?"

Her face fell. "Well, we thought he sprained his ankle yesterday, so he took a taxi to Rabanal to rest." Pointing to the women surrounding her and laughing, "I stayed back with them—it's like having six moms!"

One "mom" added, "We just got word his ankle is *broken*. Sadly, this ends their *Camino.*" His daughter unsuccessfully tried to sound upbeat.

"I'm getting a taxi in the next town to meet him. We're going home." The young girl couldn't hide her disappointment. "I've learned so much walking with Dad, and these women are so awesome. I'm braver than I thought! Dad says I've handled things like a champ." I barely knew her, yet I exulted in her accomplishments. I felt compelled to share, "I've gotta say, you remind me of myself at your age."

She laughed, "Well, that's funny cuz when we were in Orisson, my dad and I noticed how much you look like my mom! It made us miss her even more. She was too nervous to come along." We smiled at the synchronicity of the resemblance and meeting again today.

I wanted things to be different for her so she could complete her *Camino*, but I caught myself. This *was* her *Camino*. It hadn't been cut short. Some journeys are complete well before the self-imposed finish line of Santiago. I'm reminded of *Camino Message #4*: *Each pilgrim's Camino will be as it should be.*

All too soon, we arrived in the next village, interrupting our chat. There was more I wanted to ask. Her guardians called a taxi as I grabbed a bag of chips, pinning my lightheadedness on low blood sugar. I turned to catch Gina and Brad ending their rest break, preparing to return to the trail. That evening we'd discuss the next day's climb to the Iron Cross. They took off, leaving me to look at this from a new angle. I'd felt this fuzzy sensation in the past, always when Emma wanted my attention. Was she near?

The summoned taxi pulled up as I pondered the familiar feeling. *What if this is a puzzle piece? Is it Emma's way of telling me I'm getting warm? But warm to what?* Then, actual words streamed through my mind. *Yes, I'm here. You've got this. You're on the right path. Keep going.*

The tribe of women encircled the young girl. There were tears, hugs, and well-wishes in several languages for a safe trip home. The young girl looked at me before ducking her head in the taxi with a wide, teary smile and called, "*Buen Camino!*" It was all happening too fast.

"Wait!" I yelled. "I don't even know your name!"

She closed the door and rolled down her window. Looking me in the eye, "My name is Emma." She grinned, and they drove away.

 CAMINO MESSAGE #12

Synchronicities are major divine clues that you're on the right path.

CHAPTER 25

POP-TARTING the DOG

RABANAL

> Take mushrooms to John in Foncebadon tomorrow. Tell John you're my friend. He'll give you a free night stay with us.

Patrick's cryptic text stumped me. *Who's John? Where's Foncebadon? Mushrooms?* Bill's follow-up text clarified:

> Pat's friend, John, is a *hospitalero* in Foncebadon, five miles from you now. We're staying there tomorrow night, and bringing mushrooms for his famous pasta sauce. Hang back a day and join us!

Ahh. Clarity.

Having just ducked out of the rain into a restaurant in Rabanal, this poor-starving-pilgrim-close-to-death-on-the-side-of-the-trail needed to order food—*fast.* The Foncebadon and mushroom decision would wait.

Most waiters couldn't believe the food I could put away. "You really want all that, Señorita? You *know* that's for *two* people, si?"

"Si. I *do* know. And I'd love some pie, too. *Gracias!*"

A gravelly-voiced comment came from across the bar.

"A tall, thin, long-legged *señorita* like yourself always throws 'em off. If I were you, I'd order *three* pieces of that pie, just to stick it to him."

This striking older woman, sun-weathered with a feisty air—86 years young (from Portugal), slid to the closest barstool. This was Sophie, a nutty sage who showed up right on time of course.

A Belgian couple sitting nearby asked what I knew about the next day's ascent to the Iron Cross. Sophie, in fairly clear English, volunteered her two cents.

"You know, I sit here listening to the anxiety you pilgrims go through before the Iron Cross. As an eight-time *Camino* veteran, I say forget the warnings! It's no big deal really, that is, *if* you've got the knees and stamina for it. Though I thought I'd have to be airlifted off its damn cliffs the last time I ventured up. I'm done. You'll never catch *me* up there again!" Followed by a husky laugh. My mind gremlins went crazy unpacking her contradictory comment.

A female server jumped in to offer the straight scoop. The Belgian couple, Noah and Lilly, listened intently to my interrogation.

"Look. I don't want to overthink this, but I've been blasted with too many options. What should I *really* expect at the top tomorrow? I'm not worried about the climb; I'm wondering if my knee can handle the decent."

Gremlins chimed in. *Ditto! Your knee's stupid "I can do it" optimism is gonna get us killed!*

I hushed their chatter to concentrate on conflicting advice between this ancient crone and the young server. Each spoke over the other, disagreeing at times, but the Belgians and I got the basic skinny on the next day's challenge:

1. After *Cruz de Ferro* (the Iron Cross), decide if your knees can handle the steep, rocky descent ahead. Sophie added, "Choices at this juncture have broken many a pilgrim." The gremlins gulped.

2. If the trail seems too daunting, walk the steep, winding road down to Molinaseca instead. It's longer and grueling. The asphalt is hard on your feet and knees and slick as hell in rain and snow.

3. They emphasized: "There's no bus up there. People refuse to believe it. They get up there and ask, 'Where's a bus to take us down?' Read my lips. NO BUSES!"

4. If you reach El Acebo two-thirds of the way down, you can call a taxi to avoid the even more difficult final descent. But you might wait an eternity.

5. Hear me. With good weather and decent knee drugs, it's a mountaintop paradise you'll remember for the rest of your life. Just do it!

With our questions satisfied, I called the hostel to confirm I'd check-in by seven o'clock. Waiting for dinner, I pulled out my journal. Sophie's curiosity was piqued again.

"Writing love letters, are ya?"

I smiled. "Yeah. To myself."

"Smart girl."

"No. Actually, I'm re-reading what I scribbled down while healing my blister in Leon. I need to remind myself of a few things before tomorrow's decisions."

"More decisions? What could your Leon notes possibly kick you in the ass about that I haven't?"

"Pop-tarts™."

I got the strange look I deserved but left her hanging when our meals all came out at once. Putting aside the Pop-Tart™ topic, the Belgians and Sophie moved their dinners to my table. We set out to learn about our very different lives. I was grateful for their English skills, but felt sadly pitiful in my one-language existence.

During dessert, Sophie asked "what's that pop-tart thing?" Was this a can of worms too big to open with language barriers? On the other hand, it had everything to do with our Iron Cross decisions. I decided to dump the whole damn can of worms.

First worm: I explained the literal breakfast pastry meaning of Pop-Tart™ and encouraged them to stick with me as I attempted its metaphorical meaning, keeping Google Translate handy.

"You know those personal development trainings that challenge you to stretch beyond your limits, right? They push you where you tend to take short-cuts, especially when no one is looking. This Pop-Tart™ story is about that."

Noah, a retired Olympian skier, said "I've done such trainings in my competitive years."

"I never guessed this silly story would call me to task on a mountaintop in Spain. But here I am." I relayed the story as I best recalled it:

> In the final days of his leadership training program, a businessman receives the dreaded call from his assigned life coach. Every coaching call followed the standard procedure: the coach (out of the blue on any given day) calls to present a challenge to the trainee, who's then challenged to complete it in the allotted time frame. The challenge always targets a weak area in their lives that still needs work. Once completed, the trainee calls the coach back to report the challenge as "done." No explanation is required, at this point of the training. They trust your word is good, and the task has been handled in the spirit it was intended.
>
> The trainee was told his assignment: "Heal a relationship in the next three hours." He hangs up, paces, and scratches his head. His typical avoidance routine. Kidding himself, he thinks, "Heal a relationship? Can't think of one that needs that." Who's he kidding?
>
> He walks to the neighborhood store, hoping for an idea. On the way, passing a neighbor's yard, he's startled by a dog that charges the chain-link fence, growling and snapping, making him grateful for the metal fence barrier.
>
> Once at the corner store, the guy buys a box of Pop-Tarts.™ Heading home, munching his snack, he passes the same dog that charges him again. Backing up, he breaks off a corner of his snack and tosses it over the fence. The dog gobbles it up and calms right down. He tosses him another piece. The happy dog,

wagging its tail, follows him excitedly as he walks along the rest of the fence. Then, the guy tosses a whole Pop-Tart™ over the fence to the former vicious, now ecstatic, dog. Arriving home, an idea hits him. The guy calls his coach and reports: "It's done. I healed a relationship."

The coach replies, "Well done! Thanks for the call."

Assignment done? Not even close.

"What a lying knucklehead!" Sophie piped in. Noah chuckled. Lilly looked confused, trying to make her English-to-Dutch translation.

I finished the story's point: "Handling a situation by lamely dodging the spirit of a commitment is called 'pop-tarting the dog.' Or a pop-tart for short."

Noah loved the metaphor and explained its nuance to Lilly in slower English. "The problem, honey, is no one will ever know this guy blew off the challenge, violating the spirit of the assignment. But *he* knows he did. He cheated *himself.* Who knows, completing that challenge could have changed his whole life." Lilly understood.

I added, "We've all done it. But too *much* pop-tarting eats away at our integrity and self-trust."

Sophie commented, "After pulling that trick enough times, you darn well know you're full of shit! My ex-husband was one big walking, breathing pop-tart. The jerk took every cheap shortcut possible in life. Thought no one noticed. Ha! If I knew where the son-of-a-bitch was, I'd send him a box of damn Pop-Tarts™!" After a good laugh, Noah shared his thoughts.

"I've coached athletes who pop-tarted, but I never had a name for it—until now! Ever notice when you pop-tart something, it registers in your gut? We try to convince ourselves it's no big deal. I've heard potential Olympic skiers claim a lame achievement to be 'good enough.' That *good enough* attitude is a big pop-tart, and trust me, they didn't make the team."

"We pop-tart when we're overwhelmed, afraid, busy, or too lazy to see a commitment through, or we do some weenie action pretending to have met the challenge."

I shared a basic example. "Last Christmas, I watched a well-to-do mother give her child a single penny to put in the charity bucket. *That's a pop-tart!*"

"That cheapskate bitch! The karma axe is comin' down on her for sure!" Sophie never failed to amuse.

Now approaching seven o'clock, I returned to my point in bringing all this up.

"There's pop-tart potential at every turn here on the *Camino.* Only *we* know if our decisions have been playing to win, playing not to lose, or playing as small as we can get away with, which equals a pop-tart. I don't want to pop-tart anything tomorrow. Just saying this out loud to you helps me plant a firm sense of 'playing to win' in my gut *now*, so tomorrow, I can relax and trust that *whatever* decision I make—trail, taxi, road, or helicopter—it's the wisest win for me."

Surprising tears streamed down Lilly's face. She confessed. "That's exactly how *I* feel. I'm fairly athletic but not hardcore like my husband. I have a back injury, and tomorrow scares me. I hate feeling weak compared to you (pointing to Noah). I don't want to pop-tart tomorrow, either. I know you're not asking me to, Noah, but I refuse to do anything stupid just to prove something to you."

Before our eyes, we watched their relationship "playing to win" skills unfold as they talked it through, mainly in Dutch. I told Lilly about Orietta from the Shire pounding the table to make her point about the *Camino* having more tools than just feet. "Lilly, if your body calls for the tool of a taxi tomorrow, trust you'll find one. Listening to your gut *is* playing to win."

"Good God," Sophie piped in, "you three sure don't mess with usual pilgrim talk, do you? Ya know, like, 'How much does *your* pack weigh?' Or 'Ya got any blisters yet?' No, you three get right down to it!"

Roman's "get dirty" comment flashed in my mind. This unexpected conversation about personal integrity felt like wrapping ourselves in holy dirt.

Sophie continued. "Explain *playing not to lose,* Mr. Olympic hotshot."

Noah took her on. "When playing to win, you do everything you can using a winning strategy. Your mindset: no barrier will stop me, versus a *playing not to lose* strategy where you do the least you can to win, while pretending "to do what it takes." You're over-cautious to avoid mistakes. You wait for perfect conditions before risking a move. It sucks the life out of any chance at satisfaction."

Lilly tossed out a question. "Is protecting my back from re-injury playing not to lose?" Noah offered his two cents.

"No. Guarding your healing progress is playing to win. Playing not to lose often looks like pushing too hard, conveniently re-injuring yourself, and (maybe unconsciously) being relieved of others' expectations." Yikes. I heard that.

I regretted leaving these new friends, but my hostel called. Sophie announced, "I have to get home too. My cat and I missed our five o'clock shot of whiskey."

Standing next to me, she measured with her hands our similar height and leg length.

"We're kindred spirits, dear. Looking at you, you're who I used to be, which means I'm bound to be your future. You could do worse." Sophie, Angel Number Ten, became one more *Camino* treasure.

She explained where to buy John's mushrooms and Michael's twisted gift. Then, wagging her finger at us, she warned in her gravelly tone: "If I catch anyone pop-tarting up there tomorrow, I'll sic that pop-tart dog on you! And trust me, there's no damn bus up there! My cat needs her whiskey, but this was delightful, kids. *Buen Camino*!" And she was gone.

The Belgians and I also parted, leaving me feeling a *Camino*-inspired kinship.

Disappearing into the drizzly night, Sophie's words of caution hung in the air. I compared her dramatic words to an ominous movie plot—not unlike the film, *Alien*:

SOPHIE: a movie where nobody listens to the wise old woman, and they all die except for the old woman and her drunk cat. Four stars.

SOPHIE — ANGEL NUMBER TEN

ANTICIPATING THE DELUGE

Don't Rain On My Parade

~ Barbra Streisand

I stared out my hostel room window at the dark curtain of fog. Hiding behind it, the highest point of the *Camino—Cruz de Ferro*. An unsettling message from the Aussies chimed in. Snow, rain, and wind severely hampered their day. Yikes. Snow? Pablo reported:

> Descent after Iron Cross is extremely slippery with rain and snow. Very difficult. Gabby took a bad fall. Hard on knees. Think carefully before doing it. It's dangerous.

Ugh. I unzipped my pack pocket to put in Michael's new treasure. Michael and I, both having Catholic school memories (many begging to be forgotten), often shared our nun war stories. You know, the sadly false Jesus tales they laid on us back then. We honored Jesus, but not their stories about his manipulative love. As adults, we shake our heads. As children, we were duped.

Michael was a master of irreverence. My new gift—a four-inch purple plastic Jesus statue—matching the colorful stories once shared. I trusted Jesus winked and smiled along with me. I zipped it securely in the assigned pocket, warning, "Michael, STAY!"

Before bed, I did a rare thing. Though I'd posted pictures on Facebook in recent weeks, I hadn't had a spare minute to engage with followers. Now, opening my page, I wanted to say—*something*. No words came. To try to explain crazy Sophie, how Emma showed up, or why the thought of walking the descent in rain or snow scared the hell out of me, or to explain why I, in my mind, declared reaching the Iron Cross as my ultimate victory, all seemed too far removed from home for anyone to understand. So, I simply posted:

> *This might work, it might not. There's no simple way to quiet the noise in my head about tomorrow's knee-chewing descent after the Iron Cross. And, at the moment, I intend to do it anyway. Good night.*

I needed to declare it to anyone listening (at this hour, likely no one). But comments surprisingly streamed in. I felt the love from an early-rising, cheering section back home. Tears welled reading their encouragement, concerns, advice, and respect for my journey. All seemed to understand making it to the Iron Cross held something worth fighting for.

Lying in bed, I let the connections made that day sink in. As I've grown older, belonging and inclusion melded into a more significant word—connection. My standards around connection became more transparent. I declared the exploration of belonging complete.

The next day's plan was loose. Arriving in Fancy Bones with or without Gina and Brad I'd find John's *albergue* to deliver the mushrooms. Pat and Bill were clearly out of the loop on Foncebadon's correct pronunciation. I wouldn't be walking with them the following day or stay for the pasta feast. Yes, I turned down food, shocker, I know. My knees braved grossly long needles and (too) many morning margaritas in exchange for this private Iron Cross moment.

Drifting off, I considered the different people, beliefs, and judgments I'd let sabotage past dreams. Making it to the Iron Cross would *not* be one of them. I fell asleep to the faint but determined words of a favorite power anthem, "Don't Rain On My Parade."

CHAPTER 26

CRUZ DE FERRO
(The Iron Cross)
THE ASCENT

Up To The Mountain

~ Chrystal Bowersox

"It's easy, it's fun, and it's guaranteed to work. Of course you can do it. All of that is true except for the part about easy, fun, and guaranteed." ~ Seth Godin

Being a pilgrim calls for never being 100 percent comfortable. I've heard some pilgrims claim they came to regain control of their lives. I questioned if I wanted such control. I preferred the idea of somewhere between control and foolishness, I'll create magic. And, hoped the *Camino* would provide.

Brad and Gina, unable to sleep, hit the trail before sunrise. Gina's message reported she'd do the full descent with Brad. High-five to my "Another-Fucking-*Camino*-Lesson" sister! Lilly and Noah were departing late. I was antsy to start. After all, my knees endured morning margaritas and needles anticipating this moment. I laughed at the head trip we all worked ourselves into about this day.

MUSHROOM DELIVERY

The damp, rich, earthy smells walking through the woods out of Rabanal intensified the energetic high. The morning fog lifted off the valley, revealing the surrounding mountains. Only ten minutes on the trail, one might wonder how I could possibly trip and fall—over nothing (seriously, *nothing*) executing a 10.0 full-body sprawl. No René. No camera. No kidding. I assumed this was the "never being 100 percent comfortable" part.

Sitting dumbfounded in the wet leaves, my friend Karen's parting advice echoed.

Don't fall on the Camino. You've gotta watch every step. If there's a view, stop walking. Then look.

I did a body scan. My throbbing thumb was slightly out of joint, having tangled in my pole strap. Everything else registered as simply dirt-covered and stunned.

Earlier that morning, after sending my pack to Molinaseca, I shared a heart-to-heart with Mother Mary-Who-Art-Buried-In-A-Suitcase about staying close by this day. I felt inspired to invoke another guardian as well. I couldn't shake the mesmerizing chapel I stopped in just before Astorga. This small chapel, a shrine to the Divine Feminine with gold-covered walls and archways, held predominantly statues of spiritual women figures. One made the hairs on my arm rise—a statue of Mary Magdalene. Not in her false prostitute image, but as the powerful first apostle and confidant to Jesus that she was. The chapel's obvious honoring of the Matriarchy graced every woman who entered with a powerful blessing.

So, on this morning, I had the audacity to invite Mary Magdalene to join Mother Mary and me. Only if hiking was her thing, of course. What a force we'd be! I imagined they humored me and followed along, and that, somewhere in the ethers, there's a celestial Polaroid shot of my fall in the woods. Very funny, ladies.

Three more miles delivered me to the small town of Fancy Bones (Foncebadon). Finally locating John's *albergue,* I recognized him from Pat's pictures.

"Hi, John, I'm Molly. I'm Patrick's friend." Deadpan, without missing a beat, he responded, "I'm so sorry." We immediately bonded.

We sat and talked about life in a one-street town, the "no bus up there" rumor, and what to anticipate ahead. John eventually accepted my decision to miss the pasta feast and move on solo. After tasting his famous sauce simmering on the stovetop, he offered a tour of the adjacent tiny chapel. Like most ancient chapels, its simplistic energy stirred something profoundly mystical.

John explained the mural on the front wall that depicted ancient pilgrims passing through Foncebadon, the last stop before Cruz de Ferro. He pointed out various historical figures and their significance. My heart skipped a beat when he commented, "And the woman over there speaking to the group—that's Mary Magdalene."

Whoa. The hairs on my arms again stood in awe. Signs like this told me, *you're on the right path. Keep going.* After thanking John for an enlightening hour, I did just that, I kept going.

LONG-AWAITED MOMENT

The sun broke through. I chalked up my weather luck to purple plastic Jesus in my pocket. Climbing out of Fancy Bones, I sensed the alchemy of my body and spirit merging into a sweet spot, strong as steel. My intuition had GPS accuracy and solutions flowed like honey, with synchronicity at every turn.

The jury wondered what decision I'd make at the top. The climb continued. Then, without fanfare or signage, I rounded a corner, and there stood the long-awaited Cruz de Ferro. The history of this mound of over a thousand years' worth of offerings held burdens laid down by millions. Though palpable, it wasn't a heaviness, but rather lightness and relief.

A cyclist group mounted their bikes and rode off in silence as I approached. Except for a few lingering pilgrims taking in their experience, the Iron Cross was all mine. I pulled out my items, slipping one of Linda's beaded bracelets from my wrist to add to the collection in my hand. I thought this moment might be dramatic. Possibly highly emotional. Neither was the case.

With a light heart, I handed my phone to a man who kindly offered to take my picture. At the top of the mound, I held the pole like the ancient ones before me. Sensing my ancestors peering over my shoulder, I laid the offerings down, one by one. First, the memory stone honoring my parents. A purple flower picked along the trail for Emma. Bren's prayer card. And, with a smirk, Michael's purple Jesus. Last and most poignant, the sparkling Herkimer crystal honoring my body's perseverance. Touching the final item, I hesitated. I wasn't ready to release Linda's bracelet. Not yet. Not until I made peace with the Great Blue Heron. I'd know when the time was right. I slipped it back on my wrist.

I loved all those whose path had crossed mine in this lifetime, bringing me to this moment. And that was it. A touch. A nod of gratitude. A quiet chuckle and a few knee injections. All honoring a life well-lived with so much more ahead.

Taking one final look at the Iron Cross mounted 4,934 feet above sea level, a decision coursed through my veins, so strong my knees trembled: *I'll finish the ascent. Then, I will do the descent, at least to El Acebo. Yikes!* I delegated the brunt of the impact of the upcoming twelve miles to my walking poles, and to the Advil I popped in my mouth.

I left this final place where a taxi could be summoned, and I located the yellow arrow marking the point of no return Sophie dramatically mentioned.

SOPHIE'S LIE

Whistling up the next leg of the ascent, warm thoughts of my whistling Italian friend, Andrea, crossed my mind. As did Bren, his prayer card now safely with the ancient ones. Then Sophie, to whom I sent a telepathic message affirming there were indeed no buses up here nor any sign of pop-tarting. Before focusing on my mission, I sent good ju-ju back to Lilly and Noah, and ahead to Gina and Brad.

Eventually, the trail spilled onto a narrow, paved, winding road. Rounding a blind turn, there, parked and taking up the whole damn road, was a huge flippin' BUS! Yes, a bus. The driver and some passengers stood chatting, and others meandered down from a wildly decorated hostel/café on the hill. The bus clearly broke all reality's rules.

I stopped to meet this lively Norwegian tour group, some of whom occasionally walked short sections of the *Camino* as the rest waited in the next town, drinking and yucking it up. These were clearly the yuckers. Hearing the gist of my goal and dubious knee situation, they encouraged me to hop on their bus for a leisurely ride down to Molinaseca. The idea registered as a big pop-tart, but I carefully took in the reality of a freakin' bus miracle that wasn't supposed to exist. *Is that faint celestial laughter I hear?* This scene had their suspicious fingerprints all over it.

Thanking the Norwegians for their kind offer, I took one last look at the magic, and asked out loud, "Linda, is that the biggest damn bus you've ever seen or what?" as tears streamed down my face. Her strong presence on the trail walking beside me, was slowly fading the past week. She seemed to hover rather than walk by my side. I felt like tethering her to my pack. It was as if she was saying, *you've got this. You no longer need me.*

The climb passed a simple rock cairn with a small cross and engraved plaque for a pilgrim who died on the trail three years before. I'm reminded this was not a Disney ride attached to some track. My feet were my sole engine, to be planted carefully with each step. I affirmed Scott M. O'Neil's saying, "Be where your feet are."

ARMED AND DANGEROUS

Don't be fooled. It wasn't all gutsy fearlessness. Case in point. Amidst the huffing and puffing and careful foot placement on sliding rock, an eerie sense of isolation enveloped my nervous system. An intuitive alert.

I stopped and scanned the hills ahead and the wooded area I'd just come through. I spotted him. A large man below on the trail, no pack, picking his way up the rocky ascent. I froze in fear. *What the hell was I thinking—being out here alone?* Wild thoughts vacillated between *nothing to worry about,* and *if he's trouble, I'm dead.* My brain's amygdala registered the beach attack forty years before and rejected any logic that this could end well, while simultaneously my Warrior Archetype declared, *this time I will not be the victim.* My heart raced with terror.

Climbing closer, I heard him angrily swearing as he slipped on the rocks and aggressively regained footing. My previous upbeat spirit flipped into high-defense mode. Scrambling through the brush I perched myself on a large boulder several yards from the trail. I added a long sharp stick to my walking pole arsenal and closely watched him approach.

The man finally stopped at my rock. Breathing hard, he stared. My pounding heart likely matched his. With as merry a "*Buen Camino*" greeting as he could muster while still gasping for oxygen, he smiled, waved, and trekked on.

Relief washed over me. Adrenaline slowly drained from my body as he disappeared over the ridge. Once I had my wits about me, he registered as harmless. However, considering my gathered arsenal, *he* may have questioned his *own* safety. I looked at my weaponry and laughed. *Had* I been attacked and pushed over the cliff—and found still firmly gripping these weapons, reports would at least reflect my defense as a courageous one.

SOPHIE'S REDEMPTION

I slid from my perch and continued climbing. The many false summits were mentally tiring. My reward finally came. The true summit. Cramping hamstrings and calves temporarily dissolved. As Sophie promised, I glided on air through wildflower heaven with endless shades of green and gold—shades not recalled in *my* childhood Crayola crayon box.

Resting in the grass, I performed my sock-changing ritual. Massaging my injured thumb joint, I questioned how much pressure it could take when gripping the poles during the coming descent. My best defense: chase my protein bar with more Advil.

An Irishman thoughtfully called from behind to not startle me as he approached.

Smart man. Maybe word of the "highly armed warrior woman on the boulder" had spread. We chatted about this electric day, took pictures of each other with the stunning backdrop, and he trotted on. The saying "we're all just walking each other home" lived in such fleeting moments.

Walking the meadow paradise, a mystical sound of the wind slipping through tall grasses, one never heard before, engulfed the fields, flowers, and me as if all one entity in this ethereal portal. I smiled thinking what this scene might look like from a distance. To one with exceptional psychic vision, trailing behind me, they'd see the presence of a woman in flowing ethereal robes Who-Art-Rolling-Along-In-A-Suitcase. A female angel in compression socks with a Great Blue Heron circling overhead. A young girl with a ponytail picking flowers along the trail. Next, a caring older gentleman keeping pace with a blue parakeet perched on his shoulder. And, a music man with a huge smile and guitar, playing a Spanish tune, keeping our steps in rhythm.

This imagined silhouette of my Dead-Friends-*Camino*-Support-Army, constantly reminding me of who I am, never handling anything I couldn't handle myself, filled me with—butterscotch.

Together, we'd been called to this moment, the vision forever etched in my memory. *Excuse me while I kiss the sky.*

 ### CAMINO MESSAGE #13
Be where your feet are.

CRUZ DE FERRO:
THE DESCENT

The mountaintop paradise slowly gave way to a noticeable downhill slope, which snapped me out of my fantasy. The guidebook reported: "*The path now descends (very sharply!),*" with "very sharply" printed in red. Yikes. The choice I'd made hit home.

My cadence: slow but sure. Unstable rocks, slide-triggering gravel fields, and deep two- to three-foot boulder drop-offs drowned my thumb pain as

I leaned on the poles to stabilize. When I sensed great progress, usually I'd gone only a short distance.

Two hours passed. Then three. In a trance, my eyes rarely left the next spot to place my foot. My swollen right knee begged for our destination. Pablo and Gabby doing this in the rain and snow was unimaginable. Approaching hour four, wincing whenever I landed wrong on my knee, I wondered how I ever thought this was a good idea.

The trail veered close to the road. I crawled down a dirt embankment to the relief of pavement. Later, I climbed back up to join familiar pilgrims above, enjoying the first conversation since the Irishman. However, one twisted her ankle, and unfortunately, they needed to retreat down to the road.

The ridge gave way to another hour of rough descent. Finally, my knee exhaled with the sudden sighting of El Acebo. The four-and-a-half-hour descent zapped all reserves. Exhausted, hungry, out of water, and in pain (did I leave anything out?), I walked through the seeming ghost town. Spotting a flashing red neon light through a frosted window, I recognized it as a beer sign. I pulled the heavy wooden door, which opened to the sound of rowdy laughter. My eyes adjusted to the restaurant's low light as a round of applause erupted. My busload of Norwegians! And the standing ovation was for *me!* Realizing what was happening, I dropped into the nearest chair, my body letting go like a tight rubber band unwinding, and cried. Hard.

Upon arrival at the end of many long days, most of my *Camino* victories were private with me, myself, and I happily acting as my own cheering squad. Or, I walked into town with friends equally as tired. So, having strangers acknowledge, "You're rockin' this!" was something I hadn't experienced. They showered me with beers, water, lunch platters, and almond cake. The thoughtful bartender even offered an ice pack for my knee. I graciously received it all.

The bus driver, the only sober one in the bunch, vigorously shook my hand in congratulations (ouch, my thumb), saying the ride offer down to Molinaseca still stood. The gremlins calculated the almost five miles of steep descent this would cut from our day. Not one hint of pop-tarting existed in my answer "YES!" "Getting dirty" won the day.

The driver explained he'd parked the monster bus at the edge of town when a handful of riders decided to walk part of the stretch I just completed. That's the only reason the bus made this unplanned stop. *Thank you, purple Jesus and two Marys!*

Finally getting a cell signal, I updated Gina and Brad on my progress and the miracle bus. Ecstatic, they promised a six-pack of Spanish beer upon my arrival.

Consuming a crazy amount of food and drink, I glanced at my newly acquired friends, and shook my head at how my deserving knee had a miraculous ride down the mountain. Synchronicity and I were *simpatico*.

Their walkers arrived, and I, along with my collective Angels (Number Eleven), walked to the bus, savoring a box of juicy ripe cherries from the market. I sank into the plush front seat of the luxury air-conditioned bus next to the woman holding the cherries. I play to win. My muscles decompressed, knowing our twelve-mile adventure (which felt like fifty) was over.

The inner voices all agreed. This day had been tough. But we were tougher.

THE NORWEGIANS – ANGELS NUMBER ELEVEN

 CAMINO MESSAGE #14

Sometimes, just staying the course is an adventurer's act of defiance. Refusing to go numb. Refusing to pop-tart the dog. Feeling it all.

POST - CRUZ DE FERRO MISCHIEF:
CARBONATED HOLINESS

Holy Now
~ Peter Mayer

"Laughter is carbonated holiness."
~ Anne Lamott

Maybe the wine with dinner added to the slap-happy exhaustion, but something drove us to a laugh attack customarily reserved for a kid in church on Sunday. Knowing you need to get it under control only makes it worse. This phenomenon is called carbonated holiness. There's no coming back from it.

After Gina and Brad greeted me in Molinaseca with the promised six-pack, we celebrated our victory dinner with *Camino* friends. Finishing my meal, I glanced under the table. Several large pieces of lettuce were strewn about my feet. Odd. How the hell, and when, had they kamikazed off someone's plate? I nudged Gina, nonchalantly pointing under the table. She eyed the suspicious greens. Her face, ready to burst, searched mine for an explanation. This is when it began.

Our cat-that-ate-the-canary expressions caused Brad to check under the table. Spotting the escaped lettuce, he looked directly at me, eyebrows raised.

Why am I always suspect? My stupid, deadpan explanation spilled. "First day with my new hands."

Brad spit out his drink. Gina's forehead dropped to her plate, shoulders shaking.

Things escalated. A few in the group eyed us for hints of what they missed. Jack was out of the box and there was no putting him back.

Carbonated Holiness Rule #1: Never attempt to explain what triggered a laughing fit to clueless bystanders. Doing so, the supposed humor risks losing its holiness.

We paid our bill, managing to squeak out a "good night, see you in the morning" to the others. Tears streaming, we exited the restaurant, trying to catch a full breath. Composure eventually came, given we didn't make eye contact.

Running down the narrow lane, Brad, figuring we're the last pilgrims to return to the albergue, urged us: "Hurry, lights out at 10:00!" Rushing in the front door, Gina looked at her watch. "Yikes! Four minutes to brush our teeth and get in bed!"

In a flurry, Brad and I dove into our bunks. CLICK! The room went black. Damn, Gina didn't make it. She groped for her lower bunk, "shit" she mumbled, tripping over her pack in the dark, triggering our laughter—again.

Brad, trying to whisper, offered commentary from the top bunk, "First day with your new feet, Gina?" Our bunks shook with attempts to stifle the hysterics.

If you're wondering, *what's so funny here?* Exactly. Welcome to the highest level of carbonated holiness. The several "shhhh!" gestures from other pilgrims only exacerbated things. The holiness that washed over us in the dark finally calmed. Brad and Gina slipped into dreamland.

Before fading myself, I reflected on the day's indescribable beauty. Nature infused every sense with colors as if mixed on an artist's palette. I tried to recall the rich, earthy smells. And, oh, the sound. The breeze that kissed the tall grass and wildflowers on that mountaintop made a sound I'd never heard in nature before. Describing it as effervescent is close, but falls short.

In this twilight space, a revelation came. As the wind swept over the field's colors earlier, a sixth sense woke and opened a sensual portal. As with music, the whole is greater than the sum of its parts here. The holy dirt magic stirring under my boots intensified, generating mystical visuals and sounds. I can't say where that crazy-sounding knowing came from exactly, but it felt true.

Another wave of insight downloaded. The heartfelt laughter we'd experienced at dinner that had infused joy into every crack of our being, tapped the same sixth sense portal as the sound of the mountaintop wind. Eureka! At first, the two energy patterns (laughter and the ethereal sound) seemed an unlikely match in frequencies. But then I got their kinship to my bones. Embedded within both, lies the presence of grace. Within grace, butterscotch lives.

Author Anne Lamott understood this language of the soul when she deemed laughter as "carbonated holiness." Admit it. You've laughed uncontrollably in a front church pew, too.

This Iron Cross day highlighted our personal best. Dragons were slain. Poles and sharp sticks were raised, then laid down against old nightmarish fears. And damn, a forbidden flippin' bus appeared! All strengthened my faith: I'm always guided—*if* I stay present and allow *something to happen.* Can we just forget my morning faceplant in the woods, please?

I'd hold this day close. The theme of a sweet tune I often heard sung by my good friend Joe Uveges drifted through my sleepy fog: *everything is holy now.*

Carbonated holiness trail pals: Gina & Brad

PART SIX

ACT TWO

CHAPTER 27

IT'S a WRAP! (not)

MOLINASECA TO VILLAFRANCA DEL BIERZO

The Weight
~ The Band

It wasn't a conscious decision, but at some point, it was made. And it almost became the kiss of death for "My *Camino*, Act Two."

It's all part of good screenplay writing. In the second act of any movie, the Hero appears to have conquered its foe. Everyone exhales. Oh. But wait. The closing credits are far from running. Hollywood writers' rule: everything the Hero *thinks* he's gained to this point must and will fall apart. His true love is actually a Russian spy. The alien isn't really dead. Everyone makes it out of the burning building alive, but, uh-oh, the dog is missing. Our hopeful outcome is in jeopardy. We exhaled too soon.

So it is in life, and, on the *Camino*. Rushing Act Two and believing it's over and tied up in a neat bow, is wishful thinking. Example: two years prior, I declared completion of the Iron Cross as where I'd plant my victory flag, convinced everything after that would be a gift and smooth sailing.

Assuming a cakewalk when still up to my neck in Act Two, the *Camino* can only respond, *Hold my beer.*

Following the riverwalk overhung with trees and flowering vines, Gina, Brad, and I walked silently that next morning. Occasionally, we'd chuckle to ourselves about nothing. Clearly, a carbonated holiness hangover.

Speaking of hangovers, I learned the hard way that miles and alcohol don't mix well for me. Days ago, I helped four hilarious Swedish women finish drinking several morning carafes of sangria. Never again. So, when Gina and Brad decided to join a wine tasting festival in full swing (ahhh, youth!), I declined. We parted, with a plan to reconnect that night in Villafranca. Looking back, I'm happy our last several days together were so darn rich, as our rendezvous wouldn't come to pass.

The *Camino* has a way of creating, then filling voids. A few miles past the wine festival, in the middle of whimsical, ancient-looking vineyards, I stumbled upon six new walking buddies from various countries, all speaking different languages. But music, the universal uniter, worked its magic.

Only I, and one other, spoke English. Regardless, all knew a fair amount of the English lyrics for many popular tunes. Together, we found a musical common ground to lament the approaching dark clouds and the increasingly heavy load on our shoulders. Our most entertaining song (well, *we* were entertained anyway) was "The Weight," by The Band. Though our verse lyrics were hit or miss, our chorus harmonies rocked! The spirit of this rowdy sing-along eased our load for miles. Seven pilgrims singing off-key, all with the hope of "taking a load off," proved that musical comradery is king—no matter the language.

Miles later, I urged the group to push on without me. A surprising, aggravated Achilles tendon was slowing me down. The Iron Cross descent took its toll.

I stopped to share a weathered bench with another walker on his cell phone. He yelled over the static to his listener about how the hilltop provided him a rare cell signal. His volume felt jarring. "Well, I've been at it four days now. Boiling this whole *Camino* thing down to one word, I'd have to say it's "HELL!" Ahhh, memories of René's and my first few days.

I quickly tucked a bandage between my boot and socks to protect my tender Achilles, hoping it wasn't too late. Leaving, I heard the guy's loud closing comment to his listener. "I guess that's just the way it is…hell."

The line, "that's the way it is" stirred an old familiar memory of former TV news anchor Walter Cronkite. Decades ago, he'd end his half-hour news broadcast every evening with, "And that's the way it is…" as though the brief thirty-minute version of reality provided the total world picture. I was tempted to yell into the phone to whomever the guy was complaining to, "That's *not* the way it is at all!" Instead, I let it go and laughed. It seemed alchemy began running my operating system. The old seemed to be folding and melting into itself, transforming into something new. It's too early to say into *what*.

The Achilles pain pushed my old blister anxiety button. But I checked my self-talk. Yes, this new pain was disappointing. But that was it. This problem registered as "Life on the *Camino*. Shit happens. Period." I heeded the past learned lesson: catch trouble early and address it.

The black clouds descended fast, hanging like a dark, heavy blanket over the endless rows of grapevine. Torrents began dumping before I could find cover, leaving me soaked, limping, and shivering. Adding insult to injury I recalled, given our early morning exit, we hadn't made reservations for Villafranca. Ugh. Act Two was a downward spiral.

Under a covered bus stop, I removed my boot to examine "the problem." Typically, I'd refrain from graphic descriptions, but, a fluid-filled sack of skin hung off my Achilles tendon, like a water balloon filled with an unknown liquid. Freaky. No way would this foot squeeze back into that boot. Gross. I pulled out my Tevas. No go. The back strap directly hit the sack area. "Ouch!" The only option: my shower flip-flops.

I bandaged the tendon, then flopped along in one flip-flop and one boot. The step, flop, step, flop look and rhythm were extremely attractive. I could only endure. Aggravated, I thought, *and that's the way it really is, Mr. Cronkite.*

Hoping to command this problem to end, Einstein's famous words jeopardized that directive. "You can't solve a problem at the same level of consciousness that created it."

Clearly, he wrote that while sitting at his warm, dry, neurotically messy desk, and not when he felt miserable, rain-soaked, pissed off, and needing to stop every three minutes to scrape mud and pebbles from between his toes. But I knew Albert was right. My thinking needed a definite reset to resolve this problem.

I got thinking about prayer. A worthy diversion. I also thought about my Dead-Friends-*Camino*-Support-Army and how, since the Iron Cross, they'd faded. It smacked of my old "I have to do this all myself" habit. I called a huddle with them to ask for help. I confessed to the army my careless theory: *Now that the Iron Cross is complete, it's all easy street from here.* They chuckled. Cruel (but fair).

Back to prayer. I recalled Angela's (my Colorado friend) prayer technique for emergency situations. It was an easy one to dredge up in a pinch: "God, DO THIS!" Her technique would soon come in handy.

In my early *Camino* days, *playing to win* meant raising the challenge bar higher each day. Screw that. Now, it meant extracting myself from this ugly situation. ASAP.

Linda, the treasurer for our celestial Dead-Friends-*Camino*-Army Team, flipped a coin. *Heads, you suffer. Tails, you free yourself from this style-impaired, flip-flop travesty.* The map presented two options: road or trail. Linda whispered, *road.*

Five minutes down the road, four miles out from Villafranca, a vehicle approached. A taxi! I flagged it down and got inside just as the next downpour dumped. A nod to my army and Einstein. Act Two showed promise. Riding into town, I was reminded: everything's always working out for me. Eventually.

Villafranca is essentially slippery cobblestone. Seeking "room at the inn" while wearing one boot and one slippery flip-flop is not only dangerous, but ridiculous. In the chilly drizzle, looking like a drowned rat, I inquired with hostels and hotels for vacancies. Nothing. Now past 7 p.m., with low blood sugar woes, I felt an inkling of panic.

I, and my freezing cold flip-flop foot found cover, put on dry socks, and eased the water balloon blister into my boot. I thought I might pass out.

Latching onto some passing muse, my mind snagged a specific John Lennon quote I'd read once in *Rolling Stone* magazine, perfect for this dire moment:

> *"When it gets down to it, when you're drowning, you don't say, 'I would be incredibly pleased if someone would have the foresight to notice me drowning and come and help me.' No. You just SCREAM."*

Thank you, John.

The damp church bells had a cold, mocking tone. Standing in the square, I tried out Lennon's and Angela's combined prayer method—"God, DO SOMETHING DAMN IT! Amen."

Not a minute passed before a female voice called, "Molly? Is that you?" It was the two Canadian friends, Claire and Kathleen. I met them exploring Leon two weeks before. How they recognized the drowned rat version of me is a miracle. With the help of their warm, dry, clear thinking, I secured a hotel room a block away, complete with bathtub. Prayer rocks!

Once checked in and my muddy, wet clothes were handed over to laundry service, we headed for dinner. These amusing two characters claimed to be walking "The Queen's *Camino.*" Their tour service booked all accommodations in high-end hotels, and their suitcases of stylin' attire were sent ahead each day. "No backpacks in Queen's World," Claire chuckled. Their "Queens on the Trail" stories were hilarious. I was grateful for these loving women (Angels Number Twelve) placed on my path in the nick of time. I got it. I didn't have to solve every problem on my own. Connection. The harmonies of my earlier international singing clan played in my head, as did its message. *I unloaded my weight of worries and allowed myself to put the load on another for a while. Maybe I'm finally getting it?*

Once in my hotel, (did I mention the bathtub?) I sank into two hours of bubbly bliss. The bells sounded much friendlier once inside my Queen's haven. The soaking marathon provided a quiet void. Not yet wanting to fill it with my next day's Achilles dilemma, I indulged in rewinding my thoughts to the start of my *Camino.*

It seemed so long ago I'd limped through St. Jean Pied de Port. I still heard the French gentleman's question in my head: *Why are you here?* I recalled rock-sitting in the Pyrenees, reviewing my roots and the forty years that led me to the *Camino*. Those years dared to create a life of adventure, freedom, and creative whirlwinds. But what *kind* of freedom? Until now, I felt I'd maybe *leased* freedom, but never *owned* it outright. This rattled my cage. And a cage can't equal freedom. My thought: *How does one know when she owns freedom?* An odd oxymoron.

Gina and Brad's late-night message said they'd arrived and likely scored the last two beds in town. They'd be high tailing it out at sunrise at an accelerated pace to get to Santiago in time to make their flight home. I missed them already.

Having soaked myself into a prune, the receded water balloon left behind a fiery sore. Sitting in my white, plush Queen's robe, I pulled out the bandages I'd stuffed into the empty pocket originally designated for Iron Cross offerings. As I did, something hard fell to the floor. "Wide-eyed awe" best described my face as I reached for what had dropped. Sparkling in my hand—Michael's "lost" rock. I heard my Dead-Friends-*Camino*-Support-Army's celestial applause for this very clever Iron Cross avoidance scheme, acknowledging, *nicely done, Michael!*

The rock miracle required a good night's sleep before truly appreciating how much this plot twist surely beat discovering my true love to be a Russian spy, or an alien creeping through the air vents. I still worried about the dog from the fire though.

Choosing to wait until morning to ponder the day's footwear woes, I crawled under the comforter that felt like frosting on the Queen's cake. *Holy shit, what a day.* I felt tempted to declare, "Act Two is a wrap!" But not so. The alien still lurked. And the dog was still missing.

Completion isn't king here on the *Camino*. Anticipation rules the day. We ride at dawn.

QUEENS KATHLEEN AND CLAIRE – ANGELS NUMBER TWELVE

CHAPTER 28

NO STRAIGHT LINES

VILLAFRANCA TO TRIACASTELA

The streaming morning light illumined the tough three choices waiting by my backpack. Do I wear hiking boots? Flip-flops? Tevas? Tevas won—plus heavy bandaging. Today, I'd enter the gateway to Galacia Provence with the mountain destination of "My Sombrero." Or, for those going strictly by the book, O Cebreiro.

For weeks, I'd counted on my body being battle-hardened in time for this steepest climb yet. I *was* ready, minus the Achilles issue. Several miles in, I ditched the Tevas and walked in only my purple toe socks. It garnered curiosity, but no one needs to justify anything in this utopian world.

The day's sweetest gift—a white cat with a calico face joined me. No, she *led* me. Cats (domesticated and feral) on the trail are common. Some aloof, some curious. This whimsical one walked just ahead for almost two miles. She frequently looked back as if asking, "Are you coming, purple socks?" Sometimes she'd turn to say something in cat-talk. I seriously considered she might be conversing with Petey, who could very well be perched on my shoulder proudly explaining my sprinkling birdseed on his dead body—twice—because, well, you never know.

Eventually, she stopped and looked up. One eye was noticeably blue. Heeding the warnings not to pet feral cats, I thanked this noble beast for the safe passage, and she scampered away. Note to self: Google calico and white cat totems.

Countless toe-sock steps later, at a café in Herrarias, I read about the steep ascent to O Cebreiro. I'd guarded my heel all morning from strap irritation, so this climb might be feasible. Sitting at an outdoor table, my nose in the guidebook, I felt the nudge of a hot plate of french fries and heard in broken English, "Ketchup?" I looked up to discover Gentleman Jade from Albania.

Ditching the book, I gratefully accepted and shared my too-frequent *Camino* food group. Quickly, our talk evolved from introductions and "Yes, ketchup, please," to how he considered it good fortune in the long run, to have been orphaned at age eleven and raised in an Albanian fishing village by his older brother. Next, he inquired about my shoeless status, given the three pairs dangling from my pack. I reluctantly shared the battle in my head: Achilles versus the looming mountain ahead. His brother and friends joined us with a pitcher of beer, and after introductions, were curious to view my tendon before any food came. *Seriously?* Removing my toe-sock, and bandages revealed the fluid-filled balloon. Dramatized gags followed, Jade speaking as if into a microphone, "Houston. We have a problem here." The others sat back, ready for his predictable interrogation.

Jade, a sharp, handsome 68-year-old with chiseled cheekbones and a thoughtful demeanor, played Twenty Questions (the mystery object appearing to be *me),* asking about my *Camino* so far, my beliefs, and my history. I provided the shortened version, but did include my ghost friends sharing the trail, including Petey the parakeet. No one ran away. His brother leaned in, whispering, "Can't you just hear his mind clicking the puzzle pieces together? Get ready, it's coming." Indeed, Jade's well-packaged, wildly accurate monologue followed.

"So, Molly Ann...I've tracked what's led to your sitting here in those lovely, filthy, purple toe-socks—one that's hiding an oozing balloon—at the base of the mountain you know would be foolish to climb today. Yet, you sit here, with all the data you need, still pretending you haven't decided. Why is that?"

A rhetorical question.

"You're smart, beautiful, and don't fall for your own bullshit. However, if you took care of yourself here, Molly, and skipped this mountain, you'd fear looking weak."

There was no place to hide with this guy.

"You didn't come to conquer every mountain. You came to watch, listen, and keep things real. To keep things paced, and walk in your purple toe-socks because you damn well feel like it. And hear this. You are NOT the same woman who missed the Pyrenees. She faded somewhere on the meseta."

Another round of ale was poured, knowing Jade's oration wasn't over.

"Anyone will tell you, those Tevas would chew your Achilles to shreds halfway up that mountain, and you'll kiss the rest of this pilgrimage goodbye. It could heal enough in a day or two, but the *Camino* doesn't care if you wait it out here, or taxi to the other side of the mountain to catch up to your Aussie friends. Which idea delivers you joy?"

Pointing to his friend, "Ronas over there stayed behind two days ago to handle a business issue. Then taxied two stages to catch up to us. Who cares. His *Camino* lesson: don't live in either/or. Learn to blend business and fun when needed. Molly, you have bigger fish to fry than kilometer counting."

Propping his feet on the railing, Jade wrapped up his inquiry. "Tell me, Molly Ann, are you here to connect the dots, or merely collect *more* dots? Because it seems you have all the data needed to make your decision. You just don't like the answer. Okay, I'm done. You need another beer and lunch."

A stunned silence hung in the air. His timely message echoed that of my Pyrenees angels, and Orietta of the Shire. Only now, with more miles, tears, and miracles under my belt, my inner overachiever heard it at a new level.

A message chimed from Pablo & Gabby, still one day ahead:

> Left O Cebreiro this morning, heading to Triacastela tonight. Would love you to catch up to us. We could walk into Santiago together, yes?

Enter Emerald City with my kidnappers? Hmmm. Tempting.

Back in Sahagún, when the doctor warned me what would happen if I didn't stop walking, it felt prudent to skip an entire stage to heal. *Was this different? Would it be a pop-tart?*

Bringing this analytical head noise to a screeching halt, I warned the gremlins, *knock it off already!* Immediately, my dots aligned, producing a clear decision. I'd jump ahead to Triacastela. I booked a bed online, excited to surprise my friends from Down Under.

The Albanian guys toasted my wise decision. The older brother filled me in that Jade's uncanny gift of insight stems from years as a psychologist. His local radio call-in show earned him the name Gentleman Jade, and the reputation of "the Tony Robbins" of their area. Leave it to the *Camino* to deliver me a brilliant shrink who could only finagle my attention using hot french fries.

These men strategically made this town their stopping point the day before, leaving the climb to O Cebreiro by sunset their only goal for today. Jade leaned in with one last question. "*I* knew that *you* knew darn well wearing those Tevas up that steep climb today couldn't happen. I'm curious. Was my guess right? Was it fear of looking weak that kept you from speaking the obvious?"

"Much of what you said, Jade, was spot on. Especially the 'I'm beautiful and smart' part. But you didn't nail my biggest fear. Don't feel bad. Even Tony Robbins couldn't guess it. I didn't fear looking weak. For the first time on this journey, I feared that I might be pop-tarting the dog, which would be unacceptable."

Everyone's heads turned. "Pop—WHAT?"

The term fell out too easily. This time with an even rowdier crowd than Sophie, Lilly, and Noah. I filled them in on the pop-tart guy who lamely passes off taming a growling dog using a Pop-Tart™ as his "heal a relationship" completion.

The guys' humorous bantering on this idea of short-changing the spirit of integrity required three more pitchers, a full lunch, a whole almond cake, and Google Translate to cover all angles of pop-tarting 101. I'm proud to say the phrase "pop-tarting the dog" crossed yet another international border, making the world safer from avoidant chicken-shit behaviors.

Two hours later, as the guys prepared to head up to O Cebreiro, I climbed into a taxi headed for Triacastela. Another *Camino* goodbye that weighed heavy. Especially with Jade.

Buen Camino, Angel Number Thirteen.

The taxi driver pointed out from the highway the distant steep ascent I was missing. It looked outrageously ominous and beautiful. But whether to risk walking up *that* day was never the hard question. That clearly couldn't happen. My potential pop-tart quandary: do I hang back to heal a day or two to stick with the guidebook's step-by-step order of things (O Cebreiro being the next step), causing my friends to now be *three days* ahead and likely not see them again? Or do I chalk O Cebreiro up to "not in the cards this time" and prioritize reconnecting with friends? The tough question: if I choose the latter, is *that* a pop-tart?

Our path in life is never a straight line. Rather, it's an ever-overlapping spiral. However, the *Camino* guidebooks could be technically viewed as taking a straight-line approach: "You're *here*. Now you go *there*." Though at choice about where and when to stop and rest (or stop for good), it lays out a fairly set course to Santiago.

The driver tapped the dashboard to the radio beat as I contemplated the inner battle with my overachiever. For someone who appears free form, sometimes I'm a stickler for dotting every "i" and crossing every "t." Both played into my decision process earlier. And when made, it landed strong. It wasn't a pop-tart. For another pilgrim, maybe. Not for me. I chose connection over a straight line.

Wow, this was the freedom I pondered last night in the bathtub. This was the freedom I could own! One where, in times of uncertainty, I make a decision, then, make that decision right.

Whatever lessons may've awaited me on the climb to "My Sombrero" would need to recalibrate, chase me down, and be delivered in a new way as I followed this no-straight-lines journey.

For now, I had soul friends to surprise and a tendon to soak. I asked the driver to drop me off in the next town.

GENTLEMAN JADE — ANGEL NUMBER THIRTEEN

 CAMINO MESSAGE #15

Are you working to connect the dots (make a decision)? Or, are you merely collecting more dots (quit stalling)?

Journal Notes

June 8, 2019
Triacastela

Camino...Please bless Gentleman Jade (and friends) in their destination of O'Cebriero tonight. I warmly thank him for the timely arrival of his slap upside the head. Good night.

MORE HELPFUL CAMINO TIPS

1. Who says you can't have fried eggs, french fries, and beer for breakfast?

2. I've learned to greet ailing pilgrims on the trail with "Do you have what you need?" rather than "Buen Camino." Cuz when you're trailside doctoring your blister, and you just checked the map to find you have 11 km. left to go on your painful foot and about then another chipper, pain-free pilgrim bounces by and greets you with a cheery "Buen Camino!" You don't say it, but you think it. "Buen fucking Camino to you, you little Pollyanna." And then, with guilt on top of the blister, you realize you're probably going to burn in hell.

3. You know you're "in the zone" when a pilgrim asks, "So, what do you do for a living back home?" And you find you have to stop and think.

4. When you're hungry and in a hurry to get on the trail but aren't sure what the Spanish menu says—just show the cafe person your gutsy Google Translate message stating, "I'll take any egg breakfast that doesn't have cheese, wheat, or shrimp, please. Gracias." And then you pray. "Please, God, don't let it be octopus or baby pig liver in my eggs. Amen."

5. There should be a special word reserved for that feeling of panic—then relief—when you reach for your passport, wallet, or phone in your pack and it's not where it usually is. But then you find it right where you tucked it. Breathe.

6. Does your path have heart? If not, the creed you're reciting in the cavernous Girl Scout gymnasium of life will echo back: "This is BS." Listen.

7. If You Meet The Buddha Cat On The Road (and you will)

   Per Google:

   - Cats appear as a reminder about balance, knowing when to stop, reflect, and listen to your instincts.

   - Calico Cats are considered lucky charms and can bring good fortune.

   - White Cats symbolize purity, rebirth, happiness, prosperity, and healing. Their mission is to help you grow spiritually. Take special note of any white cat with one or two blue eyes. They are rare indeed.

8. Our soul doesn't develop in a straight line. It needs assistance in navigating unexpected turns. And so it is on the Camino. Alone, we are sometimes lacking, but on this winding path, together we shine.

CHAPTER 29

TUNNEL of GRACE

TO TRIACASTELA, SAMOS, SARRIA

TEA TIME

It's a fact. Watermelon and sticky lemonade will draw ants. I didn't know an herbal solution of marshmallow root and white oak bark could attract *aunts* as well. I'm talking about three quirky aunts from London. The nutty kind that movies are made of.

The elder aunties reached their day's destination of Fonfria, where my taxi ride ended. My plan: walk the last six miles into Triacastela. My rendezvous with the auntie's was surely destiny.

Finding a bucket in a *mercado,* I set my sights on soaking my Achilles. I couldn't quite picture entering a Colorado café with a bucket, removing my boots and smelly socks, and asking the waiter, "Can you fill this with hot water for my slimy herbs (to soak my Achilles water balloon, of course)? "Oh. And some fries with that, please." It just wouldn't work.

The aunt infestation happened while discreetly soaking my foot. Mesmerized by the slime in the bucket, they gawked as if passing a terrible accident scene. Then, pulled up three chairs. It was British teatime, and I was in for a bizarre rest stop.

These cousins, from one large UK family, never married. Don't confuse "not married" with "old maids." It took them but two minutes after pouring the tea to broach their favorite subjects—men, and sex. The best description of these women: *The Golden Girls* meet *Beetlejuice*.

Hearing the contents of my herbal concoction, they quickly compared it to an herbal douche they highly recommend. The conversation went downhill from there. Next topic: their disastrous patterns in romantic relationships. *Now* I had skin in the game.

After spilling their repetitive love woes, I joined in. "The unhealthy relationship pattern I used to attract over and over in my younger years was HISSCARDS." That understandably drew a "deer-in-the-headlights" look.

"It's an acronym, ladies," I explained how three friends and I broached the topic decades ago: why do we keep repeating the same detrimental pattern in relationships? And what exactly *is* our pattern?

Our friend John jumped in and confessed his. "My problem is I go for BUAPs. *Bright Underachievers with Awesome Potential.*" He explained, "I always attract insecure women. I stroke their egos and support their best qualities. They start believing in themselves, followed by breaking things off and heading for brighter horizons with new-found confidence, leaving me in the dust licking my wounds." We shared a good, compassionate laugh back then over his sad but true tale.

He insisted we fess up to *our* patterns. Liking the acronym approach, Hal volunteered next. "That's easy. My downfall is CABs. *Compulsive Athletic Blonds.* You know the type. Sporty ponytail bouncing as she crosses the finish line, beating the most recent marathon record. I'm a sucker for their 'come hither' look, but in the end, they squash me like a Red Solo Cup."

I could see the three aunties' wheels turning as I shared the final two acronyms from that night long ago. Inspired by the guys' honesty, Sheryl (my roommate) and I reported our particular brand of neurosis. Sheryl sheepishly announcing hers. "My pitfall is HIPWICHs. *Highly Intelligent Professionals, Whom I Can't Have.*" Being her roommate, I'd seen it play out too many times. She'd go for the GQ men who weren't a fit for her outdoorsy, nature-loving self, always ending with her on the kitchen floor in a heap of tears, holding her broken heart. I coaxed her up with a pint of Haagen Daz™ more than once.

My turn. "*My* kiss of death are HISSCARDs. *Humorous, Intelligent, Supposedly-Sensitive Charmers, Able to Rationalize Deception.*" My friends' acknowledging moans recalled my "loves" that crashed and burned. My road to ruin was the "supposedly sensitive charmer" part—where my blinders missed self-centered, insensitive cues. Pitiful, yes, but the reveal is the first step in recovery, right? Laughing about it, the second.

Giddy heckling erupted from the British aunties as they rushed for pen and paper to determine theirs. It's a train wreck you can't help but scrutinize. The aunties proudly produced their results as I wiped off the herbal slime, bandaged my tendon, and put on clean socks. Theirs required keen phonic skills, but their point was made. Seriously amused, I saved them in my phone notes.

Auntie #1: "JAFILEBPAAB. *Just As My Future Is Looking Ever So Bright, Promises Are Always Broken.*" Her cousins lavished her with hugs and kisses and insincere "Awww, pooor baby" comments, then looked to see who would go next.

Auntie #2: "MAROWASCKO. *Men Attempting Romantic Overtures Without Any Sense of Communication, Kindness, or Orgasms.*" Given the aunties' momentary stifled snickers, I figured that one was recent and still pretty raw. We trusted the next auntie wouldn't disappoint.

Auntie #3: "ATDP. *All Talk. Disappointing Penis.*"

Was their laughter true amusement or a tough British cover for resignation? Doing this in our twenties left room to improve our wayward hearts. But identifying downfalls in your sixties and seventies leaves room for only a self-forgiving shrug and a laugh, except for *these* women. No shrugs. They ate pain for lunch and laughed about it for dessert.

I hated to leave but left them in a cackling huddle, preparing to move from teatime to happy hour shots. *Buen Camino, wonderful crazy aunties.*

Walking alongside stunning valley views, I reflected on my HISSCARD confession of decades past. Or was it more current than I wanted to admit? I gave the standard self-forgiving shrug and laugh. This self-deprecating gesture obviously didn't sit well with *the Voice,* who suddenly appeared after days of silence. It came to let me have it.

Hold on, Sista. First, you're not dead yet! So, what's up with this shrug thing? Second, spoiler alert. A revised relationship standard is brewing in that heart of yours. Once you sort it out, this old HISSCARD shit just won't fly anymore. The Voice faded.

THE PERFECT MISTAKE

The surprise reunion with my Aussie pals felt like coming home. Having spent more time in the herb elixir than out, by morning my bandaged tendon was ready for the 21 km (11.5 mi) ahead. Weight-dumping time. I donated my first-acquired Tevas to the hostel's "take what you need" shelf. When leaving, I overheard a guy call excitedly to his wife, "Honey, look, my size Tevas—just what my blister needs!" She undoubtedly replied, "The *Camino* provides!" *I hope they deliver you relief as they did for me.*

The Aussies and I couldn't say why we turned left when we'd planned to take the shorter trail to the right, but our plan to arrive early in Sarria to kick back was foiled. However, we had no desire for any course correction. This other-worldly longer route toward Samos, somehow lured us. Maybe only I would label it as *magic.*

I blame Mister Ed. Yeah. The TV talking horse. At the impressionable age of six, he blurred my world of fantasy and realistic possibility. He was my gateway drug to wanting my personal *Puff the Magic Dragon, My Favorite Martian,* or *Flipper.* Was a fantasy friend too much to ask? This desire faded as life became more adult-serious. Putting it in "Puff" language, "painted wings and giant rings made way for other toys." Confession: this secret fantasy never completely faded.

Somewhere between Triacastela and Samos, a version of my fantasy came to pass. Maybe *My Favorite Martian* alien didn't exactly move in over my garage. Still, I swam in the magical feeling that such an occurrence might conjure.

Entering the tiny village of San Cristobo, we were transported into a mystical time warp. Though the ancient-looking stone cottages appeared inhabited (curtains blowing in open windows, full watering cans next to cascading flower boxes), we saw no one. The boarded-up church and many deserted homes, alongside inhabited ones, spoke to a diminishing community.

Possibly, children are grown and gone, leaving the elders to live out their days. Our theory was confirmed when we found a cemetery with headstone graves and crypts. The engraved dates ranged from over a century ago to present. In the stillness of this seeming ghost town, I felt my own mortality. The circle of life before us moved me to tears. Grateful tears. To have life. To be walking. With no idea what lay ahead, and trusting the way.

Taking one last look at this snapshot in time, I wouldn't forget these people we never met. I find myself even now wondering—*How are they doing? Did they wake up another day to water the flower boxes and deadhead the blooms? Did their adult children return for Christmas with grandchildren? Had anyone been inside as we walked through that day, wishing we'd called out to say 'hello?'*

We then entered a seemingly private forest. A canopy of trees towered over an endless woodland trail, fit for gnomes and fairies, like an arbor for pilgrims beckoned here, to this tunnel of grace.

Crunching gravel was replaced by a thick magic carpet from thousands of years' worth of layered, soft, decaying leaves. Birdsong in the still woods seemed the soundtrack for a dream state. Had we stepped through a portal like the one at the top of the world above the Iron Cross? It made up for every Mork or Flipper fantasy for which I'd felt shortchanged. The babbling brook danced alongside our trail and disappeared underground (I assumed to the hidden world of fairies and Gandalf), only to reappear, guiding us to Samos.

The woodlands finally opened to a road overlooking a lush river valley, the town of Samos, and a breathtaking view of its enormous ancient monastery, Monasterio de Samos, the oldest and largest of the Western world. It's still inhabited by monks walking the halls with ghosts of sixth-century Desert Fathers who followed ancient Benedictine Rule.

Descending into town, a hushed reverence lingered among pilgrims at the café. I wish I'd asked the other pilgrims, "What did *you* sense back there? Did you feel under a spell as well?"

At our patio table, caught somewhere between the portal of grace and serious hunger, a thoughtful surprise text came through from my Colorado friend, Jan. As if delivered through the portal, her wish for joy on my journey reconnected me with the bigger world out there, which allowed the coexistence of grace and the devouring of scrambled eggs, bacon, and french fries. All equally sacred players in this holy dirt game.

Heading toward Sarria once again, I wondered: *Could anyone whose feet touch down in this tunnel of grace—a tunnel having listened to the dreams, secrets, and longings of millions—possibly have missed the woods whispering, "Be still and know that I am God?"*

I refer here to any wide interpretation of "God," whether the power in nature, Buddha, the wind, Spirit, a universal force, or an omniscient Mother/Father. Whatever works. I sensed anyone unable to feel the earth's pulse and profound grace here would likely alert The *Camino* Angel Squad. This squad, likely wearing compression socks and headlamps, swoops in to inspire hearts whose worries and hurriedness prevent them from fully experiencing this hidden portal.

In the quiet miles to Sarria, pondering the idea of angels in socks and whispering woodlands, I couldn't deny the existence of magic any longer, or of talking horses. Who doesn't crave magic in this sometimes too-cynical world?

So, Mister Ed, I'm no Wilbur, but if you're out there listening, I'm open to a conversation whenever you are. I'll be waiting.

TRES KILOMETERS (NO. REALLY.)

By mid-afternoon, I hit the wall. So badly my energy, blood sugar, and legs pleaded, "We can go no farther! Call Triple-A Roadside Service! Send helicopter with almond cake and french fries to resuscitate woman in ditch wearing bright-pink t-shirt."

We'd just walked a never-ending fairytale-like country road through scenic farmland, tall grasses, and flower-filled fields towering over our heads. But the map's reported distance seemed way off, so we asked a passing farmer, "How far to the next town?"

He pointed down the road, "Three kilometers." Phew. Do-able. We walked *four* kilometers. No town.

We waved down a smiling local on his tractor. In Pablo's flowing Spanish, he asked, "How far to the next town?"

"*Tres kilometers. Buen Camino!*" And he drove off. He'd looked so kind. But he was a snake. No such town in *tres* kilometers. My fuel-deprived brain detected a conspiracy.

Our next encounter seemed innocent enough, though we eyed her with suspicion. A sweet elderly Spanish woman carrying a large bouquet of wildflowers greeted us, happily saying, "*Buen Camino! Se lo llevo a un amigo!*"

Gabby interpreted. "I'm taking these to a friend." Not having seen any home for miles, we wondered where the hell she and this friend lived. In a cornfield?

Pablo asked her, "How far to the next town?"

"*Tres kilometers.*"

At first, Gabby's snarly expression matched mine. Then I realized the *Camino* had an insistent message for us, and we hadn't been listening: *Why do you doubt and question distance all of a sudden? Asking doesn't make it shorter. You simply walk until you're there.* The *Camino* aimed to return us to a state of flow. I'm reminded of the words of thought leader, Marcia Wieder:

> "*If you have not dealt with your own doubt and you meet another doubter on the road, their doubt will magnify yours.*"

The threat of seriously hitting the wall loomed. Had either said anything even resembling, "Don't worry, the *Camino* will provide," they likely would've found my phone embedded in their foreheads. Low blood sugar has its dark side.

Then it appeared. A seventeenth-century *pension* oasis tucked in the woods. A *pension* is a small boarding house with a central kitchen, sleeping rooms, and often dreamy claw-foot tubs. There were cascading flower boxes and brightly colored umbrella tables with pilgrims sitting outside devouring soup, sausage, cheese, and fresh bread. A mirage?

"Gabby, we haven't seen a soul since Samos, where'd all these people come from?"

The owner invited us to sit. Within minutes, our own table overflowed. A hearty bowl of Galacian soup answered my hunger pangs. How'd she know to serve me first? Possibly, she didn't go for the phone-in-forehead look?

With renewed bodies and spirits, continuing our way to Sarria seemed a long, joyful walk in the park. Dare I say—at the risk of an implanted phone—the *Camino* provides.

CHAPTER 30

BELONGING

SARRIA TO PORTOMARIN

"Bring out your dead!"

I awakened in a stiff, lifeless state, and clearly a candidate for the body cart in the Monty Python movie scene. It didn't seem too far-fetched. I swore I heard that creaky cart rolling under our *albergue* window. My non-functioning muscles made forgetting my ball bag in Triacastela the day before a harsh reality. Fortunately, they'd be kindly retrieved by my friend Bill when passing through town, but that didn't save me now.

But hark! A *Camino* miracle! From dead-on-the-cart to an easy walking pace in just one hour's time. It happened frequently these days: Rise with the sun. Complain joints don't work. Walk anyway. Think about life. Eat french fries and eggs. Score a very cool stamp in a remote café. Be in awe that stiffness is gone. Talk with pilgrims about their lives. Resist your bored gremlin's temptation to say you're a Russian spy. Revel in the flowers and tall grasses, recalling colors in Italian. Find patience with clicking walking poles with no rubber tips. Think about unimportant things—they usually end up most important. Know you belong here. Struggle to calculate the euro-to-dollar value in your pocket, while recalling how your math phobia began in third grade. Walk farther. Forgive your math teacher. Sense something is changing inside (what, you're not sure). Consume half an almond cake while walking. When greeted with "Great day, eh?" respond, "It's butterscotch!"

The man's question came mid-thought at a café. "Do your feet ever just plain—hurt? Not like a blister hurt. Not my-shoes-are-too-tight hurt. I'm talkin' down to your bones hurt. You know what I'm sayin'?" This Belgian man on the bench next to me, pulled off his boot and rubbed his foot. A trail newcomer, his expression begged for encouraging news.

"Oh, sure. It's always terrible this time of day. At least, I *think* it is. I'm not even sure anymore."

He couldn't fathom my vagueness. "You *think*? How could you not *know*?"

I smiled, not at his pain, but at realizing aches were so baked into my big-picture experience, it no longer registered as a problem. My feet ached to the bone. *So what, now what?*

I could've told him the truth. "Oh, just wait, *this* is nothing! Give it five more days. You'll wanna gnaw your foot off!"

Instead, I played the advice card. "Change your socks twice a day to avoid heat blisters. They're a bear. At night, lay on your bed and put your feet up high on the wall to allow them to drain."

"Really? Will that stop the pain?"

"No. But it's a great photo op."

He didn't see the humor. It was *day two* of walking for him. *Week five* for me. Our funny-meters were universes apart.

Many pilgrims begin walking in Sarria, 100 kilometers (62 miles) from Santiago. Completing a minimum of 100 kilometers earns your *Camino Compostela*. The guidebook and experienced pilgrims warn that when church and school groups begin here, fresh on the trail and chatty, they're oblivious to weathered pilgrims who have cherished quiet for weeks.

I made a parting suggestion to the ailing gentleman. "Try owning your footache as your pilgrim badge of honor. Because it doesn't go away. But something waits beyond that ache, making it all worthwhile. *Buen Camino!*"

I continued westward, until a familiar female voice called from behind.

"Hey, PopTart!" No question who it could be. I turned to meet Lilly's warm hug, our smiles wide enough to fit a *whole* Pop-Tart™. I'd last seen

Lilly and Noah that rainy night with Sophie before the Iron Cross. I flashed back to dissecting the downfalls of pop-tarting the dog, and Lilly confessed her frustration keeping up with her Olympian husband. Brief messages exchanged back then reported we each survived Iron Cross day, but no details.

My first question, "Where's Noah?" I figured he'd walked ahead, and she was catching up to him. The reality—he'd bused a couple days ahead for a respite to heal a badly bruised rib and groin pull suffered in a fall on the Iron Cross descent. After they'd made their stone drop at the Cross, Lilly and others successfully taxied to Molinaseca. Noah pushed on with another group. My best guess, I was a couple hours ahead of him that day.

He slid on a gravel field on their descent, and landed hard. Lilly's earlier questioning of her abilities, and Noah's opinion of this trek being a "piece of cake" was turned on its head.

"Your words that night in the bar, Molly, really stuck. They changed everything. I'm not a pop-tarter. But I feel the difference now between playing not to lose and playing to win. I know whether I'm focused on "Yikes, what if I screw up?" or "Who gives a shit. Just do it, Lilly."

I shook my head. "Who are you, and what did you do with Lilly?" She wasn't done. "Remember how I wasn't sure I belonged here? I'm learning playing to win can look different for each of us. Who knew complete rest would ever be Noah's win?" Her words spilled out in half-Dutch/half-English, but I got the gist. All this stemmed from a silly rainy night conversation.

We walked the next hour sharing our solo adventure insights—moments we were called to weigh common sense against pop-tarting, our safety and well-being versus coddling, and, most of all—silencing the self-critic.

Rolling with their current situation rather than panicking was new for Lilly. Though grateful for his recovery, they understood the odd gift in Noah's mishap. The way the two handled it was the source of her smile and new strength. She'd walked solo since Molinaseca. Her humbled Olympian husband surrendered to a bus, leaving his wife to soldier on. She could've accompanied him but opted to go solo, emerging with a bold new confidence.

Lilly would get a taxi and jump a full stage in the next town to meet Noah. He'd healed enough to walk the last two days into Santiago.

Mysterious grace took hold. The quickening connection effect fascinated both of us in this magical vortex of *Camino* dog years. We felt connected for a lifetime.

Hugging the new, kick-ass Lilly goodbye, my heart sank as she disappeared into a taxi. She continued waving until out of sight. A strange question rose in my aching heart. *Once out of sight, do we stop belonging? Where did that concern stem from?*

Trail traffic became noticeably heavier. For the first time, I skirted a chatty youth group taking up the whole path. This was re-entry. The *Camino* asked: *Are you able, even in the midst of chaos, to hold onto the butterscotch? That's your test.*

Ahead of the herd, I found a semi-quiet pocket. Knowing glances exchanged with the other long-familiar pilgrims seemed to express, *Peace was nice while it lasted, eh?* Connection.

Pablo, Gabby, and I found each other, as always. We walked a magic carpet of mostly ease toward Portomarin. A fairytale pure-white horse with its flowing mane stood stoic in a field, as if aware its image would land in every passing pilgrim's photos. A cool babbling brook under a canopy of trees brought relief from the midday sun. We visited old churches in ancient hamlets, passed donkeys making appeals to be petted, and finally, emerging from winding woods, heard a faint, distant tune. A bagpipe called like sirens to sailors weary from the sea.

Its volume grew as we descended into the valley. In full Highland dress, the handsome bagpiper stood playing trailside, winking as we dropped euros in his case. I imagined, for a moment, Bren in his genuine Scottish kilt. *Sigh.* As quickly as it came, the magical tune faded behind us.

Approaching Portomarin, my curious question to Pablo fell out. "How far to the next town? I need a water refill."

"Three kilometers," he replied.

When no town appeared, I asked again. I hadn't yet caught on.

Again, he answered, "Three kilometers."

Gabby and I stopped in our tracks and glared. Duped by friendly fire! This trickster from "The Land Down Under" got us good. Gabby poked him hard with her walking pole. Rightfully so. Of course, he just smiled and gave me a Vegemite sandwich. Well, not really. Couldn't resist.

We turned off the road onto a supposed shortcut. Ugh. Shortcuts don't necessarily mean *easier*. We met other pilgrims bottle-necked in a narrow rocky gully, experiencing the same shortcut remorse. Single file, we gingerly navigated the narrow, steep descent. The descent stirred a new sensation in my knee. Nothing a rolling pin couldn't fix. Oops. Never mind. Once down safely, we laughed at our wrong decision from hell.

A bit scraped up, feet aching, we were greeted with an unexpected entrance to the city. Nothing says "Welcome to Portomarin" at the end of a long, tiring day like a steep, cement, 75-step stairway up to the main part of town. *C'mon. Really?* I rarely heard Gabby swear up a storm, but this eleventh-hour cruel test in endurance gave her a justified reason. I trust her spicy choice of words boldly spoke on behalf of the masses.

Journal Notes

June 10, 2019
Portomarin

Dear Camino,

Molly here.

Hey, a wellness check—on myself. We're on the home stretch. Is there anything I've missed that you need me to know? You've been whispering things in my ear, but, hell, I've been busy with shoelace management and unexpected parakeets to bury. Anything I should know about my life? Relationships? Dreams? Purple toe-socks? I'm listening.

Thank you. Carry on with whatever the Camino does when off-duty.

Signed,

Your over-achieving pilgrim

CHAPTER 31

TAKE ME to CHURCH

SOMEWHERE OUTSIDE PORTOMARIN

Take Me To Church

~ Hozier

Leaving a café, I spotted the woman on an old, weathered bench, face buried in her hands. By this point, I'd sharpened my intuition of who prefers to be left to their thoughts and who calls to be approached. I sat next to her.

"Do you have what you need?"

She lifted her head and looked away before speaking.

"I'm a terrible person. I need someone to take this guilt from me."

Oh God. Envisioning dead bodies, Clorox-scrubbed surfaces, and a one-way escape ticket to Spain, I took a deep breath and responded.

"Well, I personally don't need anyone *else's* guilt, but thanks anyway. Is there a reason you want to hold onto *yours*?"

"Yes, I'm a mom of three. A wife. A daughter…"

My thought—*Uh-oh. Which one did she off?*

She continued. "I've cleaned, baked, loved, packed lunches, soothed heartaches, cleaned out my-mother-the-hoarder's garage from hell and chauffeured her to doctor appointments, thrown graduation parties, and on behalf of my husband's wimpy ego, I've cursed boss after boss for being wrong and unfair. Even when they were justified. I lost myself in all that somewhere. Listen to me. I'm a walking cliché!"

By this point, I identified her as Swedish. Her name, Klara.

"Okay. And you feel guilty about all that because—?"

"Because I'm doing the *Camino* alone. Here, I don't belong to *anyone*. No one expects anything from me. There've been times I've felt alone in my own home, like I didn't belong, even at the family dinner table. But *here,* I'm alone and feel I belong, and, I hate to say it, I'm so happy."

She looked me in the eye, awaiting judgment. "It's all wrong. *That's* why I feel guilty."

It wasn't my place to absolve her of guilt or push another way of thinking. I'd let *her* decide whether or not she totally sucked as a human being. We learned about each other's lives as we walked into the next town together. Spotting a little church, I pulled Klara inside. Having the quaint holy place to ourselves, I motioned for her to join me in the pew. I spoke out loud.

"God, this is my new friend, Klara. She's a terrible human being, and I don't know what we should do with her."

Klara's eyes widened. She looked around to ensure no one heard me. I continued.

"Let me tell you how awful she is. She's raised three smart kids. Did all the mom things. Took them to ballet classes and soccer practice. One of them played violin with the Stockholm Symphony at fifteen. What kind of mom is she, anyway? That daughter is allergic to almost everything outdoors and has been stuck inside most of her life. So, Klara here—you know, the bad-mom pilgrim—got some bright paints, and the whole family painted murals of flowers, fields, trees, and butterflies on the walls throughout the whole house so her daughter could feel like she was outside. I'm telling you, she's evil, and shouldn't be cut any slack. And let me tell you what this bitch did *next…*"

Klara cupped her hand over my mouth for speaking that word in church. We laughed as I wrestled her hand away. I considered it professional immersion therapy, overdosing her on her own silly thinking.

"And another thing, God, her three kids are pretty much grown and aren't showing much gratitude for all she's done. She doesn't feel she belongs there anymore. Can you believe she's also whining about ironing her husband's underwear? What's up with that?"

That *really* made Klara scope the church for eavesdroppers.

"So Klara came here to the *Camino*, God, to take stock of her life. No demands on her. She eats almond cake for dinner (if she wants) and confessed she had french fries and a beer for breakfast. Pretty barbarian, don't you think?"

When the church door creaked open, Klara slid down in the pew and whacked me across the shoulder to shut me up. I continued.

"And get this, last night Klara confessed she had TWO carafes of sangria with friends and had to sneak into her *albergue* after lights were out. She's a heathen, I tell you! Worst of all, she's having fun, liking her own company, and hasn't been this happy in years. It's disgusting. She *should* feel guilty! So, I need to know, should she die by Templar firing squad or maybe a stoning here in the church square?"

In a giggling fit, Klara pulled me out of the pew and out the church door. Reaching the courtyard, she surrendered. "Okay! Okay! I'm done feeling guilty!"

A strong case of carbonated holiness dropped us to the ground giggling.

"Klara, finish your *Camino* with all the happiness you can tap, and there's a good chance that same *Camino* energy will spill over into your family when you get home. Not because your home has changed, but *you* will have. And that's gotta affect the whole!" My final suggestion: "Please, Klara, stop ironing your husband's underwear already. That's not a club you should belong to!"

Having only three more days of walking seemed too quick of a journey to Klara. At that moment, she decided she'd walk the three extra days after Santiago to Finisterre on the coast with her new friends. After all, she had flexibility with a one-way ticket. Which reminded me. I confessed to her my vision of dead bodies and empty Clorox bottles when she first mentioned her heavy, unforgivable guilt. I thanked her for being able to add "Klara the Murderer" to my list of *Camino* buddies, right next to the "Kidnappers of Roncesvalles."

She hurried to meet her new friends in a more hopeful state than when I found her, just as so many angels did for me. But I doubt I'm considered her angel. I'm thinking angels don't call someone a bitch or heathen while sitting in a church. If my angel status was jeopardized, I could at least exit town on the sacred path of *my* preferred church—the kind with no doors and blue skies. With that prayer, my feet shuffled out of town to a powerful and fitting song playing in my head, *"Take Me To Church." Amen to that!*

Buen Camino, Klara. Thank you for this silly moment of belonging.

Journal Notes

June 11, 2019
Palas De Rei

Occasionally, the music that creeps into my head is, regrettably, the theme from Jaws. Ugh.

Tonight, after dinner, I froze (in fear), staring down the dark, deserted street, noting my hostel was eight long blocks into the blackness. I'm brave. But not stupid. As the Aussies and I parted for our respective hostels, Pablo read my grim expression and kindly said, "I'd be happy to walk you to your hostel." Relief.

Now safely in my room and under the covers, journal in hand, my pen takes an unexpected direction. One mostly unspoken motivation to walk this journey alone had been to face whatever angst remained buried from the assault forty years before, and to break free of over-reactive caution. For years, I've learned to guard myself when called for, and walk through the fear when unfounded. But being alone in a foreign country stirred the caution pot.

Regarding men as predators, in general, is nowhere on my radar. Forgive the cliche—many of my closest friends are men. At times on this walk, I've stopped to gauge my comfort factor around a man (or men) I didn't know. My well-trained gut registered a green or red light. I responded accordingly.

Thinking back to the beginning of this journey until now, most potential problem situations have drawn to it some kind, thoughtful man who appeared right on cue to support my well-being. Interesting.

I've certainly had powerful, supportive women step up as well. Yet, it has leaned heavily

toward the male species showing up for this healing dance of mine—the very species I've possibly held (subconsciously) as somehow suspect. These gallant men hold a special place in the weave of my Camino tapestry. A place that's triggering this grateful, steady stream of tears at the moment, making a mess of this journal page.

Though the Divine Feminine has guided and made her strong presence known here, I've also been in the loving arms of the Divine Masculine. A resting place that hasn't always felt like home. Tonight, to Him, I bow in gratitude.

MORE HELPFUL CAMINO TIPS

1. Reassurance is unlikely to present itself on the *Camino*. Your only hope: sharpen your acceptance of *not knowing*, of *not landing*, of *not yet*.

2. If you promised bravery to try octopus, but have changed your mind, I'm happy to loan you my back-door-get-out-out-of-promise-free card. (Who's yer pop-tart buddy, huh?)

3. Before the *Camino*, waking up to a man in the next bed looking like Jack Nicholson in *The Shining*, I'd have freaked. Now, facing a frightening room full of 'em, I'm good.

4. The "real" *Camino* is whichever one you're doing.

5. Though most say, "Oh! You'll never be alone on the *Camino!*" The truth is, sometimes you just *are*. But learn to like your own company, and you'll soon call being alone—freedom.

6. It's every pilgrim's responsibility to pluck another pilgrim out of their analytical head and deliver them back into the heart rhythm of their *Camino*. Therefore, answering the heady question, "How far to the next town?" with the white lie "3 kilometers" is acceptable, and comes karma-free.

7. For your heroic actions, thoughtful responses, and for having my back, I thank the gentlemen of the *Camino*. Tonight, I lay down my sword against you.

CHAPTER 32

TAPESTRY

ARZÚA-BOUND

GRACE RESCUE SQUAD

I glanced around my sparse *albergue* room, appreciating its simplicity. The awkward vulnerability I'd awakened with, mixed with this appreciation, made for strange bedfellows.

Except for the bag in my hand filled with "everything blister," I was ready to leave. The night before, I'd met a young French woman doctoring some pretty nasty blisters. I left the bag outside her door and headed out. Three days to go.

A surprise message chimed after the Aussies and I connected. Then each found our own pace leaving Palas de Rei.

> Hey, Molly! Where ARE you? We miss you! Jade and the guys are pop-tarting at every damn turn. You gotta straighten these losers out!

A series of laughing emojis followed. This message from Gentleman Jade's brother triggered a funny series of defensive counterattacks from the accused parties.

In these final days, several other trail friends sent "we miss you" messages, as did I *them*. Knowing my presence was missed warmed the cold vulnerability I'd awakened with.

Weeks of spontaneous meetups made us all trail cousins in dog years. But in this countdown to Santiago, we couldn't count on those serendipitous meetings. That hit hard.

Breathing steadily on the hills, my dangling, swinging boots, and the rhythm of my trekking poles created a metronome beat. I'd miss this. I'd miss *everything*.

I recalled an afternoon walking with a wise Argentinian sage wearing a beautifully loom-woven shawl on this (her third) *Camino*. As a weaver myself, I appreciated the love and time put into it. I grasped what this elder sage tried to tell me that day.

> *"Anyone who touches your journey in a meaningful way is woven into the tapestry of your Camino. If someone leaves the trail or slips through the cracks, there's a gap left in your weave. Though their absence is felt, they haven't truly gone. Grace soon appears to carefully knit the tear and the fabric back together, leaving an imperfection in the weave of your soul where the hole had been."* She pointed to her own shawl. *"This irregularity is like the one left in your soul, meant to remember that person by. Until grace arrives, you need to be okay with everything that doesn't feel okay. It's all part of your Way."*

Maybe that explains my melancholy this morning—I have holes in my soul.

Until these messages came in, it hadn't occurred to me that I'd made a difference in another's experience here, or could leave a hole in their sacred tapestry. *Maybe belonging is a spontaneous wash of grace from cherishing honest connection. No assurances. No membership card. Just a "happy to be with you right now" kind of love.* I now see it's *all* love.

Trail friends I may never see again came to mind. The wise sage's perspective on loss and how the "Grace Rescue Squad" steps in to hold their place in the weave felt reassuring. I liked the thought of my life tapestry, with its losses, holes, and imperfections, simply being proof of grace at work, and of lingering hints of belonging.

The *Camino* challenges us on this pathway of St. James to recognize grace with the same precision we've come to know doubt and pain. Given the thousands who deeply touch others (then depart), there's much hole and heart-mending to be done here. The *Camino* keeps grace very busy indeed.

IN DEFENSE OF BOOTS

"These Boots Are Made For Walkin'"
~ Nancy Sinatra

Naked turtles. Boots. Motorcycles. Guns. And ugh, octopus, sum up today's vocabulary.

Before engaging such words, that morning, I had a talk with the *Camino*.

Hey, Camino! Weird. I woke up raw, vulnerable, and anxious. And I'm thinking nutty things like—the long-awaited destination is finally around the corner, but I wanna put on the brakes. And I'm questioning everything. Did I miss any important lessons when distracted by Compeed bandages or drinking morning sangria with the Norwegians? Cuz time's running short. Shouldn't I be feeling fireworks about now? Or have I read too many sappy Camino memoirs? Please advise.

Signed, your Camino Overachiever

I envisioned the *Camino* shaking its head at these late-in-the-game doubts, plucking me off the game board to place me back at the base of the Pyrenees to try this—One. More. Time.

My two Irish trail pals, Jiminy and Mara, caught up with me. Jiminy admitted his red curly-haired head was crammed with second-guessing *his Camino* as well. His thoughts spilled.

"So, what gives? Am I expected to arrive in Santiago with some big life-changing vision or what? 'Cuz, I don't have one. Does Santiago bar entrance until you spew your epiphanies? Hey, ladies, feel free to jump in any time to calm my neurotic worries!" His Irish brogue made the lamenting even funnier.

I confessed that so much had been chiseled away in these five weeks—my belongings, old thoughts, priorities, attitudes—I felt exposed and vulnerable like a naked turtle without a shell.

THE GOOD STUFF

Jiminy usually posed excessive questions, but every time he ran into me, his first question: "Why don't you ditch those crazy boots swinging from your pack?"

I'd always explain one more time. "I'm keeping the boots, Jiminy."

"But they betrayed you. Dump 'em on the side of the trail, stick in a few poppies, you know, like an altar to slaying the dragon!"

"The blister wasn't their fault. *I'm* the one who didn't change my socks. We've bonded. I gave up my magic shoes and one pair of Tevas. The boots stay."

Badgering was Jiminy's middle name. "So, what big goals will your naked turtle tackle when it gets home?"

"Well, I don't do goals or New Year's resolutions. Instead, I declare a new *standard* for my life. Instead of *quitting* something, I *create something* new. A new bar to live up to. Sometimes ridiculous stuff. Know what I mean?" They wanted examples.

"Okay. A couple years ago, I declared my new standard to be 'I'm a woman who says *yes*.' When building my business, I became a hermit. My response to almost anything was "no." No to socializing and recreation, no to spending money, no to reading anything other than "how-to" business books. Wise boundaries became restrictive. So, my new standard became

"YES." Yes to more happy hours, romantic encounters, snowshoeing, and kayaking. Even yes to my friend Diane's 'come to Croatia with me!'"

I asked, "What scares or intimidates *you*?" Mara answered. "Easy. Heights and clowns. Both creep me out." Jiminy, avoided my question, and asked what intimidated *me*.

"Aside from refusing to eat octopus here, I used to say I'd never drive a motorcycle. And the thought of shooting a gun scared the hell out of me. But with my new standard of YES, I signed up for a motorcycle training class, and went to the shooting range with my friend, Bill, to face my fear. After my day of target shooting, word on the street was 'to be safe around Molly, in the unlikely event of her wielding a gun, just stand squarely in front of her. You'll be perfectly safe.'" Smart-asses. All of them.

This "standards" thing fascinated Mara. Jiminy's interrogation continued.

"So, Molly, what's your standard in relationships?" Still feeling vulnerable, I said, "I'll need to sort that out. I promise to journal about it, and get back to you."

Mara was curious. "Who planted this crazy standards thing in your head, anyway?

"My mother. It first came up in grade school when balking at my parents' rules about my sisters and me not being allowed to go on any school bus field trips if snow was predicted (which happened a lot). My mother explained, 'It's not a rule, it's a standard. We won't change our minds on this because it didn't come from our minds, it came from our hearts.'"

I didn't understand back then, but I get it now. Standards are about staying aligned with what's true for you. *Like burying the parakeet,* I realized.

Saying our goodbyes, Jiminy gave my dangling boots his usual parting shove, sending them into a spiraling tangled mess, which triggered Mara's usual punishing slug to his arm. I'd miss their antics, but they'd remain woven into my tapestry.

MORE BOOTS

Walking on, thoughts of my mother lingered. An old memory surfaced. According to family lore, one winter morning, my mother ignored the doorbell as she frantically searched our house for child number three (me), age three. She searched every possible hiding place on each floor, then headed up to the attic—my favorite hiding spot. I loved to string out and plug in all the Christmas lights. She continued to ignore the doorbell and reported going into self-beat-up mode while searching. She'd just turned her back for *a minute* to put in a load of wash when I went MIA. The doorbell continued ringing. This was no time for a salesman or neighbor to demand attention! Returning to search the first floor again, she glanced to see a small figure at the front door. There I stood, naked on the front porch, wearing only winter boots, hair covered with a light dusting of snow, as I peered through the glass door on this 25-degree wintry day. Do I at least get points for putting on boots before venturing out?

As my mother whisked up my shivering naked body, her eyes followed my bootprints in the snow that ventured well beyond our neighbor's property. A mother's nightmare. She most enjoyed repeating this story whenever a new boyfriend came to dinner. Paybacks are a bitch.

How does this story relate to this moment? Quite a bit. Currently, I faced a confusing sense of feeling naked and vulnerable, my boots again playing a starring role on yet another risky adventure. My three-year-old's purpose for heading out naked into the snow? She heard the call. Now, sixty years later, boots remain the story's centerpiece as I said "yes" to the *Camino's* call.

Boisterous high school girls from Madrid approached from behind, interrupting my thoughts. I adopted a new attitude about these high-energy trail newcomers that morning. A new standard, you might say. Some say their loud music, chatter, and walking for only a week, make them not "real" pilgrims. Not true. Their presence is as purposeful as anyone's. When tempted to feel superior to the ways of others, Wayne Dyer reminds us, "Always remember. There's undoubtedly someone, somewhere, in therapy *because of you.*"

I hardly cringed at their music speakers and loud sing-along while they passed our gaggle of weathered pilgrims who, after almost 500 miles, looked to be held together with duct tape and gorilla glue. The *Camino* was messing with me. The song blasting from their speakers earned the next spot in my *Camino* soundtrack—Nancy Sinatra's "These Boots Are Made For Walkin.'" Its relevance to the day's boot theme wasn't lost on me.

I caught up to the girls singing at the top of their lungs and asked if they knew how old this song was. "No way!" was their shocked response to the tune's 50+ year history rather than being a current American hit, as they assumed. Not to brag, but I knew all the lyrics.

Hitting repeat on the song at full blast, the girls herded me to the middle of the pack—my dangling boots swinging to the beat—where I joined in mid-verse. These girls (50 years my junior) wanted to learn the correct lyrics and pronunciation *from me*, of all people. *Camino* connection knows no age.

A handful of my familiar fellow pilgrims stepped aside as we passed, singing our hearts out. A few spotted me in the pack, their surprised looks accusing me of making a deal with the devil and going to the dark side.

There I was. Vulnerable and stripped bare. Feeling a little lost. But mostly found. Happy to be in my 60s, acting sixteen again. A naked turtle standing before the gods as Nancy Sinatra, music (and boots), had, once again, saved me.

CHAPTER 33

READY...OR NOT

SOMEWHERE BEYOND PALAS DE REI

A Swedish man paused by my resting rock to catch his breath. He eyed the hill he'd just climbed with a look that begged for compassion. I had plenty to give.

"It wasn't even that steep," he lamented, breathing hard, "I'm four days in. I just wasn't ready for this. Were you?"

I laughed. "I don't think any of us are ever *really ready.* But we come anyway."

He smiled and trudged on.

Saturday Night Live producer Lorne Michaels, famously said, "The show doesn't go on because *it's ready*—it goes on because it's *11:30.*"

"Ready" is a curious word in various contexts. I begin each of my seminars with a relaxed mindset because—I'm impeccably ready. If any group opts to go down an interesting, unexpected tangent, my inner GPS always knows the way back.

There's also *this* flavor of ready: If you insist on having all your ducks in a row before beginning anything, your train will leave the station without you.

"Being ready" and "the *Camino*" have their own peculiar relationship. I hadn't rushed to Denver to catch my Paris flight six weeks ago because *I was ready.* I left because it was May 10th. Nor will I arrive in Santiago in two days because *I'm ready.* I'll arrive because metaphorically—it'll be *11:30.*

Rock-sitting turned into a thing. As it was in the Pyrenees, so it was near the grand finale. Again, overlooking a valley, the lush shades of green and the rich smells of wet farmland soil in the heart of Galacia seemed like candy to the senses. The guidebook suggested having ponchos ready for the spring rains here. But this day bragged blue sky with white cottontail clouds. The darker, more threatening clouds on the periphery floated away from us, thankfully headed elsewhere. I'm reminded—*something will happen, and, simultaneously, everything is always working out for me.*

Perched on the rock, massaging my knee, I reflected on my unexpected early morning reunion with several *Camino* family members. Our reunion unleashed a group-think-out-loud session about what insights gained would ask of us once back home. Mostly, we marveled at the mystical force present here. A force of perseverance when we'd have otherwise given up.

We all found each other mid-morning. I'd come upon an old, rustic, whimsical table in the woods with a do-it-yourself stamp. It was there, stamping my *Credential,* I heard the unexpected familiar refrain. "Hail, the Queen!" I beamed ear to ear at the best gift ever—a walking reunion with my Kingsmen.

Soon, Emma's women pals appeared and joined us. Our conversation eventually landed on a familiar subject. The guys poked fun at, while admitting the truth in, the common *Camino* phrases repeatedly heard. Taking turns standing on a rotted tree stump like Roman orators, they proclaimed one *Camino* saying after another—prefaced with "as *they* say."

The first one up started, of course, with the most popular.

"As *they* say, the *Camino* provides!" The Kingsman's small but loyal audience responded with eye rolls and approving nods and claps.

Next man up. "As *they* say, everyone's *Camino* looks different. To each his or her own!" Finger-pointing and laughs all around. A member of Emma's group took her turn on the stump.

"You know what *they* say, it's not the destination, but the journey that counts!" Bravos! from the gallery. The Kingsmen's leader, Benjamin, mounted the stage, dramatically raising his orator finger before his court.

"*They* say, it's your road, and yours alone. Others may walk *with* you, but no one can walk it *for* you!" His Roman crowd erupted in cheers.

Laughing and walking on, Markus from Germany posed a curious question. "Who are *they* who say these things, anyway?" Though drowned out by the many languages being spoken, I heard his interesting question. The phrase "as they say" rolls off our tongues so quickly. Who *are* "they?" A true authority? Do their pearls of wisdom pertain only to this trail? He and I continued to overthink our overthinking.

Markus' great English skills allowed us some fun with his curious questions. Together, we plotted the various degrees of "they" on a continuum—from the lowest level of ridiculous idioms to the higher-level sayings that we take more to heart. Starting at the bottom, we laughed our way up the scale: from "as *they* say, never wear white after Labor Day," or "as they say, an apple a day keeps the doctor away," to "*they* say you can kill two birds with one stone." We unanimously nixed that one due to the implied bird abuse. Markus' replacements: "He was, as *they* say, mad as a hatter!" and, "*They* say, a fool and his money are soon parted." *Who woulda thunk one word could make these miles pass so quickly?*

We then felt drawn up the scale to examine where this conversation began—*Camino* sayings. We agreed their rare, unique substance earned a position at the highest point on our continuum. That's where the rubber meets the road for pilgrims. The farther along the trail we get, the more these sayings speak truth. None of our banter answered who "they" were. But it did put *what* "they" say in a hierarchal perspective.

My squirrelly knee eventually begged for a break when it spotted the sitting rock. Though I told the group I'd catch up to them later, we held our goodbye hugs extra tightly, knowing we couldn't count on reconnecting.

From my rock, I watched the Kingsmen and Emma's clan wind down through the serpentine paths below. A precious mix of *Camino* families. I wondered: *Are the spirits of thousands (from Caminos-past) walking alongside them? Beside me? What about our ancestors? Are they shadowing our walk, whispering to us that we can unravel the patterns they passed down through generations?* Pretty cool to think about.

If they *were* with us, I hoped they would also celebrate the tenacity and strength they instilled that's kept us going.

My mind kept probing. *What the hell were we doing here anyway? 500 miles! Are we nuts? Why do we forge on beyond exhaustion through wind, rain, mud, and snow? Is there a bigger picture we don't see? (As they say) many report "hearing the call" to come. If that's true, who sent the invitation?*

I recalled René's request in our final late-night-talk-in-the-dark before she left. "Molly, promise me, you'll let me know what all this is *really* about. It's gotta be more than just fucking walking."

Then, I heard it.

Well, I say *heard* it. Actually, it wasn't a sound. Not one that reaches the ears anyway. Like a lava lamp, the three words floated and oozed through the middle of my mind's eye:

YOU are THEY

Say WHAT? They WHO? was the only response I could muster. The hairs on my arms raised. A sure sign to pay attention. Had I just received a possible—albeit cryptic—answer to *Why are you here?* But it made no sense.

Though grammatically challenged, my response seemed to summon yet another message. This time, it oozed in as a thought download.

DOWNLOAD #1

I'm referring to YOU, as in the collective YOU. All Camino pilgrims. You each hold the potential to serve in the peaceful army of THEY.

From The Kingsmen and Klara the murderer, to barstool Sophie and the hot soup guy in the Pyrenees. All of 'em. Including the thousands bonding at this moment on the Way. Ultimately, however, acting as a THEY is each pilgrim's choice.

My inquiries spilled out loud to whomever, whatever, planted these words in my head. *Choice? To do what? To walk? Someone is a THEY because they walk? Odd you've chosen to use the word THEY, given we spent the morning picking apart that very word. Am I making all this up? Too many french fries and morning Sangrias?*

My questions were met with the following surprise, rapid, itemized response.

DOWNLOAD #1 CONTINUES

I'll take your questions in order:

Question 1. *It's every pilgrim's choice whether or not to examine their Camino experience, and to use their insights once back home.*

Question 2. *No. General walking does not a THEY make. Only those who answer the call to walk here. Here, where a buzzing line of energy (a ley line), embedded for centuries, infuses each pilgrim's steps with its robust spark. It's optional for a pilgrim to put that energy to use.*

Question 3. *You asked why we used the word THEY. Because we knew you'd relate. Take the highest level of that word from earlier today and up it ten notches. That's the level of THEY integrity we speak of. Though it's not about spouting sayings from tree stumps, I admit you all were pretty entertaining.*

Question 4. *Yes. Your curiosity is indeed inviting these intuitive downloads. But are you making this up? No. Your mind has already stirred up enough shit to chew on until the end of time. You really didn't need more. Yet, here we are. I think you're ready to move on to bolder questions, such as—When is a pilgrim ready to become a THEY? What do THEYs do exactly?*

Me—ready? Nothing made me *ready* for this strange exchange. The source of these messages? Not a clue. They seemed loftier than what my dear Dead-Friend-*Camino*-Support-Army would cook up, or my intuitive *Voice*. Yet, it's doubtful I alone held any clout to attract some cosmic message from on high. I, a mere former "accident waiting to happen" who'd shed her shell and was, at the moment, a naked turtle. Though not exactly *ready*, maybe metaphorically, it was 11:30.

Regardless of whether I made them up, the odd messages continued to stream in.

Ready or not.

CHAPTER 34

THEY

PROGRESS TOWARD ARZÚA

I finished my rosemary alcohol and socks ritual. As pilgrims passed, I acted like everything was normal. Privately, I eyed each one suspiciously. *So, are you a THEY?*

These out-of-left-field messages compounded the inner struggle since waking that morning. *Or were they my own thoughts?* Adding this strange new information to the struggle I was already experiencing about reaching the finish line in two days, felt like a trying-to-get-all-my-grocery-bags-into-the-house-in-one-trip kind of struggle.

Sanity check. They weren't voices. More like downloaded bundles of information. Information my intuition, surprisingly, ushered in as credible. My informant never made its identity clear. Given my childhood talking horse fantasy (Mr. Ed), for ease of relaying this info, I'll refer to my source as *Camino* Ed. Ed for short. I bet it's getting easier to believe I left birdseed behind for my dead parakeet, huh?

Ed's response to my questions came in *his* preferred order and timing over the next twenty-four hours. I've reduced them to manageable bites.

But first, a disclaimer.

Mind you, these gems weren't delivered on stone tablets to some wise prophet. They were downloaded to one who waited days before checking an infected blister, believes her parakeet to be a member of her Dead-Friend-*Camino*-Support-Army, and interjected "pop-tarting the dog" into international relations. But a whacko, I'm not. Nor a psychic. Sure, my meditations have been known to get oddly interesting, and dead friends steal rocks from my pack. But I'm not a spiritual channel. Truthfully, I get pitifully distracted just trying to meditate. My mind drifts to such critical thoughts as: *At what nano-second, and at what proximity to the ceiling, does a fly know to stop flapping its wings to flip its little dangling legs upside-down to plant them on the ceiling?* Admit it. Now you're wondering too.

So, see, I'm fairly normal. And yet, this woo-woo stuff downloaded through *me*—sitting on a rock, kneading my muddy calves, and questioning everything. Not exactly a celestial Virgin Mary apparition in some mystical grotto.

My point: these messages from *Camino* Ed—you can take 'em or leave 'em.

Changing focus from the weird shit going on in my head, I noticed my friends disappeared from the landscape below. *How long was I talking to a horse?* My synchronistic meet-up with Pablo and Gabby was overdue.

I began the slow descent, inviting Ed to continue our exchange. One advantage of walking alone is being free to converse aloud with any talking horse that appears along the trail.

Okay Ed, spill it. When does a pilgrim become a THEY? Is there a membership card? A secret handshake? Whoever Ed was, he likely thought, *Ha-ha. Another funny American. Not.*

ED DOWNLOAD #2

Pilgrims come here for many reasons. Adventure. Depleted spirit. Dreams to sort. Healing. Soul searching. A broken heart. Many believing, "If I could just fix this. Then I'll be alright." But eventually, you learn—very little unfolds here according to plan.

Weathering this gauntlet, a phenomenon slowly unfolds.

Thousands of years' worth of ancient energy radiates up into the soles of pilgrims' feet, inviting them to stay present to where they are, not where they hope to get, as that may never come. Perspectives begin to shift. Experiencing this microcosm of life, the pilgrim finally connects the dots: "Ahhh. This is how it works in our larger life as well!"

Instead of expecting a break, a fix, or equilibrium—when faced with yet another trail challenge—the battle-hardened pilgrim surprises even herself with the solution: "I'll create magic!" With this new mindset, the portal opens. Spiritual trajectories reset.

In only weeks, down to her bones, the pilgrim has been emboldened.

Many vow to carry this magic home for safe keeping.

Now having been made "ready," the pilgrim rises to the level of THEY.

It took only seconds to absorb Ed's long message. One minute, I was in the dark. The next, I just knew. *So, Ed, what are THEY actually up to? Do THEYs only hang out here on the Camino? So what, now what?*

ED DOWNLOAD #2 CONTINUES

A backpack, smelly socks, and a selfie at the Iron Cross aren't necessary to wear the badge of THEY. THEYs have existed for eons, worldwide, long before pilgrims received the formal call.

At every moment...

There are Buddhist monks in high mountain temples endlessly reciting mantras to ease suffering, deter catastrophic world events, and encourage the flourishing of your happiness.

Cloistered nuns kneel in endless vigil, praying for the Holy Spirit to light the world's darkness.

Simple farmers tend the land, their hard work serving as a prayer to end hunger.

Somewhere, a musician listens intently to their muse to write the next beautiful song.

A wise boss empowers workers, offering the rest of the day off for a project well done.

A woman, just this second—singing and kneading bread— whispered a prayer for world peace in earnest.

THEY are out there. You can sense when one is in your midst.

Specific faces appeared in my mind. *Yeah. I've definitely known a few THEYs in my lifetime—mind-blowing ones, and quiet changers. But I'm confused, Ed. Sounds like THEYs have things pretty well handled. Why are pilgrims needed?*

ED CONTINUES

First, some background.

*As our world evolved, long-existing cultures showed
foundational cracks.*

*Following huge shifts after World War II, for a short time, THEYs
held their own to support the massive social changes.*
*But energies were spread thinly. Their weary spirits, unable
to shore things up alone, declared, "We're losing ground.
Send reinforcements!"*

The time was right. Camino gods stepped up to answer the call.

Naturally, they declared, "The Camino will provide!"

New game.

*This promise upped the ante for every pilgrim arriving here from
that point on.*

Pilgrims are called to become THEYs—on steroids.

Think: "Camino Special Forces."

*Pilgrims gain a mysterious gift here that other THEYs can't access
easily on their own.*

That being—an infusion of magic through the holy dirt.

The dots for the underlying meaning of "the *Camino* provides" began connecting. Recognizing my need to let all this settle in, Ed pushed the pause button as I entered a tiny village. Predictably, I stumbled onto the Aussies inside an old barn that offered welcome shade, the miracle of almond flour cookies, and our final synchronistic meet-up.

Together, we'd take on the rollercoaster hills ahead. Over the weeks, our whining took on a customized style. Instead of expressing complaints verbally, we'd developed "a look."

Whenever Gabby reached *her* fatigue threshold, she'd turn part-way up a hill leaning on her poles, glare at us with squinty eyes, let out a heavy sigh, and forge on. Pablo coped by pausing, planting his poles firmly while looking up to the sky, then back at Gabby and me as if to relay he just garnered enough strength from the heavens to support us both. When my back, knees, or low blood sugar offered their nasty opinions, I'd stop, plant my poles (always suitable for dramatic emphasis), and shake my head. My signal for: "What's the name of this crazy show anyway, and where's the escape hatch?" But there was no escape. Only the road ahead.

Leaving the ancient hamlet, competing with oxen and cattle dogs for road space, the French gentleman's question asked in St. Jean Pied de Port whispered again in my ear: *Why are you here?*

I hoped buried in Ed's messages might be the answer. I sensed my talking horse was still hanging in the wings of my personal desert, now close to completion—patiently waiting with his final bits of information. Information that would enhance the new shell reconstruction process for this naked turtle.

CHAPTER 35

THE MAIN SAIL DROPS

THE ENDLESS 29 KM ROAD TO ARZÚA

Lagging behind my friends, Ed jumped in again. He's not one for small talk. More of a straightforward kinda horse. His formerly slow, oozing communication style changed as he further explained the *Camino* Special Forces idea. The best I can describe the style change is to compare it to the stunt my brother-in-law, Greg, often pulls with newcomers to his sailboat.

At day's end, when taking down the sails, Greg requests their help. He directs them to go down the steps into the cabin. Standing above on the deck, he informs them he's about to lower the mainsail *very slowly* into the pit, and as it comes down, the helper should fold the sail carefully, back and forth, keeping the folded edges even. With arms up, they give an anxious nod they're ready for the sail's slow-motion descent. At that point, Greg releases the sail, which plummets into the hole in a heap, burying the person who was just duped. Funny guy.

That best describes how Ed's remaining deliveries came down. Fast and furious, burying me in jumbled thoughts. But once out from under the heap, I understood the necessity of his final addendum. It connected the dots. But first, I had a question.

Okay, O great talking horse, when does THEY-ing begin? Here in Spain or back home?

ED'S RESPONSE

Yes, and yes.

You recall the trials and wins you've personally experienced on the trail, yes?

Spoiler Alert: they weren't solely personal.

A pilgrim's energy field gets charged with every determined step, and every trial faced.

This charge magnifies and radiates far beyond their body and the trail.

In addition, every laugh with a fellow pilgrim, every bonding toast at a pilgrim's dinner, each yellow arrow missed, causing miles of backtracking, every breakdown where you claimed you couldn't go on, but did—generates powerful momentum that spills over into the holy quantum field, like a prayer blanket.

The quantum field transports the same healing energy you've created for yourself to another individual or group, possibly far away, in need of a matching strength and resolution.

Your magnified energy inspires their spirit to push beyond limitations toward their own proverbial Santiago. The world's in urgent need of more spill over prayers, Molly. This is what the Camino vowed to provide.

Ha! And you thought you were just going for a walk.

This sent my mind spinning. *Wow. The Camino influence goes way beyond what I imagined. And I thought the biggest secret here was toe socks.*

So, do I have this right, Ed: the energy of my keepin' on, of recovering from my pitiful meltdowns, of finding strength when it seemed gone, is enough to spill into this quantum field and inspire some stranger, maybe a country away, and they have no clue where their burst of possibility has come from? And Ed, tell me, what happens to this quantum field when we go home?

Now, he *really* began dropping the massive main sail. *Dang, Ed, one sure doesn't fall softly into transformation here, do they?*

ED'S MAIN SAIL DUMP

Pilgrim THEYs return home with an advantage—a knowing that:

1. Miracles do happen.

2. Magic is real and is always within reach.

3. Angels (not necessarily the winged kind) will show up when all resources seem exhausted.

Home will look the same. What's changed is you.

You'll be tempted to tell everyone about the magic.

But they won't get it. Nor should they.

They aren't the ones who juggled morning mash while applying Compeeds, persevered day after day through a proverbial desert, nor did the holy dirt ever radiate its sacred energy up through their aching feet.

Taking the Camino home is both simple and complex. No need to speak of its magic. Just live it. Live simply, wholeheartedly. Chop wood, carry water.

Don't feel defeated when things crumble. Magic and crumbling can co-exist.

Watch for arrows. There will be signs.

As on the trail, aim to change no one. But do drag a friend or two into the proverbial church now and then to remind them of their greatness.

Live generously so the vibrant qualities you've gained here will continue to spill into the quantum field. Our intention? This Camino love-drenched spillover will flow into hungry hearts across towns, countries, and continents.

Sounds kinda lofty, Ed. I'm afraid I'm not exactly your ideal saintly type. I'm more the analytical, dairy-free rebel who leaves birdseed for dead parakeets.

ED CLARIFIES

You misunderstood. Sure. THEYs are exceptional, but also normal. They have their shitty days.

Off-script, wild times. Negative spirals, weird adventures, and have been known to polish off a quart of ice cream in one sitting.

The Camino (and home) calls for facing problems head-on.

You know when THEYs are off their game. They'll avoid inevitable, healthy conflict, claiming a phony superior spirituality. It's all avoidance and frosted poop.

As on the Camino, it's not about getting it right.

It's about knowing how to offer yourself and others grace when out of alignment.

Fortunately, pilgrim THEYS are self-cleaning ovens. You self-correct when you've missed an arrow, then return to center. No doubt you'll lose your way again.

And again. The holy dirt continues to guide you back to your True North.

I assured him I heard every word. *I wish I could've written all of this down, Ed. I'm afraid it'll be swallowed up with the excitement of Santiago, or fade flying home over the ocean.*

Ed: *Not to worry. The only direction you'll ever need is already written down. Need an arrow? Just look at your journal notes. It's all right there. Once you even scribbled one on your t-shirt so you wouldn't forget it! I think you washed it, though. Too bad.*

Me: *Wait. Are you talking about the Camino Messages in my journal? Aren't they my guidelines for the trail?*

Ed: *What? You thought you'd check them at the border when you left Spain? As on the Camino, so it is at home. Now, go find your friends.*

My head buzzed as it all began to click. *Was this why I'd been gathering the Messages along the way? Sure, they guided me here, but they'll also serve as arrows back home?*

Wow. That brought up a curious question.

Hey, Ed, have you been feeding me those Camino Messages all along…since that first morning in St. Jean Pied de Port? Ed? Are you still there?

(Crickets)

Geez. He disappears as quickly as he comes.

I promised myself to sort all my scribbled messages. Oh dear. I also promised Jiminy (and myself) that I'd journal on my relationship standards. *Let's face it. I'll suck as a card-carrying THEY.* With only two days left, progress seemed unlikely.

Catching up to Gabby and Pablo, we walked through the town of Rabid Dog (or per the official guidebook: Rabidiso). Our destination of Arzúa waited at the top of a steep, almost two-mile hill. Ugh. We could only offer each other "our looks." To his delight, Pablo could make a truthful declaration this time: "Only three kilometers to go."

At the top, Google Maps clarified our hostel locations. Crap. Mine was up another steep hill. Gabby and Pablo unexpectedly had to taxi five miles to theirs. We parted, planning to meet the following evening in Pedrouzo, for our final night before Santiago. I trudged up the hill, unaware I was about to enter yet another sitcom-worthy *Camino* episode.

CHAPTER 36

THE SISTERS, TEA, and ME

ARZÚA

Knocking on the heavy wooden door, two Polish sisters in their 80s enthusiastically greeted me. Each wore a different, strong perfume that brought tears to my eyes. The first one, who spoke better English (proudly identifying herself as the younger of the two), led the way up the wooden staircase toward my third-floor private room. The sisters—one in front, one behind—bickered in Polish to the second floor. The younger sister continued with me to the third.

I lit up seeing the antique-filled, European-style room. I understood most of her English as she pointed out the large window. "There's a nice restaurant one block that way. My sister and I live on the fourth floor. Push our buzzer if you need anything." She patted me on the shoulder. "Take a shower, dear. You've earned it."

Opening the door to leave, her sister almost fell into the room from the hallway, obviously eavesdropping. The same bickering kicked in. The older sister changed her mood on a dime as she turned to me with a big smile, holding a basket of shampoos, soaps, and lotions. "For you, dear. They smell wonderful." Given the encouragement to shower, and now all these, I wondered, *did I smell that bad?*

I wanted to close the door and collapse on the bed, but the sisters stood nitpicking about something in Polish. The younger one explained her sister wanted to ask questions about America and Hollywood, but she warned her I'd had a long day.

"After my shower, I'll be happy to answer questions on my way to dinner."

"If our door is open, do come up. Otherwise, we're eating dinner," the younger sister instructed. The older one added, "Yes, come up for some tea, dear." They continued bickering up the steps to their apartment. Family dysfunction knows no international boundaries.

Ahhh, finally, silence. But short-lived. Their mystery shower's hot/cold controls wouldn't change temperatures. I dressed *again*, and rang their buzzer. Arguing at the door as to who would show me the ropes of the shower, the older sister took my hand, saying, "*I* show you how. My sister's an idiot!" Then, flipped her sister the bird. This got more entertaining by the minute.

After explaining the shower trick, I escorted her to the door, but she planted herself firmly inside my room (perfume wafting) and asked about Hollywood movies. Sister #2 came to my rescue and dragged her out by the sleeve, triggering another tiff as they climbed the stairs.

I can't say how long I stayed under hot running water, but all steep hill memories melted down the drain. Relieved to see the sisters' door still closed as I left for dinner, I almost made my getaway. Reaching the front door, a cackling laugh and voice called from the landing. "Molly, honey, we're here! Do you want to come up for some tea?"

The younger sister rushed down, and, not unlike a vaudeville show where the act is pulled off stage by the large hook, the elder sister abruptly disappeared out of sight with a sideways jerk. I wondered if either would live the night.

Halfway through dinner, I pulled out my journal, phone notes, and notebook that stored my "Camino Messages." While consolidating and sorting my notes, thoughts drifted to my odd hostesses. The memory of an old-time classic movie with Carey Grant, *Arsenic and Old Lace,* played in my head through dessert and consumed my walk back to the hostel. It's a dark comedy where two old, nutty serial-killer sisters poison the tea of unsuspecting, unmarried, male house guests as a favor to put them out of their assumed lonely, family-less misery. Their bodies were "buried" throughout the house. Remembering the younger sister's questioning as we climbed the steps earlier made me wish I had lied. "Are you married, dear? Do you have family and children?" Uh-oh. I answered, "No."

Tiptoeing up the three flights, my stomach did an anxious twist when I smelled strong perfume. I found a note on my door. "*Please come up for tea when you get back, dear.*"

Eeeek. What's with the tea thing? The serial killer movie replayed in my head. My overactive imagination wondered if I were the only guest in the large house. I noticed the old antique lace covers on every wooden table, dresser, and overstuffed chair for the first time. *Creepy.* I found a pen and left a note on their steps. "*Thank you for the kind invitation. I would, but I'm so tired I'm ready to fall into a dead sleep.*" Dead joke for my own amusement intended.

With everything packed for the morning, I crawled into the large plush poster bed with my journal. The page initially earmarked for "relationship standards" begged for Ed's downloaded information. Just as I began to summon Ed for questions, a knock at the door startled me.

"Yes?"

"Fresh towels for morning, dear."

I opened the door to accept the older sister's stack of towels, knowing I wouldn't use them. She remained there with a broad smile, staring. Creepy again. I didn't understand why she lingered, but I thanked her and closed the door, admittedly, somewhat in her face.

Crawling back under the quilt, I resumed organizing my notes and realized unraveling these could take weeks, maybe months. I'd normalized sensing Ed reading my interpretation of his downloads over my shoulder. Now, *I* was the creepy one. Like a whisper inside my mind, I sensed when he wanted something reworded, or added. I recorded it all, closed the journal, and turned out the light.

In the dark, I pondered everything and everyone. First, this whole bizarre Ed thing. Where'd he come from? Is it my own mind dumping its beliefs? I thought of angels, like Orietta and Acacio in the Shire. *Are Brad and Gina doing okay? Lilly and Noah? Does this night find Bren holding his young son? Gloria (of Long Island) messaged she had to return to the US for a family emergency. Will I see my Kingsmen again? And what about the old sage woman with the woven shawl?*

She was right. So many I'd lost track of. Was their memory truly woven into my tapestry for safekeeping? And, as always, the question still hung: *Why am I here?*

The sound of distant bells rode the light breeze outside my open window. I'm not complaining, mind you. I'm just stating a fact—the bells were ringing.

I chuckled in the dark, thinking about the nutty *Arsenic and Old Lace* movie doubles abiding above me as I drifted to sleep. That is, until my eyes popped open. A paranoid gremlin emerged from retirement, forcing me to get up and drag my bone-tired self across the room, where I firmly locked the deadbolt with a loud click. *Now,* I was ready for that dead sleep.

JOURNAL NOTES

June 12, 2019

Ed's like my math teacher, always checking if I'm "showing my work" as I consolidate his downloads about returning home. The hovering horse added a few comments:

When feeling lost in the jungles of time and space back home, ask yourself:

- What would I do if I were on the Camino right now?
- Am I allowing myself mistakes?
- When exhausted and defeated, do I extend myself grace?
- Remember, the Camino is simply a microcosm of the larger Universe. Now, you must trust "the Universe will provide."

I squeezed in a question: "Otherwise, the hundreds invested in Compeed bandages, french fries, and giant Tevas were for naught?" Sensing his affirming nod and about to close my journal, Ed adds a final thought:

Returning to your day-to-day roles, life's expectations will be jolting, maybe disappointing.
You'll miss it here.

Because of that, it's key to connect with fellow/sister pilgrims to relight each other's fuses and to continue filling the quantum field craving your energy.

You'll recognize each other. If you look closely, you can identify kindred Camino spirits by the residual sparkle in their eye. That gleam means they, too, remember the magic.

Good night from Arzúa

P. S. A prayer to Mother Mary-Who-Art-Buried-In-A-Suitcase, and any celestial beings in hiking boots under this field of stars:

"I'm almost there. Please deliver me safely to Santiago— in one piece. In one peace. Amen."

CHAPTER 37

CALL and THEY WILL COME

ARZÚA TO O PEDROUZO

Call Me (Come Back Home)
~ Al Green

My sunrise departure succeeded without crazy sister interference. Walking through Arzúa, enjoying the yellow hues of the sky, and eating my morning mash, I didn't expect Ed so early.

One more download. Quick and easy, whenever you're ready.

In thirty-six hours, I'd walk into Santiago. I counted on this last stretch being an easy, blank-slate thinking day. I hoped Ed's final ideas would contribute to that ease.

Just ahead, more walkers entered town where their northern coastal route—The *Camino Del Norte*—merged with the *Camino Francés* for the final stretch into Santiago. Though the air was thick with anticipation, I felt resistance to the approaching finale. I then recalled the *Saturday Night Live* theory: "We don't go on because we're ready. We go on because it's 11:30."

Ed hovered, happy to see an opening.

 ### *ED DOWNLOAD FINALE*

One last thought.

We hear it said a lot in Camino world: "The numbers coming to walk are growing like crazy!"

As though it's somehow worrisome. I'm here to tell you it's a good thing. A necessary thing.

You're now ready to learn the bigger picture.

The numbers are growing. Exponentially. Not because this is a hip, luxurious vacation spot. But because so many—from every corner of the world—are hearing the call.

They come because they can't NOT come.

Face it. It's not normal to say, "Hey, gimme a heavy pack; let me walk through exhausting heat, boot-sucking mud, and bitter cold winds, 'cuz that sounds really fun." But sign up, they do.

They act on "the call," some clueless they've even received one.

Whether it takes three months or three decades, they get here.

And more are coming.

Even those who think they're not ready.

Whether in the holy dirt for a week, or for months, all contribute to the healing prayer blanket filling the quantum field.

We'll continue to call, and THEY will come, only to then be called back home.

Ready or not.

Because, for this fragile world in need of healing, it's 11:30.

This would be Ed's final message.

Sitting down on a bench to let it sink in, a buzzy calm came over me, like a warm blanket of bubbling grace. Feeling new respect for each passing pilgrim for answering the call, I wondered what distant soul in the quantum field they'd inspire through their perseverance. Shouldn't they *all* know about this *THEY* stuff? As with any spiritual thread running through the ethers, I trusted this knowing would hit the right ears, at the right time, as it has through the ages, and now mine. Many reading this likely already knew long before I did. It's unclear if having a Mr. Ed or Flipper fantasy is a prerequisite.

Speaking of the right ears, WhatsApp delivered delicious news. Gentleman Jade was only a couple kilometers behind me, asking my whereabouts. I told him I'd wait.

Our reunion brought happy tears (mine) and a shit-eating grin (his). Clearly, it's a case of pre-Santiago melancholy/joy syndrome.

I'd wondered how long my Ed encounter would incubate before sharing it with anyone. I imagined years. Or never. But *the Camino* thought differently. It summoned this ideal sounding board. Jade and I caught up on our respective tea-serving, serial-killer hostel stories and other such adventures before I spilled the *Camino* Ed story. Jade's very nature left no choice but to tell all. Our walking brainstorming session sorted through the possible meanings in Ed's downloads.

I pulled out my journal notes and *Camino* Messages. Scribbled and ink-smudged, I opened the rough draft as if unscrolling some secret charter. I read out loud each *Camino* Message collected over five weeks, followed by my shitty first draft of guessing how each might translate to our lives back home. Aside from my own touches of sarcasm and irreverence, I felt Ed's messages to be concisely recorded.

I hadn't expected Jade's emotional reaction. He sensed, as we all did, *something* mystical going on here. But his psychologist brain explained it away as fatigue mixed with anticipation. He now understood why he sought my whereabouts. He needed to hear this.

Jade broke his quiet contemplation with a chuckle. "Damn. So, how evolved are we expected to act once we get home, anyway?"

"Well, Ed never claimed we'd be saints, or even mature. Just inspired."

Each pass we took at its meaning brought more clarity, but we finally opted to let it be. Only distance, time, and living could answer our hanging questions. The *Camino* miles were dwindling, and we wanted to enjoy every last one.

In a small village, not far from the town where Jade would meet his brother and friends for the night, we stopped for a potato chips and olives lunch. Devouring them trailside, Jade scooped up a handful of gravel and dirt as he talked, allowing it to sift gently through his fingers like a waterfall. *Holy dirt,* I smiled to myself. These simple moments were rated high on the "*Camino* times I'll remember most" list.

I appreciated Jade's knack for drawing out personal thoughts without playing psychologist. Mentioning my incomplete relationship standards assignment from Jiminy, he invited me to finish the assignment with him— if I wished to. Through recent miles, the topic organically sorted itself out in my head, including the often-misinterpreted word "expectations" and where it fits (or doesn't) in relationships.

Polishing off the olives, we took our conversation back to the trail, where I offered my standards report, starting with treasured friendships.

"I don't ask a friend to 'show up' because I *expect* it. I look for a friend to show up because through our history together, they've already shown me: 'This is who I am. This is what you can count on from me. And if either gets messed up, we'll work it out.' Soul pals reassure the other: 'Hey, I'm not going anywhere.' They count on the same from me. Friends follow through because of their love, dignity, and integrity. They're good for their word. And when they aren't, they offer grace and communication to one another. We love each other enough to ask tough questions, poke the bear, have hard respectful conversations, and not let each other skate over bullshit or run away from accountability or real connection. I've left friends behind, Jade, not because they didn't meet *my* expectations, but rather, in a sustained way, they failed their *own*."

Jade clutched his gut on that last line as though sucker-punched. "Whoa. I get it. I have nothing more to ask or add. Which standard is next?"

I shrugged. "It's one-stop shopping with me. That's pretty much my standard for all relationships. What could make for a better romantic or business partner than starting with what I look for in a friend? I'd add an addendum, though. There's a grace we can forget to offer each other. Differences are inevitable. When they surface, we must remember we're on each other's side. The problem we're facing is the enemy, not each other. I have to say, by this age, anyone unwilling to meet me there is no longer interesting. He becomes boring."

Jade laughed. "I can hear it now. Your opening question on a first date, 'So, tell me, do you meet your own mature expectations, or will I find you boring?'" Busted.

Just as Jade was getting on a roll about his own standards with friends, his marriage, and work, we spotted his brother and friends enjoying a cold pitcher on the edge of town. Hugs and beers were shared all around. Recalling our last rendezvous below O Cebreiro, it felt like home to be in their midst again. Before long, toasts were made to our old friend, Pop-Tarts.™ As their bantering continued, I turned down the sound, pulled back, and took it all in.

This warm connection is what Ed said can become influential in the quantum field. Feeling foolishly inept as a *THEY*, I gave this quantum field stuff a shot. I sent this warm feeling of belonging to whomever out there might feel disconnected or on the outside looking in. Then waited. Would I sense it being received through the ethers? Nope. I felt nothing, except for the confirmation that Ed was rolling his eyes at me.

Hearing back isn't the point, Molly.

I know that, Ed. I just wanted to try it.

Jade knew I couldn't stay long. This was their destination. I still had eight miles to go to O Pedrouzo. Another tough goodbye. Jade understood that the woman who'd begun in St. Jean Pied de Port over five weeks before, wouldn't be the same woman arriving in Santiago tomorrow. And he knew in between the two lay a confusing field of shuffled dreams, rearranged priorities, standard adjustments, and mostly, how I truly showed up for myself. No one else would get all that about me. I was grateful to be seen.

As for the wild messages from Ed, with so much left unsaid, Jade's and my shared curiosity needed to be enough. I knew he'd hold the messages for safekeeping. I *didn't* know back then that, other than Jade, I wouldn't tell anyone about *THEY*, or Ed, for over three years. Let alone risk sharing it in a book.

We exchanged extra-long hugs, knowing we'd likely not see each other again. As if on cue, the afternoon bells tolled. I looked at these dear men who lived a world away. They'd been called here from Albania. I felt grateful our soles (and souls) kept this appointment with destiny.

Returning to the final stretch of my desert, tears streaming, I wondered— *Could life be any more magnificent and still painfully ache any more than it does right now?*

My exposed turtle heart cracked wide open.

And So It Goes
~ Jennifer Warnes

CHAPTER 38

MOONLIGHT SONATA AFTERNOON

CLOSE TO O PEDROUZO

Moonlight Sonata

~ Beethoven

Running into Swedish Klara (a.k.a. Murderer and Ironer of Husband's Underwear) lifted my spirits and iced the cake of the day's surprises. The memory of our church episode kicked in another laughing jag. Klara glowed with no sign of her former guilt-ridden self. Well, until she confessed, she worried she hadn't walked far enough to deserve any big celebration in Santiago.

"Seriously, Klara? It isn't how *far* you walk. It's the layers you dare to examine, sort, and release. And the joy you replace it with. You've nailed it."

She smirked. "Okay then. So, what do you think would be most dramatic when I arrive in Cathedral Square—should I collapse in a mound of sobbing tears? Or how about I stay stone silent, emotionless, for dramatic effect?"

I loved this sarcastic little shit. "What I think is, when you arrive at the cathedral, you need to offer to iron St. James's underwear as penance for overthinking all this."

She laughed, acknowledged her baseless worries, and with a warm goodbye hug and a thank you, she disappeared into a swarm of former strangers, now friends.

Good on you, Klara from Sweden! Buen Camino.

Klara's words stirred my curiosity. What would *my* response be when entering Cathedral Square? How long had I anticipated this? The idea of anticipation and dreams merging with reality brought back a childhood memory.

Around age eight, gripped by the love of horses, I mucked stalls at a nearby farm in exchange for riding their mare. My established ritual upon entering the barn: stick my head in the large barrel of grain to breathe in the calming, intoxicating scent of sweet molasses and oats. Next, pick up a brush, run my fingers over the carved leather saddles on my way to the stall, and before grooming my favorite horse, bury my head in her mane to breathe her in.

My fantasy back then: a horse of my own. At age thirteen, my mother could hardly contain herself in sharing the news that she and my dad were making my dream come true. She searched my face for a sign of matching excitement. Most would jump with giddy joy, but oddly, I could only produce a crooked smile, a deep breath, and a wide-eyed whisper of "Thank you, Mom."

At first, I felt stunned, then elated, followed by a deer-in-the-headlights overwhelm. I could go as far as thinking of the beautifully carved saddle I'd own, sticking my head in my own barrel of sweet-smelling grain, and having my initials on the brushes. But the idea of the actual horse slowly sank in later, at a pace I could handle. And sink in it did—once I owned my new horse, Rocky—with a giddy, grateful, happy dance.

To this day, any dream that comes to pass takes a similar slow-motion route through my nervous system, as if there's too much to squeeze through the joy portal all at once. I wondered: *Will I whoop and holler wildly when I walk into Santiago? Or will I need to stick my head in molasses and oats until I acclimate? Hard to predict.*

As I merged with the pilgrim traffic again, I avoided photobombing a family selfie in progress, overhearing the young son say, "Send it to Grandma! She likes to know exactly where we are at all times!"

Hearing this, an oddly satisfying realization landed. *NO ONE knows where I am right now. Between this town I can't pronounce, and the next, not a soul in my life knows exactly where I am or what I'm doing in this moment.* In the past, uneasiness would have me thinking, *Gee, I should let someone know where I am, because—well, just because.* Never had I breathed so freely while tucked into such anonymity. For some reason, this mattered.

Miles passed. Somewhere, a distance behind me, a mysterious familiar melody increased in volume, drifting from a dense stand of trees— Beethoven's "Moonlight Sonata." The volume swelled. Six young men were spilling gracefully out of the wooded area, one with speakers in his pack. Beethoven's piece gave way to "Pachelbel's Canon in D." My heart melted. These Spanish and Viennese college music majors were studying in Barcelona. We talked a while before they moved on, leaving a beautiful opera playing in their wake. They, too, heard the call. And they came. I videoed their departure. To this day, I watch and listen when I need a touchstone into *Camino* reality.

Just ahead, an intriguing gray cat with two white boots escorted me into a quaint village, then darted away. The village's old-world feel—stone buildings with dry-stacked stone walls filled me with nostalgia, feeling like I'd been there before, in another time. The sound of cowbells enhanced the feeling as a herd of oxen were led through the narrow village street. I stood to the side, mesmerized by this ancient scene, feeling transported back to the 1600s. Many pilgrims raised cameras to video the sight, just as a shiny, new 2019 sports car squeezed past the cows and headed straight for us. We roared with laughter as the "ancient" spell broke, reminding us of the time and place in which we really existed. I hope any pilgrim who also captured that video laughs with me in spirit each time it's viewed.

The church bells rang (for me, of course) as I finally arrived at our hostel in Pedrouzo, its office housed in the attached bar. The owner stamped my *Credential*, eyeing the over one hundred collected stamps, commenting, "Nice work." I beamed.

We hit the jackpot with Gabby's choice of hostel, given its winning trifecta:

1. A bar with a supply of ice. 2. A hair dryer. 3. Potato chips, olives, and beer.

Gabby skillfully booked our hard-to-come-by accommodations in Santiago as we ate our enviable junk food dinner. Did I mention she's a stellar travel agent in Australia? Knowing the final day would be crowded, we'd start before dawn using our trusty headlamps. The finality of everything called for a melancholy toast to our last night on the trail.

Later in my room, staring into the dark, I sensed my Dead-Friends-*Camino*-Support-Army's presence. Santiago was within reach, and they weren't going to miss it. Earlier, I spent time digging out chunks of holy dirt containing tiny sparkly gold flecks from the soles of my boots. Sweeping up the sparkles, I recalled a day at the gym early in my knee and ankle rehab (two years before). I'd raised the weight on the machine, put in earbuds, and pushed PLAY on my iPod. The first song: Paul Simon's "Diamonds On The Soles of Her Shoes." I smiled back then, thinking, *how perfect for my determined mission ahead. Will these soles ever actually make it?* Now they had.

Back then, I pictured myself on the *Camino* with the diamond soles of my shoes glistening in the sun. The tune became my training anthem. Now, two years later, it would accompany me on the final 21 km (12 mi) stretch toward Santiago—waiting for the perfect moment to push play.

I set the alarm for o'dark thirty, nodding to my Support Army. We—all of us—would set out before sunrise.

CHAPTER 39

DIAMONDS on the SOLES of MY SHOES

TO SANTIAGO

Diamonds on the Soles of Her Shoes
~ Paul Simon

Early morning, by the light of a tiny lamp casting a whimsical star pattern on the ceiling, I searched for my headlamp. Then remembered, I surrendered it to the packing police. All good. I'd have diamond light from the soles of my shoes, yes?

I gave my last room on the trail a final look. How many beds had I slept in these past weeks? How many nights had I questioned if I'd make it? And if I did, at what cost? Now I knew. It cost me *everything*. The person I had been, for the one I had become—a naked turtle in hiking boots.

The stars cast by the room's lampshade brought back Andrea's words: "Santiago de Compostela means 'St. James, under a field of stars.' Legend says the *Camino's* mystical road follows the Milky Way, and the stars of the Milky Way are said to be created by the dust raised by traveling pilgrims." Goosebumps accompanied my last look at the ceiling.

I met Pablo and Gabby outside, where we read a surprise text from René:

> I'm cheering you all on today as you make your way into
> Santiago. I'm there in spirit and living vicariously through you.
> Buen Camino. You're my heroes!

René's sentiment lingering, by the light from the Kidnappers' headlamps, we walked the dark street toward the portal entrance into a surreal, dense, dark, eucalyptus forest. If ever there was a Hero's Journey metaphor, this was it. Harry Potter's and Dorothy's respective dark forests had nothing on me.

Choosing to walk this pitch-black path alone, I dropped behind my friends. In the distance, an occasional flicker from Pablo's headlamp lit the canopy of trees, but mostly, it was the faint rhythm of their distant walking poles providing my bearings. Despite the disorienting, dark, three-kilometer gauntlet, my pace quickened. Knowing without seeing, intuiting without assurance, trusting each step would find solid ground. No one could see my wide smile.

In the darkness, the soul of the ancient trees breathed softly. How many thousands had they ushered through, offering the final anointing "Job well done, pilgrim?"

Like the emerging ancient Greek mythic goddess of the underworld, Persephone (you know, wearing ancient Patagonia and toe socks), I walked toward the distant pinhole of light. The volume of bird song increased as if welcoming me into the resurrection portion of my Hero's Journey.

The forest spilled out into the countryside weighted in a mystical fog so surreal I looked around for the Hollywood fog machine. But this was the real deal. My friends waited for me. With a reverent nod, we continued in silence.

Finding our pace and determining our afternoon meeting place, I walked solo. The fog gave way to blue skies, the mid-morning sun warming my back. Intuition firmly signaled: *Now!*

I obeyed, put in my earbuds, and hit play on "Diamonds on The Soles of Her Shoes." It no longer served as a carrot at the gym or as a doubt-buster. It now spoke to owning every step and *taking* my turn (not waiting for it to be *given* to me). Jumping in, even when not quite ready. Dancing with fear.

Living in the uncertainty of *things might work—they might not.* Embracing ease and discomfort, confidence and "we're all gonna die!" It could *all* happen. The ethereal girl with diamonds on her shoes and I merged as one. Tears streamed down my face *again*.

The song continued stirring an emotional cocktail. I sensed my loyal Dead-Friends-*Camino*-Support-Army once again behind me. Through all this, I appreciated their laughing along with my irreverence and free-form interpretation of their messages—even Mother Mary, who I tossed in a stuffy suitcase with smelly pain cream. They were present in full force: my dear trickster music man, Michael, with his mischievous smile and Spanish guitar, accompanied Paul Simon's song, keeping our diamond-soled feet in rhythm. Ahh, yes, keeping rhythm. The key to any journey of the soul.

After Michael, Mother Mary-Who-Art-Rolling-Along-in-a-Suitcase in her ethereal robes. Next, dear Linda, my angel buddy who braved the dusty trail, the Great Blue Heron circling overhead. And feisty Emma—daughter-turned-puzzle-loving-spirit-guide—appearing as a young girl in a ponytail. Bringing up the rear—my dad, slow but sure, keeping time to the music with a blue parakeet on his shoulder.

The song faded in my earpiece. I pondered this journey filled with myth, music, and magic. Do not adjust your sets, and warn your grammar meter, because from this point forward in my *Camino* journey, I'm purposely adding "k" to the word magic (though spell-check fights me every time). It adds a reverence to the often-mistaken interpretation of magic as being solely about wands and endless colorful scarves streaming from a stage magician's sleeve. In my world, the "k" identifies mysticism and transformation. My mind played with the distinction between the two: *What if magic speaks to that momentary spark of elation when something seemingly impossible occurs? And magick is when that spark is sustained over time. It's about sacred transformation that melts believing into knowing, and creates an agreement with the world of possibility.*

Why did it matter? Ed once mentioned the magick would follow us home only if our hearts owned it. Rather than bits of magic occurring sporadically once home, I preferred the idea of being wrapped in a perpetual blanket of mysticism—just as this trail is eternally blanketed by a mystical field of stars and holy dirt. I wasn't thinking airy-fairy here. I fully intended to chop wood, carry water. But rumor had it, even *THEYS* still trip over themselves with doubt. We'll still be painfully misunderstood and sometimes react rather than respond. Magick will be needed. The challenge: find your way back to your heart and True North. A heart that knows "something will happen" and trusts it all.

THEY often say: *Ask for what you want.* Okay, fine.

Dear Spirit of the Camino, as I return to a chaotic world, please blanket me with magick when I falter so I can quickly "straighten up and fly right," as my wise grandmother Elsie used to say. Of course, she also used to mercilessly chase us with her grossly crooked arthritic thumb.

It's all good. It's all love. Amen.

Lost in thought, I almost didn't notice the woman walking in rhythm beside me until she spoke. "Congratulations on being close to finishing your *Camino*." She looked familiar, though I couldn't place her.

I responded, "Thank you! To us both!"

She explained. "We met back in the *farmacia* in Sahagún. You were buying rosemary alcohol and were a bit cheesed off about an infected blister you needed to stop and heal."

Our connection that fateful day came back to me.

"By the way, your 'rosemary alcohol and fresh socks' ritual works. Not one blister! So, thanks."

"No, thank Gary-from-Seville! Sadly, we've lost track of him." *Please, Grace Squad, weave Gary into my tapestry and help us somehow reconnect with him so I can thank him.*

Our talk moved from blisters to the Cathedral only miles away, then to going home. She seemed overly anxious about the latter. I risked inquiring about her reason.

Her story in a nutshell—as the daughter of a minister for a new-thought church outside London, she always claimed to live a spiritual life, until arriving here and uncovering a painful truth. Her positive-talking and supposed spiritual demeanor was only a tactic to hide from being direct with people, upfront about true feelings, facing problems directly, and her "don't make waves—let's just be about peace, love, and groovy" persona. Hiding shored up her "always smiling, spiritual, peace-loving" facade.

She reached out to shake my hand. "Hi, I'm Claudia. And I'm an avoiding, spineless fraud." She laughed, though it was a serious revelation for her.

Her honest self-examination was impressive. I reached out *my* hand.

"Hi, I'm Molly. I'm a stripped-to-the-core naked turtle waiting for a new shell. I have to say, you certainly aren't avoiding *now*! So what, now what?"

"Well, first off, I'll need to clean up my act. Get honest. Welcome truthful connection with people who challenge me. Quit faking the high road when being narky or miffed would be more genuine. It's exhausting behind this 'keep the peace' mask. My father's an amazing minister. So real. He connects with people on an honest level, even when it's uncomfortable. Pisses me off. Guess the talent skipped a generation. He can skillfully call BS—but always with compassion and forgiveness. Well, I'm thinking maybe *those* two traits he actually *did* pass on to me. Guess I'll hold onto those, huh?"

"Phew. Yes! See? You're not a *total* fuck-up. What a relief!" I needed a chapel to drag this Brit into.

"Molly, it feels like I've gone through an after-death life review—in real time, only minus those fat little cherubs. I've been a smiley, agreeable doormat most of my life. With my partner and kids. My parents. Friends. My spiritual community. If I lifted the rug to show you what I've swept under there in the name of keeping this phony peace and acting all holy, you'd gag a bloody hairball." *Hmm. Clearly another British term.*

"Yeah. I'm guessing true peace couldn't breathe under that rug of yours very well, given the bloody hairball and all." Unaware that her British vocabulary amused me, she continued her confessions.

"All this holy-like crap gutted me more than facing the challenges head-on ever would have. It explains the knot I always feel in my stomach and the sleepless nights. I think who I really am is clawing to get out."

I took advantage of her pause. "I have a name for this passive cover-up of your 'spiritual practice.' The official term is 'spiritual bypassing.' I call it 'frosted poop.'" Claudia belly-laughed and typed "frosted poop" into her phone notes for later reference.

I asked, "So, now what?"

"Well, I suppose I'll sit down for an honest talk with my father about frosted poop and false fronts when I get home."

"You're not false, Claudia. You're the refreshing real deal. It's those who claim to have everything all figured out and get swept away by those hopped on guru juice that I'm wary of."

She laughed. "Guru juice. Frosted poop. This new vocabulary will definitely perk up my stodgy Brit friends back home!"

Disappointed to end our conversation, Claudia came upon the friends she'd arranged to walk into Santiago with. *Buen Camino, Claudia. Our meeting was no accident.*

Miles later, reunited with the Aussies, gazing from an overlook, we could see the city of Santiago. We swallowed the lump in our throats, not quite ready for this to end. Yet, we made the long trek into and through the city.

A smile hijacked our faces as we finally reached old town Santiago. Rounding the corner of a massive stone wall, we entered a church courtyard that revealed the back of the elusive cathedral. Its steeples touched the sky. Walking with throngs of other pilgrims, the spirit of "Diamonds on the Soles of Her Shoes" softly blended with the sound of distant bagpipes. Rumor had it, they'd usher us through the long archway, into the main square and our glorious destination.

Finally reaching the bagpipes, I wasn't sure if the sensation coursing through my veins was anxiety or excitement. We walked, I with my glistening diamond-soled shoes, through the archway tunnel, which—up until that moment—had only been a reality in my brain bubblegum fantasies.

CHAPTER 40

QUESTIONS, PATIENCE, and ANSWER HATS

SANTIAGO

Wounded Bird

~ Graham Nash

Damn. Not one barrel of oats and molasses in sight. All I could offer the bones of St. James was an inscrutable grin, and a wide-eyed whisper of "Thank you." That was followed by reverent homage to my kick-ass body. "We did it! You're an animal!" It too, needed time for all this to sink in.

Pilgrims were hugging, crying, and leaving a good dose of snot behind on their *Camino* family's shoulders. One guy lay face down spread-eagle. A sacrifice to the blister gods? I admit having the fleeting thought: *Did I do this wrong? Do I need an entrance do-over to show proper respect for this 500-mile walk?*

But I caught myself and withdrew the question. I owned that my spirit loves the *anticipation* on Christmas Eve as much as the *arrival* of Christmas morning. I cherish imagining my initials on the brushes long before my horse appears. I sprinkle birdseed on my dead parakeet because, well, you never know. I thrive best in anticipation and possibility. And that's just the way it is, Mr. Cronkite.

Don't get me wrong. There were hugs, high-fives, and picture-taking with the Cathedral backdrop. It's just that some internal reserves remained untapped.

After turning in our *Credentials,* and being told, "Come back in two hours for your *Compostela,*" next step: lunch, pitchers of sangria, and celebration. The Aussies and I raised a glass to challenges faced, and to completion. Five weeks before, they were strangers—suspected kidnappers in a van who lured me into a lifetime friendship.

The time came to pick up our *Compostelas.* Standing to leave, my right knee buckled. My body, which was good for 500 miles, finally waved the white flag. Maybe it overheard the option of walking another three days to Finisterre on the coast. My body made it clear, *Don't even think about it. We're done!* I agreed. My walking pole would serve as a handy cane for the next couple of days.

We'd all been forewarned in St. Jean Pied de Port that the Cathedral's major renovation project would mean unsightly scaffolding, limited access, no mass, and no ceremonial swinging of the gold incense-filled *botafumeiro.* Sadly, this magnificent ritual piece hung from its ropes in the sanctuary—disappointingly still.

Leaving the cathedral, I said "Thank you" to St. James, tempted to ask if my Swedish friend, Klara, came by to iron his underwear as penance for her ridiculous guilt. Given all the carbonated holiness found on his trail of stars, I'm confident St. James would've chuckled.

Compostelas in hand, one final task remained. This pilgrim had not one, but two shipped bags to reclaim. In a storage room filled with hundreds of backpacks and boxes, there they were—my suitcase sent from St. Jean and the 6.5-pound (when empty) backpack shipped from Pamplona. I wondered what inside seemed so important six weeks before.

LOOSE ENDS

"Golden Slumbers"
~ The Beatles

Alone in the hotel room with my now *three* bags, I faced everything Karen and René pried from my grip. My first mission—find the small bag tossed into the suitcase in St. Jean. Locating the smelly muscle cream hinted the bag with Mother Mary-Who-Art-Buried-in-a-Suitcase would be close behind.

I tipped the small bag, and the earrings fell into my palm. The late afternoon sun hit their sparkling stones. Any prior need for burying my head in oats and molasses dissolved. These simple trinkets broke the spell and represented everything it took to make it here. They spoke of angels, rosemary alcohol, missed turns, a rolling pin shared with the world, the sweet call of "Hail, The Queen," magick buses, and the protection this Divine Mother energy provided for 500 miles. Perhaps for my lifetime.

Raw emotion bubbled up, and a waterfall of tears finally fell. They fell for all the doubts that gave way to miracles. For the mystical appearance of fruit stands, new soul friends, learning to say "I'm feeling blue" in Italian, burying the parakeet, and soul-deep carbonated holiness. Mostly, I cried for the deep partnership forged with my body. I dedicated the snot now covering my sleeve to her, my ever-patient temple. *We did it right, my friend. We never figured out the damn rules, so we made up our own. I wouldn't do anything differently. For sticking by me, thank you. That was one hell of a desert.*

Curled up on the bed, eyes heavy from the flood of tears, I held Mother Mary—formerly Who-Art-Buried-in-a-Suitcase—close to my heart and fell into a dreamy, exhausted sleep.

Santiago Day Two. Pablo and Gabby taxied to Finisterre on the coast. I stayed to reconnect with friends one last time. Walking the narrow streets with my trusty walking pole as a cane, an unknowing witness could think: *Molly's limping yet again.* But the beginning in St. Jean and the end in Santiago weren't at all the same. To this end, never did I doubt my body's fortitude. My naked turtle slowly assimilated this loving truth into its newly forming shell. As Ed once commented: *This time, build a shell that love can permeate.*

A call came from behind. "Hey, Colorado!" Sylvia and Myra, the British Columbia sisters and I shared a hug-fest reunion. We last spoke in the backyard in Fromista, and later Sylvia had whizzed past Andrea and me on the *meseta.* I accepted their invitation to stay with them at their apartment, a block from Cathedral Square, the following night.

Eating lunch with a group of Moroccans, I again heard my name called. "Molly! You did it!" I lit up to see Kathleen, of the *"Camino* Queen Duo," who saved my soggy soul that rainy night in Villafranca. After a warm reunion, an hour later, I was pulled by another familiar voice.

"Molly? Is that you?" Unbelievable. It was Nick from Chicago, whose rock for the Iron Cross had also gone missing! The "rest of the story" spilled out. Thrilled to report he found his father-rock before the Iron Cross, he shared he'd never felt so free after dropping the weight of that relationship. We had a good laugh over Michael clearly rejecting being deposited at the Cross, and how his rock magickly reappeared soon after. The thundering cathedral bells overhead rattled our bones, and likely those of ancient ghosts who still walked these streets.

The next twenty-four hours blurred. Shopping, greeting Bill and Patrick (and my ball bag) in Cathedral Square, and yes, a sentimental final hug and salute from the Kingsmen before departing to their respective corners of the world. The *Camino's* heart is generous.

Arriving at Sylvia and Myra's apartment, we shared tales of the trail over Spanish wine. We delved further into our lives back home. I casually mentioned losing my prescription glasses just beyond Fromista. Their wide-eyed look raised my curiosity.

"Were they *purple,* by any chance?"

My jaw dropped. "YES! You found them?!"

"We did, Molly. Damn it. Walking with my sons along that long stretch of cement posts, we saw your purple glasses hanging eye-level from the fence by the trail. We stopped to try them on, checking whether they were valuable prescription glasses. We had a five-minute debate about whether to leave or take them to Santiago, hoping for a lost and found. Final vote—leave them. The owner would likely return to look for them. Oh, Molly, if only we'd known they were yours." Ugh. So close. The lesson in this would eventually surface. We talked until late. Our time together, fleeting but fun.

The next day, another hotel for my last night in Santiago. Pablo and Gabby booked a train for the following morning to southern Spain for their post-*Camino* unwinding. I'd be Portugal-bound to melt on North Beach for a week in the old-world town of Nazaré.

Following our final dinner together, surrounded by ancient stone buildings, the Aussies and I said goodbye. Like a surreal storybook tale, one where the Heroes survived—we closed the book for now. After tearful hugs, we turned toward our respective hotels, looking back for one more wave. My heart ached until sleep took me.

A toast to the end of the road and to the truth:
"We get by with a little help from our friends."
(Cheers to you, Mother Mary who-art-buried-in-a-suitcase!)

THE END / THE BEGINNING

The morning sun hit the ivy-covered wall outside my hotel window. I stored my suitcase at the hotel, my pack holding only what I'd need for Portugal. Before catching the bus, I stopped at a French café for breakfast. There, the *Camino* presented one last surprise soundtrack song. To better understand, first, some history.

Years ago, I worked as a trainer in a national conflict resolution program for school districts. I worked closely with the founder, Peter Yarrow, of the folk group Peter, Paul and Mary. At each school assembly, the kids and adults joined Peter on stage to sing "Puff the Magic Dragon." One lasting memory was the teary reaction of the adults at a certain point in the song:

A dragon lives forever, but not so little boys
Painted wings and giant's rings make way for other toys.
One gray night it happened, Jackie Paper came no more
And Puff, that mighty dragon, he ceased his fearless roar.
His head was bent in sorrow, green scales fell like rain
Puff no longer went to play along the cherry lane
Without his lifelong friend, Puff could not be brave
So Puff, that mighty dragon, sadly slipped into his cave.

The song, reminding us of lost innocence and the all-too-quick passage of time, begged the question: "Will you disappear into your cave, or roll with life and live it full out?"

That morning in the French café, I smiled to recognize the song playing, "Puff The Magic Dragon"—in French! Its sentiment about time passing and dear friends left behind seemed apropos. Before catching my bus, I texted Peter to tell him where I was, about my completed *Camino,* and how his song magically appeared. Two hours later, as my bus pulled out headed for Portugal, I received Peter's response:

💜 Carry on, my sweet survivor.

With Santiago disappearing in the rearview mirror, the chaotic traffic colliding with the racket of the noisy bus engine, jarred my nervous system. Feeling a little lost, I realized the journey left me with as many questions as it answered. *Were the answers I did get enough to sustain the gains made? Had I wrapped my whole being in the holy dirt? Did I go beyond where I once would have?* I was reminded of the passage in Paulo Coelho's book, *Warrior of the Light*:

> *"I've been through all this before,"* he says to his heart.
> *"Yes, you have been through all this before,"* replies his heart,
> *"but you have never been beyond it."*

Had this journey finally delivered me *beyond it*? Yes. Beyond all hopes. But my sense of its being more of a beginning than an ending felt even stronger. Damn. Another beginning? I'd kind of hoped the credits would run on this Hero's Journey once in Santiago, and I'd finally leave the theater commenting, "Excellent show!" At that, the *Camino* rolled its eyes.

All I knew right then was that breathing was much easier *beyond it*. Putting away the map in the bus seat pocket, a small strip of paper fell to the floor. It read:

The odd thing about the often long and lonely path of life, is that when

you get to the end of it and look back, you'll find that it was neither of these.

I unbuttoned my shorts pocket and slid the message in. Pulling my hand out, with it came a handful of damp birdseed that had been through several washes. Smiling at the Petey memory, I left the bits of seed that scattered on the empty seat, because, well, you never know. My thinking: *They might reassure someone in doubt, that they have indeed gone beyond it, buried the parakeet, and earned the Girl Scout badge.*

I laughed to myself about the massive wisdom I *thought* I'd have gained once this journey wrapped up. Much remained hanging. As for the French gentleman's question, "Why are you here?" *I think, sir, what's most important is simply that—I'm here. Period. Figuring out why I came is not nearly as important as coming. And coming was a phenomenally good idea.*

And René's curiosity as to what this was *really* about? That answer would take living in the question for a long while. Graham Nash's song, "Wounded Bird," once again whispered in my ear to patiently wait when questions linger, and the *answer hat* remains elusive.

The lack of an answer keeps us hungry. It keeps us walking forward—just three more kilometers. It makes the end of the story—never-ending.

In life. In pilgrimages. And in books.

Perhaps it's best to end with a question.

Don't you think?

Journal Notes

June 20, 2019

Somewhere On a Beach in Portugal

> "Whether I shall turn out
> to be the hero of my own life,
> or whether that station will
> be held by anybody else,
> these pages must show."
> ~ Charles Dickens

FINAL WISE TIPS, WITH LOVE, TO MY FELLOW/SISTER PILGRIMS

1. Just deal with the fact you didn't invest early in the Compeed bandage company.

2. Remember that *Camino* veteran who once said you'd only need to pack two t-shirts? And you laughed, "NO WAY!" Well?

3. Often along the Way, you see something so beautiful that you whisper to yourself, "Remember this magick. Don't ever lose it." Many such scenes are buried deep in my bones forever.

4. Stay true to, and honor, your music era. If Nancy Sinatra can show up on *my Camino*, trust *your* one-hit-wonder can make an appearance in the middle of nowhere and save you, too.

5. Once back home, you'll slip and say *"Buen Camino!"* to a complete stranger on the street, leaving a restaurant—days, maybe weeks—after finishing the *Camino*. Repeat after me: "I'm home now."

6. You'll have the urge to take and post a picture of your backpack on social media once you've completed your *Camino*. It served you well. It's family now. Others won't get it. But that's okay. Post it anyway.

7. On the *Camino,* as in life, precious people come and go. Some you thought you'd see again, but they slipped away. Trust they're woven into your tapestry always. The missed chance is a reminder: don't take magick connections for granted.

8. When you lose something (ya know, like purple glasses) avoid searching with the mindset of its being "lost." You cannot find something that's "lost." When it's lost to you, it remains lost. Expand your view—wider and higher—look for it to be FOUND. Otherwise, the *Camino* (a.k.a. The Universe) cannot possibly reveal it to you.

9. Trust things are always working out for you.

10. You will miss the bells.

I sense these are only the tip of the iceberg. Home, my own bed, and what and who I love, await me. Only then will what I've really gained and lost here be uncovered. A *THEY* testing ground for sure.

Buen Camino to all who came before me. Thank you for weaving the web of wisdom, secrets, and connection in this holy dirt. And to all who follow—for you, I've left behind as much grace as I could muster.

Most importantly, don't complain about the bells. I'm telling you.

Signing off, dear pilgrims.

May you always have "just 3 kilometers to go."

EPILOGUE

Drops of Jupiter
~ Train

AUGUST 2023

COLORADO

Many questions that surface while walking the *Camino* quickly fade, no longer needing an answer. But René's question posed in our final late-night-talk-in-the-dark before she left Spain has come due:

"Molly, if you ever figure it out, do you promise to tell me what this *Camino* thing is all about? It has to be more than just fucking walking."

Well, my friend, there was no "figuring things out." But I've reduced the whole *Camino* metamorphosis down to this one-sentence paradox:

You're inside a box,
and the directions on how to get out
are written on the outside of the box.

Tilting your head to understand its meaning might help. Maybe squint your eyes, as you would with an M.C. Escher drawing. Or butterscotch. In its complexity and whimsy, it reveals how, when we let go *of figuring it out*, transformation unfolds.

I've learned the *Camino* (and life) won't allow us to skip the beginning step-by-step stage of any challenge. But when we face it with a mighty trust, and finally give up the struggle, the edges of the box soften. I don't know exactly when I began leaning on my True North and synchronicity more than on my frustration. But, somewhere, I crossed from inside the box to find myself sitting outside of it. And there waiting were the darn directions on how to get out.

Directions I no longer needed. Cruel, but worth the outcome.

I swear, if I'd heard Glinda the Good Witch say, "You had the power all along, m'dear," I'd have snapped her wand in two. I don't believe we *can* see any path to power while struggling inside the box of our "shitty first draft." The challenge: how quickly can we give up the struggle, take the required steps, and get on the other side? Or, in true *THEY* form, don't entertain struggle in the first place.

Gentleman Jade wisely summed it up: "It's like we won the lottery a long, long time ago, and instead of checking our numbers, we kept buying more tickets." *Ahhh, paradox.*

So, dear René, through the lens of these amusing paradoxes—come along as I wrap up my *Camino* adventure with all I've uncovered. I promise, no more "fucking" walking.

RE-ENTRY

Four years have passed, and still, people ask at happy hour, a business luncheon, in the produce aisle:

"I heard you walked the *Camino*! How was it?"

"I've read the *Camino* can really change you. Is that true?"

"Wow. 500 miles. Would you do it again?"

Using brief "*THEY* speak," I respond: "Best thing I've ever done. If you ever hear the call to walk it, say *yes*."

This answer satisfies most. But my heart, ready to burst, wants to tell everything—about the *Camino's* mesmerizing rhythm, its call to get dirty, and the appearance of rogue parakeets.

In any conversation unrelated to the *Camino* (they *do* happen), my mind predictably draws some parallel to my journey. Maybe to a journal Trail Tip, a wrong turn that led to a miracle, or some distant cowbell. Any dirt pathway spotted winding into the hills still calls to me. It's an addiction. Everything here, seems to have a peculiar tie to whatever unfolded there.

Hey Ed, I didn't bring the Camino home. It followed me.

CRUTCHES

Blowing the dust off an old screenplay this week seemed a clever escape from finishing the epilogue for this book. Procrastination ruled. Mostly to avoid mentioning the crutches. Kinda like the guy who heard most accidents happen within five miles of home, so he moved.

The art of "bringing the *Camino* home" can be a harsh mistress.

Having completed the book's final chapter months ago, I initially had some pie-in-the-sky idea I'd breeze through the epilogue. I planned to highlight insights gained once home, synchronistic wins, a few tough losses, and moments when faith has been tested. I intended to toast my successful knee replacement and commiserate with fellow pilgrims how soon after returning from Spain, the pandemic upended our lives. I'd share how the hardest "letting go" reminder came with a storage unit burglary that took the box holding my treasured *Compostela* and collection of sacred *Credential* stamps. My heart sank. At the epilogue's close, I imagined the *Camino* gods cheering as I tied it all in a neat bow, allowing the Act Three curtain to finally fall.

Ha! The *Camino* continues to laugh.

Long before my *Camino*, walking was always my healing grace. Any problem to be solved, any need to stir my creative muse, was usually met with "I'm going for a walk." I happily subscribe to the Roman phrase, *solvitur ambulando.* Translation: "It is solved by walking." However, eleven months ago, that go-to solution was taken off the table.

It seemed minor—a fractured metatarsal bone in my foot. No huge deal. "Six to eight weeks, and you'll be hiking again," the doctor said. Instead, a rogue blood clot in my calf followed, which, in the end, left behind a curiously serious, damaging syndrome, leaving the bone still not healed and my lower leg and foot blue, cold, and numb. Sparing you months of puzzling details, I'll just say no medical specialist has an answer or solution. Yet.

In the ten months following the injury, I remained externally focused in order to save my foot, with Mayo Clinic being the next step. However, I knew the emotional and spiritual message underlying all this awaited me in the wings, for when I chose to turn my questioning inward. Gina and I had to ask "Where are those 'Another Fucking Lesson *Camino* Bus' counselors when you need 'em?"

The good news: I've remained my foot's unwavering ally. We've had practice at this! The old belief "I'm an accident waiting to happen" is long gone. I credit my mostly sane, steady, optimistic state during this time to the rich lessons of the trail.

Not surprising, Ed's "voice" still lingers, and the relevance of the *Camino* Messages becomes more evident. I admit, it's tough recreating the essence of the *Camino* here. Some days, I ache to sit in the weeds on some ancient Roman road once again, and cry for the mystery of it all. But *THEY* always redirect my longing, whispering: *Step up, Molly. You're being called to a higher way. But first, chop this wood, and carry that water.*

And with that, I realign with my True North. Keeping things simple. Frequently checking if I'm lugging an unnecessary can opener.

THE CAMINO MESSAGES COME HOME

One quiet pandemic evening, well before this injury, I gathered together my fifteen *Camino* Messages, each transporting me to when I first scribbled it down along the trail. Moments I didn't just survive, but thrived. Jade and I had questioned their relevance once home. Answer: they're a lifeline.

Though the full list is rich and helpful, it can feel overwhelming when the moment demands a quick arrow. So, just as the Ten Commandments could be reduced to the practical idea of: "Try to be less of a shithead," I often pare down the list to only messages relevant to the moment. Like "quick keys" for those "you gotta be kidding me" days.

I hadn't planned for my foot to play a lead role in this epilogue. But here we are. I'm learning that when a challenging, reoccurring theme in life creeps back in, I need to find inspiration that keeps it as a teacher rather than let it hold me hostage. Beyond the *Camino* Messages, another gem where I've found inspiration when feeling lost, is in these lines of David Wagoner's poem "Lost."

LOST

Stand still. The trees ahead and bushes beside you
Are not lost. Wherever you are is called Here,
And you must treat it as a powerful stranger,
Must ask permission to know it and be known.
The forest breathes. Listen. It answers...
Stand still. The forest knows where you are.
You must let it find you.

To hold onto this valuable "Lost versus Found" message, I call on the "Lesson of the Purple Glasses:" When looking for what feels lost, I raise my eyes—wider and higher—and look for its being FOUND. Otherwise, the Camino (aka The Universe) cannot possibly reveal it to me.

Of late, the following three *Camino* Messages keep my view wider and higher, trusting the forest and medical and spiritual answers will find me.

CAMINO MESSAGE #13
Be where your feet are.

Loose gravel and slippery descents remind pilgrims to be keenly present. Ed forewarned of the challenge of bringing that presence back home.

Good chance not being in the moment played into my foot injury. My monkey mind was everywhere but where my feet were, and tossed me inside a box—with no directions.

Overthinking, I had gotten caught up in how to restore my business after the pandemic shutdown. Lost in worry, and attempting to write the script for my future before it could unfold naturally. Finally waking up to my creating such interference, like a momentary skid on loose gravel, cautions me to *be where my feet are*. Only then can True North direct me.

CAMINO MESSAGE #5
When haunting questions hang in the balance, muster patience and grace until the "answer hat" is here.

WAITING is a good and actual strategy. Not the sit-on-the-escalator kind of waiting, but one that, through strategic patience, eventually accesses intuitive truth. It's futile to force an outcome when the real answer is: It's not time to know the answer yet.

It seemed easier on the *Camino* to allow the laws of nature to organize a far better result than anything I could have orchestrated. Answers came when it was time, with calm certainty.

Waiting for clarity at home is more challenging. But having gleaned wisdom from long days on the *meseta*, I'm reminded business, creativity, and healing also have their own optimal timing. And when no answer is on the horizon, stop "figuring it out," and instead muster patience and grace, until the *answer hat* arrives.

And so, I wait.

FEBRUARY 2024

UPDATE: THE ANSWER HAT COMETH

Having Pollyanna hanging out in one's soul can be exhausting. She whispers sappy things like *this storm can't last forever.* Or, *the rainbow will be awesome!* Though tempted to respond, "Stick it, Polly!" I'm eighteen months out from the injury, and Mayo Clinc and local practitioners extraordinaire have put an optimistic healing plan in motion. It appears my foot will remain intact. I finally feel freed up to turn my attention inward. Apparently, the *Camino* was still on the clock as—on cue—an angel appeared who asked one simple question that inspired an emotional and physical turning point.

An email exchange with Australian film producer and *Camino* memoir author, Bill Bennett *(The Way, My Way),* addressed the daunting hanging fear of losing my foot. Bill's words challenged me to answer the same question he posed when facing his fears on the *Camino:* "What's the worst that could happen in this situation? And can I live with that?"

His question triggered an unexpected answer. I realized what seemed the worst thing—losing my foot—actually wasn't. The true worst: to never walk again. Suddenly, I could deal with losing my foot. Though not the desired outcome, *that* one had a solution: get a really cool prosthetic, yes? Hell, I could then walk all of you under the table without ever getting another blister! *That,* I could live with. Bill's point—what seemed the worst no longer felt as dark.

Facing my own Great Blue Heron moment head-on, I then freely breathed into my next step (pun intended). Waiting there for me was the next *Camino* Message to lean into.

CAMINO MESSAGE #12

Synchronicities are major divine clues that you're on the right path.

Synchronicities. They're always there, scheming to delight us. Focusing on synchronistic happenings signals the Universe to keep them coming.

The mind-body connection is staggering. Having turned my focus inward to examine what influence I maybe had on my spiraling injury (and now on my healing), I sensed the *Camino* asking:

What if you were to powerfully own your Messages more than your fears? As on the Camino, can you trust walking confidently into your future not knowing exactly where your next step leads? (Numb or not?) Can you surrender the fear that's causing your feet to stop you literally dead in your tracks? If so, I'm seeing healing, and a very cool Girl Scout badge in your future.

Finally addressing the fears running me at the time of the injury coincided (not surprisingly) with synchronicity taking hold. Healing players and circumstances began appearing with mind-numbing precision. With that support, it isn't that the fear disappeared. I just didn't believe in it anymore.

Now, four months into a rigorous physical therapy regimen, I've traded my Master's in Shoelace Management for one in Neuroplasticity. With hours of physical therapy and spiritual practices, my rewired brain is slowly accepting this numb foot as a viable appendage. I'm giddy to be walking over two miles a day. I laugh recalling when walking that distance on foggy *Camino* mornings was considered "the warm-up before breakfast." Now, it's a feat to celebrate (and I do).

Some ask, "When do you expect complete recovery?" Pollyanna's best guess—I have three kilometers to go.

You've likely caught on—one's *Camino* never ends. The trifecta of myth, music, and magick, remain my teacher. They continually remind me I can't control everything. Okay. *Nothing.* I bow to the Great Blue Heron (along with Linda's beaded bracelets that remain on my wrist as inspiration) who taught me spiritual redirection doesn't equal betrayal or taking away, but rather making space for the soul's next calling. In laughing with friends until we cried, crying with friends until we laughed, I've come to cherish the sacred imperfections in the weave of my life tapestry. The lessons of the *Camino* live on.

This circles us back to the overarching point of "sitting outside the box." I needed these four years for it to finally sink in: It takes a million steps to reveal we don't take baby steps for the distance they cover, but to put ourselves within reach of life's magick. When we let go, the holy dirt takes it from there.

In closing, let it be known, that my new shell is kick-ass. A shell love can permeate. A kind of love I've never before felt. For myself, for you, for this life.

My personal *THEY*, who's ever-growing, ever-stumbling, ever-finding-its-way-off-the-escalator, proposes this: "What if love isn't the answer to our problems, but rather a doorway to them? Not a way out, but a way in. What if we continually ask ourselves "What magick can love and I muster here?"

Then sprinkle a handful of birdseed.

Because, well…you never know.

The End

~ The Beatles

Five years later, Linda remains my guide. And her wooden, beaded bracelets still grace my arm. May the hard-won lessons of the Great Blue Heron (that can so unexpectedly change the course of our lives) rest peacefully in our souls.

MESSAGES FROM THE CAMINO

Message #1 — Any carefully made Camino plan <u>will</u> be turned on its head.

Message #2 — Watch for angels.

Message #3 — The Camino provides.

Message #4 — Each pilgrim's Camino will be as it should be.

Message #5 — When haunting questions hang in the balance, muster patience and grace until the "answer hat" is here.

Message #6 — If I am able to master my mind, I'll find the extraordinary in the mundane.

Message #7 — When magic finds you, hold it loosely and dear.

Message #8 — Trust your True North. It's always there.

Message # — The spectacular is buried in the slow, gentle nothing.

Message #10 — This is holy dirt. Wrap your whole being in it. Get dirty.

Message #11 — The easiest path to living your integrity often hides in plain sight. Bury the parakeet.

Message #12 — Synchronicities are major divine clues that you are on the right path.

Message #13 — Be where your feet are.

Message #14 — Sometimes just staying the course is an adventurer's act of defiance. Refusing to go numb. Refusing to pop-tart the dog. Feeling it all.

Message #15 — Are you working to connect the dots (make a decision)? Or, are you merely collecting more dots (quit stalling)?

ACKNOWLEDGMENTS

To my sage editor, Jen Valentino, my deepest gratitude. Her patient, gracious support through my healing roller coaster, editing adventures, and a few wild miracles, allowed me to focus on more than one goal at a time. She wisely walked me through every word, paragraph, and intention of every sacred step of my *Camino*.

Huge thanks to my publisher Laura Di Franco of Brave Healer Productions and her team, who held the vision when I lost sight of it, and provided the grounded rhythm of getting this book to publication.

In the spring of 2020, my seminar company hit pause as the world shut down. Having recently returned from my *Camino* in 2019, many suggested, "You should write a book about it!" My usual response: "Nah, I write screenplays. I have no idea how to write a book. Besides, I could never capture my *Camino* experience on a page. I haven't even sorted it out in my *head* yet." But my writing group extraordinaire, *Writers of the Roundtable*, persisted. They pushed to hear about my journey, chapter by chapter, as they followed me through every kilometer and small Spanish village. Their encouragement saw me through hundreds of drafts and my doubts of "no one really cares to hear about all of this, do they?" I thank these dear friends: Mary Zalmanek, Barbara Bowen, Leisel Hufford, Rich Vogel, and Marylin Warner.

I knew I would know my book cover when I saw it. So I patiently waited. Ukrainian watercolor artist, Yana Shvets, swooped in and magically captured the very soul of *Holy Dirt*. For her intuitive heart, I'm grateful.

Of course, cheers to the gamblers. They being my support team and dear pilgrim family that paved wild and sacred pathways into the tapestry of my *Camino*: René Nelson, Karen Jones, Pablo and Gabby, Gina and Brad, Bill and Patrick, Roman, Bren, Klara the Murderer, Gloria and Evan, Sophie, Lilly and Noah, Gentleman Jade & Co., the sweet Kingsmen, my dear angel companion, Linda Sacha, along with all of my Dead-Friend-*Camino*-Support-Army. And of course, my *Camino* Angels who showed up in the nick of time. Thank you all.

Finally, a high-five to my wise cheerleader, thirteen-year-old nephew, Owen Robinette, who never missed a beat in encouraging and keeping my writing on track!

To the warm, supportive people of Spain, gracias. You are loving *THEYS* of the highest order. The frosting on all these acknowledgements: my trifecta of "myth, music, and magick" that, to this day, guide every step I'm (re)learning to take-out of my mind and into my body. You remain my rock.

ABOUT THE AUTHOR

MOLLY LORD. An educator, passionate storyteller, screenwriter, and pioneer in the field of music and archetypes. With her keen sense of story, she is loved by national audiences for her dynamic, humorous, and unconventional teaching style and take on life.

It all began with her first Beatles album. Age eight. The experience inspired one question that begged to be explored for decades: *what really happens when music crawls inside our heads?*

Forty years in varied fields of human behavior studies (teaching, directing non-profits, and mediating for the criminal justice system), ideally led to launching her Jungian-based seminar company, *Tuned-In Productions.* Its cutting-edge workshops, keynotes, and virtual trainings, highlight the scientific and spiritual link between behavior patterns that run our day-to-day lives and the music we love.

When not uncovering the soundtrack of people's lives, you'll find Molly burning the midnight oil on a screenplay, kayaking a mountain reservoir, or hear her hiking boots (or snowshoes) crunching in the gravel on Colorado Rocky Mountain trails.

In the midst of her creative endeavors, when she heard the unexpected call to walk the 500 miles of the *Camino de Santiago* in Spain, she initially answered with a resounding, "Are you kidding me?" But things changed. Unable to ignore the call, she packed her old injuries, fears, and a twisted desire for the unknown and found herself on a pilgrimage across the breathtaking landscapes of Spain. Molly's passionate adventure to get out of her mind and into her body (in order to survive) shaped her *Camino* memoir, *Holy Dirt*. Its rave reviews claim her stunning messages were music to their ears! Play on.

Connect with Molly Lord: mollyalord@gmail.com

www.MollyLord.com

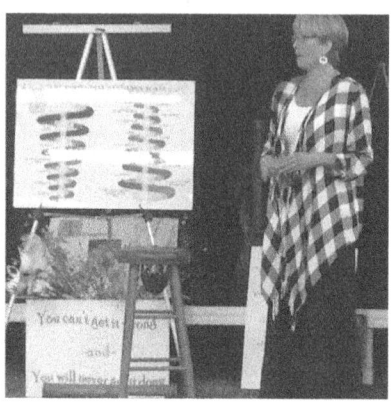

THE MINDFUL MUSIC ONLINE SERIES

Raise your frequency from self-sabotage to success,
from feeling you're falling short to a leader's mindset.

Prop your feet up, get popcorn ready!

CHANGE YOUR TUNE IN 20 MINUTES

Done-for-you playlists (partners with Spotify)
to shift your state of mind to a better feeling one!

Relief at your fingertips with the simple touch of play!

THE SOUNDTRACK OF MY CAMINO

There's A Place In The World For A Gambler / Dan Fogelberg

Somewhere / Barbra Streisand

On The Road To Find Out / Cat Stevens/Yusuf

I'll Play The Blues For You / Daniel Castro

Inner Demons / Julia Brennan

Bristlecone Pine / Michael Johnson

Old Friends, Bookends / Simon & Garfunkel

This Is It / Kenny Loggins

100,00 Angels / Bliss

The Wind / Cat Stevens/ Yusuf

Wounded Bird / Graham Nash

Brasilerias-No5-Laurinda Almeda

You Say / Lauren Daigle

(I'm Gonna Be) 500 Miles / The Proclaimers

The Promise / Tracy Chapman

Don't Rain On My Parade / Barbra Streisand

Up To The Mountain / Chrystal Bowersox

Holy Now / Peter Mayer

The Weight / The Band

Take Me To Church / Hozier

These Boots Are Made For Walking / Nancy Sinatra

Call Me (Come Back Home) / Al Green

And So It Goes / Jennifer Warnes

Moonlight Sonata / Beethoven

Diamonds on the Soles of Her Shoes / Paul Simon

Golden Slumbers / The Beatles

Drops of Jupiter / Train

The End / The Beatles

Home To Myself / Melissa Manchester

IN CLOSING

We all return "home" from our respective Hero's Journeys on the wings of sacred holy forces. In honor of these courageous returns, I'll close with this final soundtrack song.

Home To Myself
~ Melissa Manchester

For reading *Holy Dirt*, and listening
when inspired to push play,
I warmly thank you.

www.ingramcontent.com/pod-product-compliance
Lightning Source LLC
Chambersburg PA
CBHW061601120626
46550CB00004B/1567